Level 1 · Part 2
Integrated Chinese
中文聽說讀寫

TEXTBOOK Traditional Characters

Third Edition

THIRD EDITION BY

Yuehua Liu and Tao-chung Yao
Nyan-Ping Bi, Liangyan Ge, Yaohua Shi

ORIGINAL EDITION BY

Tao-chung Yao and Yuehua Liu
Liangyan Ge, Yea-fen Chen, Nyan-Ping Bi,
Xiaojun Wang, Yaohua Shi

CHENG & TSUI COMPANY
Boston

Third Edition / sixth printing April 2016

22 21 20 19 18 17 16   6 7 8 9 10 11 12 13 14

Published by
Cheng & Tsui Company, Inc.
25 West Street
Boston, MA 02111-1213 USA
Fax (617) 426-3669
www.cheng-tsui.com
"Bringing Asia to the World"™
ISBN 978-0-88727-673-6— ISBN 978-0-88727-672-9 (pbk.)

Cover Design: studioradia.com

Cover Photographs: Man with map © Getty Images; Shanghai skyline © David Pedre/iStockphoto; Building with masks © Wu Jie; Night market © Andrew Buko. Used by permission.

Interior Design: Wanda España, Wee Design

Illustrations: 洋洋兔动漫

Shanghai photos, p.52: Wu Jie

Tai Chi photo, p. 252: Jgremillot

Great Wall photo (left), p. 261: Marianna Natale

Great Wall photo (right), p. 261: Brian Snelson

Library of Congress Cataloging-in-Publication Data

Integrated Chinese: textbook traditional characters = [Zhong wen ting shuo du xie]. Level 1. Part 2 / Yuehua Liu ... [et al.] — 3rd ed.
    p. cm.
  Includes indexes.
  ISBN 978-0-88727-673-6 (trad. hbk.) — ISBN 978-0-88727-672-9 (trad. pbk.) — ISBN 978-0-88727-671-2 (simp. hbk.) — ISBN 978-0-88727-670-5 (simp. pbk.)
  1. Chinese language—Textbooks for foreign speakers—English. I. Liu, Yuehua. II. Title: Zhong wen ting shuo du xie.

PL1129.E5I683 2008
  495.1'82421—dc22

                    2008062321

The *Integrated Chinese* series includes books, workbooks, character workbooks, audio products, multimedia products, teacher's resources, and more. Visit **www.cheng-tsui.com** for more information on the other components of *Integrated Chinese*.

Printed in Canada

Expand your *Integrated Chinese* Study

with support for the whole series

Textbooks, Workbooks, Character Workbooks, Teacher's Handbooks, and **Audio CDs** *work together as a comprehensive curriculum.*

Online Workbooks, eTextbooks, BuilderCards, and **Textbook DVDs for all levels** *take study further and add flexibility to the classroom.*

INTEGRATED CHINESE COMPANION WEBSITE

More supplements for students, more support for teachers!

www.cheng-tsui.com/integratedchinese

Kù Chinese

eFlashcards

STUDENTS Sharpen your vocabulary recognition and pronunciation with new *eFlashcards* and learn fun idioms and slang with the video series *Kù Chinese*.

TEACHERS Enhance your classroom instruction with *Video Activity Worksheets* (available for all *Integrated Chinese* DVDs), sentence pattern drills, teacher-generated PowerPoints®, and additional tools for testing and assessment.

Visit www.cheng-tsui.com or call 1-800-554-1963 for more information about other supplementary materials, such as graded readers, listening comprehension workbooks, character guides, and reference materials.

Contents

Lesson 11: Talking about the Weather   1

Lesson 12: Dining   31

Learning Objectives

Relate and Get Ready

Lesson 13: Asking Directions   63

Lesson 14: Birthday Party   101

Lesson 15: Seeing a Doctor   133

Lesson 17: Renting an Apartment

Lesson 18: Sports

Lesson 19: Travel   257

More Companions for Integrated Chinese

The Way of Chinese Characters
The Origins of 670 Essential Words
2nd Edition

By Jianhsin Wu, Illustrated by Chen Zheng, Chen Tian

Learn characters through a holistic approach.

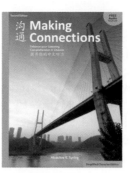

Making Connections
Enhance Your Listening Comprehension in Chinese

By Madeline K. Spring

Improve listening skills using everyday conversations.

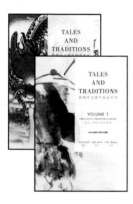

Tales and Traditions
Readings in Chinese Literature Series
2nd Edition

Compiled by Yun Xiao, et al.

Read level-appropriate excerpts from the Chinese folk and literary canon.

Readings in Chinese Culture Series

By Qun Ao, Weijia Huang

Increase reading and cultural proficiency with level-appropriate essays about Chinese culture.

Integrated Chinese BuilderCards
Much More than Vocabulary Flashcards

By Song Jiang, Haidan Wang

Reinforce and build vocabulary with flashcards.

Strive for a 5
AP* Chinese Practice Tests

By Weiman Xu, Han Qu, Sara Gu, So Mui Chang, Lisha Kang

Prepare for the AP exam with eight practice tests, tips, and more.

Cheng & Tsui Chinese Character Dictionary
A Guide to the 2000 Most Frequently Used Characters

Edited by Wang Huidi

Master the 2,000 most-used characters.

Cheng & Tsui Chinese Measure Word Dictionary
A Chinese-English English-Chinese Usage Guide

Compiled by Jiqing Fang, Michael Connelly

Speak and write polished Chinese using this must-have reference.

Visit **www.cheng-tsui.com** to view samples, place orders, and browse other language-learning materials.

*Advanced Placement and AP are registered trademarks of the College Board, which was not involved in the production of, and does not endorse, this product.

Publisher's Note

When *Integrated Chinese* was first published in 1997, it set a new standard with its focus on the development and integration of the four language skills (listening, speaking, reading, and writing). Today, to further enrich the learning experience of the many users of *Integrated Chinese* worldwide, Cheng & Tsui is pleased to offer this revised and updated third edition of *Integrated Chinese*. We would like to thank the many teachers and students who, by offering their valuable insights and suggestions, have helped *Integrated Chinese* evolve and keep pace with the many positive changes in the field of Chinese language instruction. *Integrated Chinese* continues to offer comprehensive language instruction, with many new features and useful shared resources available on our website at **www.cheng-tsui.com**.

The Cheng & Tsui Chinese Language Series is designed to publish and widely distribute quality language learning materials created by leading instructors from around the world. We welcome readers' comments and suggestions concerning the publications in this series. Please contact the following members of our Editorial Board, in care of our Editorial Department (e-mail: editor@cheng-tsui.com).

Preface to the Third Edition

It has been over ten years since *Integrated Chinese* (*IC*) came into existence in 1997. During these years, amid all the historical changes that took place in China and the rest of the world, the demand for Chinese language teaching-learning materials has been growing dramatically. We are greatly encouraged by the fact that *IC* not only has been a widely used textbook at the college level all over the United States and beyond, but also has become increasingly popular with advanced language students at high schools. Over the years, regular feedback from the users of *IC,* both students and teachers, has greatly facilitated our repeated revisions of the series. Following its second edition published in 2005 that featured relatively minor changes and adjustments, the third edition is the result of a much more extensive revision.

Changes in the Third Edition

Manageable Number of Lessons

Level 1 now contains 10 lessons in Part 1 and 10 lessons in Part 2 for maximum flexibility. Based on the reports from many teachers that they could not finish all the lessons in the Level 1 volumes within one academic year, we have, for the third edition, eliminated the chapters "At the Library" and "At the Post Office," as the language contents in these chapters have become somewhat obsolete. The chapter "Hometown" has also been removed, but part of its content has been incorporated into other chapters.

Revised Storyline

In the present edition, a new, connected storyline about a diverse group of students strings together all the dialogues and narratives in the lessons throughout Level 1. The relationships among the main characters are more carefully scripted. We want the students to get to know the characters well and to find out how things develop among them. We hope that, by getting to know more about each cast member, the students will be more involved in the process of learning the language.

Current Vocabulary

As in the earlier editions, the third edition makes a special effort to reflect students' life. Additionally, we have updated some of the vocabulary items and expressions in the hope of keeping pace with the evolution of contemporary Chinese and enhancing students' ability to communicate. In the meantime, we have deleted some words and expressions that are of relatively lower frequencies of usage. As a result, the total number of vocabulary items for the series is moderately reduced. The grammar sequence, however, remains fundamentally unchanged.

Clear Learning Objectives and Engaging Learner-Centered Approach

Ever since its inception in 1997, *IC* has been a communication-oriented language textbook which also aims at laying a solid foundation in language form and accuracy for students. The third edition holds fast to that pedagogic philosophy. On top of that, it has adopted a task-based teaching approach, which is intended to intensify students' motivation and heighten their awareness of the learning objectives in each chapter. Each lesson includes Learning Objectives and Relate and Get Ready questions at the beginning to focus students' study. At the end of each lesson, there is a Progress Checklist to be used by students in self-testing their fulfillment of the learning objectives.

It is our hope that these changes will enable students to learn Chinese in a more efficient and pragmatic way and develop their language proficiency and problem-solving abilities in real-life situations. In their feedback to us, many users of previous editions of *IC* noted that, more than many other Chinese language textbooks, *IC* was effective in developing students' abilities to use the language. While making all the efforts to retain that merit in the new edition, we have endeavored to place language acquisition in a real-world context and make *IC* all the more conducive to active use of the language in the classroom and, more importantly, beyond it.

Contextualized Grammar and Interactive Language Practice

The somewhat mechanical drills on sentence patterns in the earlier editions are now replaced by Language Practice exercises based on simulated real-life situations. In particular, we have increased the number of interactive exercises and exercises that serve the purpose of training students' abilities in oral communication and discourse formation. Similar changes are also to be seen in the *Integrated Chinese* workbook, which offers new exercises that are more distinctly communication-oriented and more closely aligned with the learning objectives of each chapter. The exercises in the workbook cover the three modes of communication as explained in the "Standards for Foreign Language Learning in the 21st Century": interpretive, interpersonal and presentational. To help the user locate different types of exercises, we have labeled the workbook exercises in terms of the three communication modes.

Linguistically and Thematically Appropriate Cultural Information and Authentic Materials

In comparison with the earlier editions, there is more cultural information in the third edition. The revised texts provide a broader perspective on Chinese culture, and important cultural features and topics are discussed in the "Culture Highlights." In the meantime, more up-to-date language ingredients, such as authentic linguistic materials, new realia, and new illustrations, are introduced with a view towards reflecting cultural life in the dynamic and rapidly changing contemporary China. We believe that language is a carrier of culture and a second/foreign language is acquired most efficiently in its native cultural setting. Based on that conviction, we have attempted to offer both linguistic and cultural information in a coherent, consistent manner and simulate a Chinese cultural environment in our texts, especially those that are set in China.

All-New, Colorful, and User-Friendly Design

Where design and layout are concerned, the third edition represents a significant improvement. We have taken full advantage of colors to highlight different components of each chapter, and have brought in brand-new illustrations and photos to complement the content of the text. The book has also been thoroughly redesigned for optimal ease of use.

Updated Audio Recordings

Throughout this book, an audio CD icon appears next to the main texts, vocabulary, and pronunciation exercises. This symbol indicates the presence of audio recordings, which are available on the companion audio CD set.

Acknowledgments

During the course of preparing for the third edition, we accumulated more academic and intellectual debts than any acknowledgment can possibly repay. We wish to express our deep gratitude to all those who helped us in so many different ways. In particular, our heartfelt thanks go to the editor, Professor Zheng-sheng Zhang of San Diego State University; colleagues and friends at Beijing Language and Culture University; and Ms. Laurel Damashek at Cheng & Tsui.

As authors, we take great pleasure in the contributions that *IC* has made to Chinese teaching and learning over the past ten years, and we also feel the weight of responsibility. In retrospect, *IC* has traversed a long way since its earliest incarnation, yet we know its improvement will not end with the present edition. We promise to renew our efforts in the future, and we expect to continue to benefit from the invaluable comments and suggestions we receive from the users.

An Overview of the New Features of the Third Edition

Chapter Opener

Each lesson opens with an illustration that highlights the theme for the lesson.

LEARNING OBJECTIVES

In this lesson, you will learn to use Chinese to

- Name some popular sports;
- Talk about your exercise habits;
- Discuss your feelings about various sports;
- Make a simple comparison between how soccer and American football are played.

RELATE AND GET READY

In your own culture/community—

1. Do people exercise regularly?
2. Are most people sports fans? Which sports are most popular?
3. Are there many sports programs on TV?
4. Which is more popular, American football or soccer?

Learning Objectives for every lesson help students focus their study and envision what they will have accomplished at the end of the lesson.

The self-reflective questions in **Relate and Get Ready** help students to reflect on similarities and differences between their native language and culture and Chinese language and culture.

Dialogue Design

Each dialogue or narrative begins with an illustration depicting the scene. For the main characters, instead of the characters' names, their avatar icons appear in the dialogue. This helps the students get acquainted with the characters more quickly.

（今天是星期四，學生餐廳有中國菜，師傅是上海人。）

Language Notes and Grammar Callouts

（李友給王朋打電話。）

王朋，你做什麼呢①？

我看書呢。

今天高小音過生日①，晚上我們在她家開舞會，你能去嗎？

能去。幾點？

LANGUAGE NOTES

❶ Apart from 過生日 (guò shēngrì, to celebrate one's birthday), the verb 過 (guò, to live [a life]; to observe [a holiday]; to celebrate [a festival]) appears in many other expressions such as 過年 (guò nián, to celebrate the New Year), 過節 (guò jié, to celebrate a festival), and 過日子 (guò rìzi, to live one's life; to live from day to day).

The **Language Notes** are clearly marked and numbered in green circles, and placed next to the dialogue for ease of reference. The **grammar points** are highlighted and numbered in red to draw the students' attention to the language forms covered in the Grammar section of each lesson.

Vocabulary Section

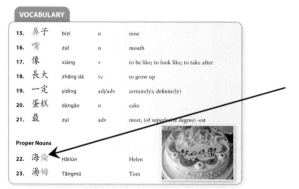

VOCABULARY

15.	鼻子	bízi	n	nose
16.	嘴	zuǐ	n	mouth
17.	像	xiàng	v	to be like; to look like; to take after
18.	長大	zhǎng dà	vc	to grow up
19.	一定	yídìng	adj/adv	certain(ly); definite(ly)
20.	蛋糕	dàngāo	n	cake
21.	最	zuì	adv	most, (of superlative degree) -est

Proper Nouns

| 22. | 海倫 | Hǎilún | | Helen |
| 23. | 湯姆 | Tāngmǔ | | Tom |

A low-frequency character that the teacher may decide not to have the students practice writing is shown in a shaded gray color.

Language Practice

A. Rules Are Rules

Parents and teachers always seem to have more rules for their children and students. Work with a partner and figure out what the rules are, based on the visuals.

EXAMPLE:

做功課的時候，不准/不能看電視。

Zuò gōngkè de shíhou, bù zhǔn/bù néng kàn diànshì.

1.

In addition to role plays and partner activities, this section also includes contextualized drill practice with the help of visual cues.

New sentence patterns are highlighted in blue.

A **Recap and Narrate** activity lets students practice summarizing the dialogues in their own words.

Customized Learning: How About You?

Beginning students need not be overwhelmed by additional vocabulary items that do not seem to be very useful or relevant to them. However, they should be given opportunities to select and learn words and phrases that relate to their own interests and experiences. **How About You?** provides this personalized vocabulary space.

Culture Highlights

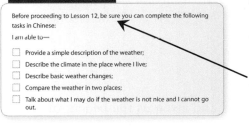

A theatrical scene from Beijing Opera

Photos or other authentic materials accompany the culture notes. In order to introduce students to the different varieties of Chinese around the globe, the textbook includes photos in both simplified and traditional characters.

Self-Reflection: Progress Checklist

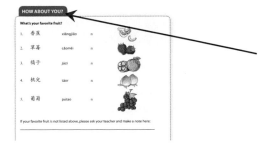

It's important for students to feel engaged and responsible for their own learning. At the end of each lesson, students are asked to check on their learning progress and evaluate whether they have achieved the learning objectives.

Functional Expressions: That's How the Chinese Say It!

After every five lessons, **That's How the Chinese Say It** provides a review of the functional expressions that have appeared in the texts. It includes additional linguistic and cultural contexts to demonstrate the use of these expressions.

Preface to the Second Edition

The *Integrated Chinese* series is an acclaimed, best-selling introductory course in Mandarin Chinese. With its holistic, integrated focus on the four language skills of listening, speaking, reading, and writing, it teaches all the basics beginning and intermediate students need to function in Chinese. *Integrated Chinese* helps students understand how the Chinese language works grammatically, and how to use Chinese in real life.

The Chinese title of *Integrated Chinese*, which is simply 中文聽說讀寫 (*Zhōngwén Tīng Shuō Dú Xiě*), reflects our belief that a healthy language program should be a well-balanced one. To ensure that students will be strong in all skills, and because we believe that each of the four skills needs special training, the exercises in the *Integrated Chinese* Workbooks are divided into four sections of listening, speaking, reading, and writing. Within each section, there are two types of exercises, namely, traditional exercises (such as fill-in-the-blank, sentence completion, translation, etc.) to help students build a solid foundation, and communication-oriented exercises to prepare students to face the real world.

How *Integrated Chinese* Has Evolved

Integrated Chinese (IC) began in 1993 as a set of course materials for beginning and intermediate Chinese courses taught at the East Asian Summer Language Institute's Chinese School at Indiana University. Since that time, it has become a widely used series of Chinese language textbooks in the United States and beyond. Teachers and students appreciate the fact that *IC*, with its focus on practical, everyday topics and its numerous and varied exercises, helps learners build a solid foundation in the Chinese language.

What's New in the Second Edition

Thanks to all those who have used *Integrated Chinese* and given us the benefit of their suggestions and comments, we have been able to produce a second edition that includes the following improvements:

▲ Typographical errors present in the first edition have been corrected, and the content has been carefully edited to ensure accuracy and minimize errors.

▲ The design has been revised and improved for easier use, and the Textbooks feature two colors.

▲ **Revised illustrations** and **new photos** provide the reader with visual images and relevant cultural information.

▲ Many **new culture notes** and examples of **functional expressions** have been added.

▲ **Grammar and phonetics explanations** have been rewritten in more student-friendly language.

▲ **Workbook listening and reading sections** have been revised.

▲ **A new flexibility for the teaching of characters** is offered. While we believe that students should learn to read all of the characters introduced in the lessons, we are aware that different Chinese programs have different needs. Some teachers may wish to limit the number of characters for which students have responsibility, especially in regards to writing requirements. To help such teachers, we have identified a number of lower-frequency Chinese characters and marked them with a pound sign (#) in the vocabulary lists. Teachers might choose to accept *pinyin* in place of these characters in homework and tests. The new edition adds flexibility in this regard.

▲ **The Level 1 Workbooks** have been reorganized. The Workbook exercises have been divided into two parts, with each part corresponding to one of the dialogues in each lesson. This arrangement will allow teachers to more easily teach the dialogues separately. They may wish to use the first two or three days of each lesson to focus on the first dialogue, and have students complete the exercises for the first dialogue. Then, they can proceed with the second dialogue, and have students complete the exercises for the second dialogue. Teachers may also wish to give separate quizzes on the vocabulary associated with each dialogue, thus reducing the number of new words students need to memorize at any one time.

▲ **Level 2 offers full text in simplified and traditional characters.** The original Level 2 Textbook and Workbook, which were intended to be used by both traditional- and simplified-character learners, contained sections in which only the traditional characters were given. This was of course problematic for students who were principally interested in learning simplified characters. This difficulty has been resolved in the new edition, as we now provide both traditional and simplified characters for every Chinese sentence in both the Textbook and the Workbook.

Basic Organizational Principles

In recent years, a very important fact has been recognized by the field of language teaching: the ultimate goal of learning a language is to communicate in that language.

Integrated Chinese is a set of materials that gives students grammatical tools and also prepares them to function in a Chinese language environment. The materials cover two years of instruction, with smooth transitions from one level to the next. They first cover everyday life topics and gradually move to more abstract subject matter. The materials are not limited to one method or one approach, but instead they blend several teaching approaches that can produce good results. Here are some of the features of *Integrated Chinese* which make it different from other Chinese language textbooks:

Integrating Pedagogical and Authentic Materials

All of the materials are graded in *Integrated Chinese*. We believe that students can grasp the materials better if they learn simple and easy-to-control language items before the more difficult or complicated ones. We also believe that students should be taught some authentic materials even in the first year of language instruction. Therefore, most of the pedagogical materials are actually simulated authentic materials. Real authentic materials (written by native Chinese speakers for native Chinese speakers) are incorporated in the lessons when appropriate.

Integrating Written Style and Spoken Style

One way to measure a person's Chinese proficiency is to see if s/he can handle the "written style" (書面語, shūmiànyǔ) with ease. The "written style" language is more formal and literal than the "spoken style" (口語, kǒuyǔ); however, it is also widely used in news broadcasts and formal speeches. Inaddition to "spoken style" Chinese, basic "written style" expressions are gradually introduced in *Integrated Chinese*.

Integrating Traditional and Simplified Characters

We believe that students should learn to handle Chinese language materials in both the traditional and the simplified forms. However, we also realize that it could be rather confusing and overwhelming to teach students both the traditional and the simplified forms from day one. A reasonable solution to this problem is for the student to concentrate on one form, either traditional or simplified, at the first level, and to acquire the other form during the second level. Therefore, for Level 1, *Integrated Chinese* offers two editions of the Textbooks and the Workbooks, one using traditional characters and one using simplified characters, to meet different needs.

We believe that by the second year of studying Chinese, all students should be taught to read both traditional and simplified characters. Therefore, the text of each lesson in Level 2 is shown in both forms, and the vocabulary list in each lesson also contains both forms. Considering that students in a second-year Chinese language class might come from different backgrounds and that some of them may have learned the traditional form and others the simplified form, students should be allowed to write in either traditional or simplified form. It is important that the learner write in one form only, and not a hybrid of both forms.

Integrating Teaching Approaches

Realizing that there is no one single teaching method which is adequate in training a student to be proficient in all four language skills, we employ a variety of teaching methods and approaches in *Integrated Chinese* to maximize the teaching results. In addition to the communicative approach, we also use traditional methods such as grammar-translation and direct method.

Online Supplements to Integrated Chinese

Integrated Chinese is not a set of course materials that employs printed volumes only. It is, rather, a network of teaching materials that exist in many forms. Teacher keys, software, and more are available from www.cheng-tsui.com, Cheng & Tsui Company's online site for downloadable and web-based resources. Please visit this site often for new offerings.

Other materials are available at the IC website, http://eall.hawaii.edu/yao/icusers/, which was set up by Ted Yao, one of the principal *Integrated Chinese* authors, when the original edition of *Integrated Chinese* was published. Thanks to the generosity of teachers and students who are willing to share their materials with other *Integrated Chinese* users, this website is constantly growing, and has many useful links and resources. The following are some of the materials created by the community of *Integrated Chinese* users that are available at the *Integrated Chinese* website.

▲ Links to resources that show how to write Chinese characters, provide vocabulary practice, and more.

▲ *Pinyin* supplements for all *Integrated Chinese* books. Especially useful for Chinese programs that do not teach Chinese characters.

▲ Teacher's resources.

About the Format

Considering that many teachers might want to teach their students how to speak the language before teaching them how to read Chinese characters, we decided to place the *pinyin* text before the Chinese-character text in each of the eleven lessons of the Level 1 Part 1 Textbook.

Since *pinyin* is only a vehicle to help students learn the pronunciation of the Chinese language and is not a replacement for the Chinese writing system, it is important that students can read out loud in Chinese by looking at the Chinese text and not just the *pinyin* text. To train students to deal with the Chinese text directly without relying on *pinyin*, we moved the *pinyin* text to the end of each lesson in the Level 1 Part 2 Textbook. Students can refer to the *pinyin* text to verify a sound when necessary.

We are fully aware of the fact that no two Chinese language programs are identical and that each program has its own requirements. Some schools will cover a lot of material in one year while some others will cover considerably less. Trying to meet the needs of as many schools as possible, we decided to cover a wide range of material, both in terms of vocabulary and grammar, in *Integrated Chinese*. To facilitate oral practice and to allow students to communicate in real-life situations, many supplementary vocabulary items are added to each lesson. However, the characters in the supplementary vocabulary sections are not included in the Character Workbooks. In the Character Workbooks, each of the characters is given a frequency indicator based on the *Hànyǔ Pínlǜ Dà Cídiǎn* (漢語頻率大辭典). Teachers can decide for themselves which characters must be learned.

Acknowledgments

Since publication of the first edition of *Integrated Chinese*, in 1997, many teachers and students have given us helpful comments and suggestions. We cannot list all of these individuals here, but we would like to reiterate our genuine appreciation for their help. We do wish to recognize the following individuals who have made recent contributions to the *Integrated Chinese* revision. We are indebted to Tim Richardson, Jeffrey Hayden, Ying Wang and Xianmin Liu for field-testing the new edition and sending us their comments and corrections. We would also like to thank Chengzhi Chu for letting us try out his "Chinese TA," a computer program designed for Chinese teachers to create and edit teaching materials. This software saved us many hours of work during the revision. Last, but not least, we want to thank Jim Dew for his superb professional editorial job, which enhanced both the content and the style of the new edition.

As much as we would like to eradicate all errors in the new edition, some will undoubtedly remain, so please continue to send your comments and corrections to editor@cheng-tsui.com, and accept our sincere thanks for your help.

Scope and Sequence

Lessons	Topics & Themes	Sections & Contexts	Learning Objectives & Functions
11	Talking about the Weather	1. Tomorrow's Weather Will Be Even Better! 2. The Weather Here Is Awful!	1. Employ basic terms for weather patterns and phenomena 2. Describe simple weather changes 3. Compare the weather of two places 4. Talk about what you may do in nice or bad weather 5. Present a simple weather forecast
12	Dining	1. Dining Out 2. Eating in a Cafeteria	1. Ask if there are seats available in a restaurant 2. Order Chinese dishes 3. Tell the waiter your dietary preferences and restrictions 4. Ask the restaurant to recommend dishes 5. Rush your order 6. Pay for your meal 7. Get the correct change after your payment
13	Asking Directions	1. Where Are You Off To? 2. Going to Chinatown	1. Ask for and give directions 2. Identify locations by using landmarks as references 3. Describe whether two places are close to or far away from one another 4. State where you are heading and the purpose of going there
14	Birthday Party	1. Let's Go to a Party! 2. Attending a Birthday Party	1. Ask a friend to go to a party with you 2. Suggest things to take to a get-together 3. Offer someone a ride and arrange a time and place to meet 4. Thank people for their gifts 5. Describe a duration of time 6. Talk about the year of your birth and your Chinese zodiac sign 7. Give a simple description of someone's facial features
15	Seeing a Doctor	1. My Stomachache Is Killing Me! 2. Allergies	1. Talk about basic symptoms of a cold 2. Describe common symptoms of allergies 3. Understand and repeat instructions on when and how often to take medications 4. Talk about why you do or don't want to see the doctor 5. Urge others to see a doctor when they are not feeling well
That's How the Chinese Say It!			Review functional expressions from Lessons 11–15

Forms & Accuracy	Culture Highlights
1. Comparative Sentences with 比 (bǐ) (I) 2. The Particle 了 (le) (III) 3. The Modal Verb 會 (huì, will) (II) 4. Adj+(一)點兒 ({yì} diǎnr) 5. The Adverb 又 (yòu, again) 6. Adj/V + 是 (shì) + Adj/V, + 可是/但是… (kěshì/dànshì…)	Temperature scale in China Climate conditions in China Western place names in Chinese Internet bars in China
1. 一…也/都…不/沒… (yì…yě/dōu…bù/méi) 2. Adverb 多/少 (duō/shǎo) + V 3. 剛 (gāng) vs 剛才 (gāngcái) 4. Resultative Complements (I) 5. 好 (hǎo) as a Resultative Complement 6. Reduplication of Adjectives 7. The Verb 來 (lái)	Principal cuisines in China Staple foods on the Chinese menu Food culture in China Western fast food in China
1. Direction and Location Words 2. Comparative Sentences with 沒(有) (méi{yǒu}) 3. 那麼 (nàme) Indicating Degree 4. 到 (dào) + Place + 去 (qù) + Action 5. The Dynamic Particle 過 (guo) 6. Reduplication of Verbs 7. Resultative Complements (II) 8. 一…就… (yī…jiù…, as soon as…then…)	Greetings in Chinese Traffic lights in China Terms for spoken and written Chinese
1. 呢 (ne) Indicating an Action in Progress 2. Verbal Phrases and Subject-Predicate Phrases Used as Attributives 3. Time Duration 4. Sentences with 是…的 (shì…de) 5. 還 (hái, still) 6. 又…又… (yòu…yòu…, both…and…)	Dinner parties in China Singing karaoke in China Gift giving in China Chinese zodiac signs
1. 死 (sǐ) Indicating an Extreme Degree 2. Times of Actions 3. 起來 (qi lai) indicating the Beginning of an Action 4. 把 (bǎ) Construction (I) 5. The Preposition 對 (duì) 6. 越來越… (yuè lái yuè…) 7. 再説 (zàishuō)	Medicine in China Outpatient visits in China Medical insurance in China
1. 在 (zài, to exist) 2. Complimentary Expressions 3. 怎麼了 (Zěnme le? What's the matter? What's wrong?) 4. 糟糕 (zāogāo, [It's] awful/What a mess)	

Lessons	Topics & Themes	Sections & Contexts	Learning Objectives & Functions
16	Dating	1. Seeing a Movie 2. Turning Down an Invitation	1. Describe how long you've known someone 2. Invite someone to go on a date 3. Make the necessary arrangements to go out with friends 4. Accept a date courteously 5. Decline a date politely 6. End a phone conversation without hurting the other person's feelings
17	Renting an Apartment	1. Finding a Better Place 2. Calling about an Apartment for Rent	1. Describe your current and ideal living quarters 2. Name common pieces of furniture 3. State how long you have been living at your current residence 4. Comment briefly on why a place is or isn't good for someone 5. Discuss and negotiate rent, utilities, and security deposits
18	Sports	1. My Gut Keeps Getting Bigger and Bigger! 2. Watching American Football	1. Name some popular sports 2. Talk about your exercise habits 3. Discuss your feelings about various sports 4. Make a simple comparison between how soccer and American football are played
19	Travel	1. Traveling to Beijing 2. Planning an Itinerary	1. Talk about your plans for summer vacation 2. Describe what kind of city Beijing is 3. Describe your travel itinerary 4. Ask for discounts, compare airfares and routes, and book an airplane ticket 5. Ask about seat assignments and request meal accommodations based on your dietary restrictions or preferences
20	At the Airport	1. Checking In at the Airport 2. Arriving in Beijing	1. Check in at the airport 2. Wish departing friends a safe journey and remind them to keep in touch 3. Greet guests at the airport 4. Compliment someone on his or her language ability 5. Ask about someone's health 6. Remind people to move on to the next event
That's How the Chinese Say It!			Review functional expressions from Lessons 16–20

Forms & Accuracy	Culture Highlights
1. Descriptive Complements (II) 2. Potential Complements 3. 就 (jiù) 4. Directional Complements (II)	Dating in China Valentine's Day in China Turning down a date the Chinese way Nightlife in China
1. Verb + 了 (le) + Numeral + Measure Word + Noun + 了 (le) 2. 連···都/也 (lián...dōu/yě) 3. Potential Complements with Verb + 不下 (bú xià) 4. 多 (duō) Indicating an Approximate Number 5. Question Pronouns with 都/也 (dōu/yě)	College dorms in China Renting an apartment in China Raising pets in China
1. Duration of Non-Action 2. 好/難 (hǎo/nán) + V 3. 下去 (xia qu) Indicating Continuation 4. Duration of Actions 5. The Particle 著 (zhe) 6. 被/叫/讓 (bèi/jiào/ràng) in Passive-Voice Sentences	"Putting on weight" in China "Football" in China Morning exercises in China TV channels in China
1. 不得了 (bù déliǎo, extremely) 2. Question Pronouns as Indefinite References (Whoever, Whatever, etc.) 3. Numbers over One Thousand 4. Comparative Sentences with 比 (bǐ) (II)	Travel agencies in China Travel season in China
1. 的 (de), 得 (de), 地 (de) Compared 2. ···的時候 (...de shíhou) and ···以後 (...yǐhòu) Compared 3. 還 (hái) + Positive Adjective 4. Kinship Terms	Domestic flights in China Beijing Roast Duck in Chinese food culture
1. 一言為定 (yì yán wéi dìng, it's a deal; it's decided) 2. "Good," "Very good," "Excellent," "Extraordinary" 3. Greetings and Farewells	

Abbreviations of Grammatical Terms

adj	adjective
adv	adverb
conj	conjunction
interj	interjection
m	measure word
mv	modal verb
n	noun
nu	numeral
p	particle
pn	proper noun
pr	pronoun
prefix	prefix
prep	preposition
qp	question particle
qpr	question pronoun
t	time word
v	verb
vc	verb plus complement
vo	verb plus object

Cast of Characters

Back Row:

Mr. Fei:

費先生

Owen Fields, Gao Xiaoyin's high school classmate.

Gao Wenzhong:

高文中

Winston Gore, an English student. His parents work in the United States. He says he enjoys singing and dancing. He is also a big fan of Chinese cooking. He has a secret crush on Bai Ying'ai.

Gao Xiaoyin:

高小音

Jenny Gore, Winston's older sister. She has already graduated from college, and is now a school librarian.

Wang Peng:

王朋

A Chinese freshman from Beijing. He has quickly adapted to American college life and likes to play and watch sports.

Helen:

海倫

Gao Wenzhong's cousin. She has a one-year-old son, Tom.

Li You:

李友

Amy Lee, an American student from New York State. She and Wang Peng meet each other on the first day of classes and soon become good friends.

Front Row:

Bai Ying'ai:

白英愛

Baek Yeung Ae, a friendly outgoing Korean student from Seoul. She finds Wang Peng very "cool" and very "cute".

Wang Hong:

王紅

Wang Peng's younger sister. She is preparing to attend college in America.

Wang Peng's parents:

王朋的父母

From Beijing, in their late forties.

Chang laoshi:

常老師

(Chang Xiaoliang): Originally from China, in her forties. Chang Laoshi has been teaching Chinese in the United States for ten years.

LESSON 11

Talking about the Weather

 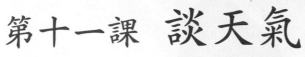

第十一課　談天氣

Dì shíyī kè　Tán tiānqì

11

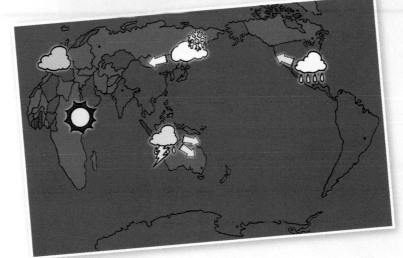

◆ LEARNING OBJECTIVES

In this lesson, you will learn to use Chinese to

• Employ basic terms for weather patterns and phenomena;
• Describe simple weather changes;
• Compare the weather of two places;
• Talk about what you may do in nice or bad weather;
• Present a simple weather forecast.

◆ RELATE AND GET READY

In your own culture/community—

1. What is the typical weather in spring, summer, autumn, and winter?
2. Where do people get information about weather?
3. What weather-related outdoor sports are popular, if any?
4. How do people feel about rain or snow?

Dialogue I: Tomorrow's Weather Will Be Even Better!

(Gao Xiaoyin is looking out the window.)

  今天天氣比^① 昨天好，不下雪了^②。

我約了朋友明天去公園滑冰，不知道天氣會^③怎麼樣？

我剛才看了網上的天氣預報，明天天氣比今天更好。不但不會下雪，而且^❶ 會暖和一點兒^④。

是嗎？太好了！

LANGUAGE NOTES

❶ In a sentence with the 不但 (búdàn)···，而且 (érqiě)··· (not only…, but also…) structure, the conjunction 而且 (érqiě) in the second clause is generally required, while the conjunction 不但 (búdàn) in the first clause is optional.

你約了誰去滑冰？

白英愛。

你約了白英愛？可是她今天早上坐飛機去紐約了。

真的啊？那我明天怎麼辦？

你還是在家看碟❷吧！

❷ 碟 (dié) means a small plate or something that resembles a small plate. It is now often used to refer to DVDs. The phrase 看碟 (kàn dié) thus means to watch a movie or TV series on DVD.

Jīntiān tiānqì bǐ① zuótiān hǎo, bú xià xuě le②.

Wǒ yuē le péngyou míngtiān qù gōngyuán huá bīng, bù zhīdào tiānqì huì③ zěnmeyàng?

Wǒ gāngcái kàn le wǎng shang de tiānqì yùbào, míngtiān tiānqì bǐ jīntiān gèng hǎo. Búdàn bú huì xià xuě, érqiě❶ huì nuǎnhuo yì diǎnr④.

Shì ma? Tài hǎo le!

Nǐ yuē le shéi qù huá bīng?

Bái Yīng'ài.

Nǐ yuē le Bái Yīng'ài? Kěshì tā jīntiān zǎoshang zuò fēijī qù Niǔyuē le.

Zhēn de a? Nà wǒ míngtiān zěnmebàn?

Nǐ háishi zài jiā kàn dié❷ ba!

VOCABULARY

1.	天氣	tiānqì	n	weather
2.	比	bǐ	prep/v	(comparison marker); to compare [See Grammar 1.]
3.	下雪	xià xuě	vo	to snow
4.	約	yuē	v	to make an appointment
5.	公園	gōngyuán	n	park
6.	滑冰	huá bīng	vo	to ice skate
7.	會	huì	mv	will [See Grammar 3.]
8.	剛才	gāngcái	t	just now; a moment ago
9.	網上	wǎng shang		on the internet
10.	預報	yùbào	v	to forecast

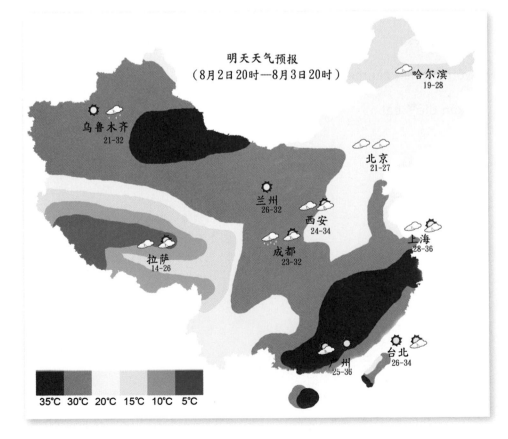

天氣預報
tiānqì yùbào

VOCABULARY

11.	更	gèng	adv	even more
12.	不但⋯，而且⋯	búdàn..., érqiě...	conj	not only..., but also...
13.	暖和	nuǎnhuo	adj	warm
14.	冷	lěng	adj	cold
15.	辦	bàn	v	to handle; to do
16.	碟	dié	n	disc; small plate, dish, saucer

世界主要城市天气

城市	天气	气温(℃)	城市	天气	气温(℃)
华盛顿	☀	33/21	新德里	☁	36/28
纽约	☀	31/21	德黑兰	☀	36/26
芝加哥	☁	30/20	莫斯科	☁	23/15
洛杉矶	☁	25/18	圣彼得堡	☁	23/15
旧金山	☁	21/13	伊斯坦布尔	☁	30/22
温哥华	☀	23/13	雅典	☁	35/22
蒙特利尔	☀	28/18	布拉格	☁	22/7
多伦多	☀	30/17	日内瓦	☁	26/14
阿卡波克	☁	23/12	法兰克福	☀	23/9
巴西利亚	☁	17/11	柏林	☁	21/10
里约热内卢	☁	21/16	慕尼黑	☁	23/8
布宜诺斯艾利斯	☁	13/5	巴黎	☀	23/12
圣地亚哥	☁	14/4	里昂	☀	29/20
东京	☁	29/11	都柏林	☀	22/12
曼谷	☁	34/26	伦敦	☁	23/11
新加坡	☁	30/25	斯德马尔摩	☁	22/13

紐約今天會不會下雪？
Niǔyuē jīntiān huì bú huì xià xuě?

Grammar

1. Comparative Sentences with 比 (bǐ) (I)

Specific comparison of two entities is usually expressed with the basic pattern

A + 比 (bǐ) + B + Adj

 李友比她大姐高。

Lǐ Yǒu bǐ tā dàjiě gāo.

(Li You is taller than her oldest sister.)

❷ 今天比昨天冷。

Jīntiān bǐ zuótiān lěng.

(Today is colder than yesterday.)

❸ 第十課的語法比第九課的語法容易。

Dì shí kè de yǔfǎ bǐ dì jiǔ kè de yǔfǎ róngyì.

(Lesson Ten's grammar is easier than Lesson Nine's grammar.)

There are two ways in which the basic comparative construction may be further modified: a) by adding a modifying expression after the adjective:

A + 比 (bǐ) + B + Adj + 一點兒/得多/多了 (yì diǎnr/de duō/duō le)

❹ 今天比昨天冷一點。

Jīntiān bǐ zuótiān lěng yì diǎn.

(Today is a bit colder than yesterday.)

(4a) *今天比昨天一點兒冷。

*Jīntiān bǐ zuótiān yì diǎnr lěng.

 明天會比今天冷得多。

Míngtiān huì bǐ jīntiān lěng de duō.

(Tomorrow will be much colder than today.)

❻   紐約比這兒冷多了/冷得多。

Niǔyuē bǐ zhèr lěng duō le/lěng de duō.

(New York is much colder than here.)

Note that the modifying expression must be placed after the adjective, not before it.

(6a) *紐約比這兒很冷。

*Niǔyuē bǐ zhèr hěn lěng.

"Much colder" is 冷多了 (lěng duō le) or 冷得多 (lěng de duō), not 很冷 (hěn lěng, very cold).

b) by adding the adverb 更 (gèng) or the adverb 還 (hái) in front of the adjective:

A + 比 (bǐ) + B + 更/還 (gèng/hái) + Adj

❼   昨天冷，今天比昨天更冷/今天比昨天還冷。

Zuótiān lěng, jīntiān bǐ zuótiān gèng lěng/jīntiān bǐ zuótiān hái lěng.

(Yesterday was cold. Today is even colder than yesterday.)

跟 (gēn) and 和 (hé) can be used in another type of comparative sentence:

A 跟/和 B（不）一樣 + Adj (A gēn/hé B {bù} yíyàng + Adj)

However, unlike a comparative sentence with 比 (bǐ), a comparative sentence with 跟 (gēn) or 和 (hé) only indicates whether two things or persons exhibit the same degree of an attribute, without specifying which of the two exhibits it to a greater or lesser degree.

Compare (8a) with (8b) and (8c) with (8d).

❽ **a:** 這個教室和那個教室一樣大。

Zhè ge jiàoshì hé nà ge jiàoshì yíyàng dà.

(This classroom and that classroom are the same size.)

b: 這個教室跟那個教室不一樣大。

Zhè ge jiàoshì gēn nà ge jiàoshì bù yíyàng dà.

(This classroom and that classroom are not the same size.)

c: 這個教室比那個教室大。

Zhè ge jiàoshì bǐ nà ge jiàoshì dà.

(This classroom is larger than that classroom.)

d: 這個教室比那個教室大得多。

Zhè ge jiàoshì bǐ nà ge jiàoshì dà de duō.

(This classroom is much larger than that classroom.)

---

2. The Particle 了 (le) (III): 了 as a Sentence-Final Particle
[See also Grammar 5 in Lesson 5 and Grammar 5 in Lesson 8.]

When 了 (le) occurs at the end of a sentence, it usually indicates a change of status or the realization of a new situation.

 下雪了。

Xià xuě le.

(It's snowing now.)

 妹妹累了。

Mèimei lèi le.

(My sister has become tired.)

 我昨天沒有空兒，今天有空兒了。

Wǒ zuótiān méiyǒu kòngr, jīntiān yǒu kòngr le.

(I didn't have time yesterday, but I do today.)

❹ 你看，公共汽車來了。

Nǐ kàn, gōnggòng qìchē lái le.

(Look, the bus is here.)

When used in this sense, 了 (le) can still be used at the end of a sentence even if the sentence is in the negative.

 我沒有錢了，不買了。

Wǒ méiyǒu qián le, bù mǎi le.

(I don't have any money [left]. I won't buy it anymore.)

Remember that to negate 有 (yǒu, to have), one uses 沒 (méi), not 不 (bù).

3. The Modal Verb 會 (huì, will) (II) [See also Grammar 9 in Lesson 8.]

會 (huì) indicates an anticipated event or action.

 白老師現在不在辦公室，可是他明天會在。

Bái lǎoshī xiànzài bú zài bàngōngshì, kěshì tā míngtiān huì zài.

(Teacher Bai is not in the office now, but he will be tomorrow.)

❷ A: 你明年做什麼？

Nǐ míngnián zuò shénme?

(What will you do next year?)

B: 我明年會去英國學英文。

Wǒ míngnián huì qù Yīngguó xué Yīngwén.

(I'll go to Britain to learn English next year.)

 他說他晚上會給你發短信。

Tā shuō tā wǎnshang huì gěi nǐ fā duǎnxìn.

(He said he will send you a text message this evening.)

The negative form of 會 (huì) is 不會 (bú huì):

 小王覺得不舒服，今天不會來滑冰了。

Xiǎo Wáng juéde bù shūfu, jīntiān bú huì lái huá bīng le.

(Little Wang is not feeling well. He won't come ice skating today after all.)

 她這幾天特別忙，晚上不會去聽音樂會。

Tā zhè jǐ tiān tèbié máng, wǎnshang bú huì qù tīng yīnyuèhuì.

(She is very busy these days. She won't be going to the concert tonight.)

❻ 天氣預報說這個週末不會下雪。

Tiānqì yùbào shuō zhè ge zhōumò bú huì xià xuě.

(The weather forecast says that it won't snow this weekend.)

4. Adj+（一）點兒 ({yì} diǎnr)

The expression （一）點兒 ({yì} diǎnr) can be placed after an adjective to indicate slight qualification. 一 (yī) is optional.

❶ 前幾天我很不高興，昨天考試考得很好，我
    高興點兒了。

Qián jǐ tiān wǒ hěn bù gāoxìng, zuótiān kǎo shì kǎo de hěn hǎo, wǒ gāoxìng diǎnr le.

(I was very unhappy a few days ago. I did very well on the exam yesterday. I am a little bit happier now.)

❷ 我妹妹比我姐姐高一點兒。

Wǒ meìmei bǐ wǒ jiějie gāo yì diǎnr.

(My younger sister is a bit taller than my older sister.)

❸ 你得快點兒，看電影要晚了。

Nǐ děi kuài diǎnr, kàn diànyǐng yào wǎn le.

(You'd better pick up the pace a bit, or you'll be late for the movie.)

❹ 今天比昨天冷點兒。

Jīntiān bǐ zuótiān lěng diǎnr.

(Today is a bit colder than yesterday.)

❺ 老師，請您說話說得慢一點兒。

Lǎoshī, qǐng nín shuō huà shuō de màn yì diǎnr.

(Teacher, would you please speak a little bit more slowly?)

（一）點兒 (yì diǎnr) does not precede the adjective. The following sentences are therefore incorrect:

(2a) *我妹妹比我姐姐一點兒高。

*Wǒ meìmei bǐ wǒ jiějie yì diǎnr gāo.

(4a) *今天比昨天一點兒冷。

*Jīntiān bǐ zuótiān yì diǎnr lěng.

(5a) *老師，請您說話說得一點兒慢。

*Lǎoshī, qǐng nín shuō huà shuō de yì diǎnr màn.

Language Practice

A. Let's Compare

a. Shopping for Shoes

You are helping a friend decide between two pairs of shoes. Please compare their colors, styles, and prices.

size: 8 $90   size: 8.5 $100

b. Blind Date

You are out on a blind date. Your date is telling you his/her preferences, and would like to know yours. Let's see how compatible you and your date are.

EXAMPLE: **Your date**

    >

好吃 (hǎochī, good to eat; delicious)

我覺得美國菜比中國菜好吃。你呢？

Wǒ juéde Měiguó cài bǐ Zhōngguó cài hǎochī. Nǐ ne?

1.   >   好喝   hǎohē (delicious to drink)

2.   >   難   nán

3.   >   慢   màn

B. Healthy Lifestyle Choices

Little Zhang decided to change his old habits in order to lead a healthier lifestyle. Let's see how he does things differently these days.

EXAMPLE:

past

present

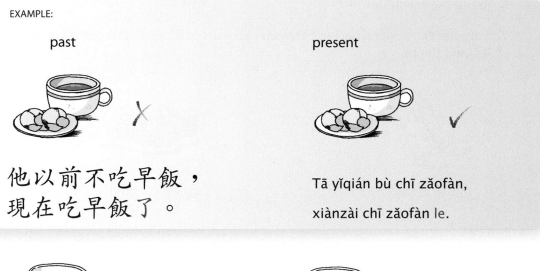

他以前不吃早飯，
現在吃早飯了。

Tā yǐqián bù chī zǎofàn,

xiànzài chī zǎofàn le.

1.

2.

3.

C. Are You a Fan?

If you are a fan of Wang Peng, Li You, Bai Ying'ai, or Gao Wenzhong, and you know everything about them, what will you say when others ask questions about them? Let's practice using the structure 不但···而且··· (búdàn…érqiě…).

EXAMPLE:

Someone asks

A: 王朋帥嗎？ 高   Wáng Péng shuài ma?   gāo

You, as a fan, will answer

B: 王朋不但很帥，   Wáng Péng búdàn hěn shuài,
而且很高。   érqiě hěn gāo.

Someone asks

A: 王朋喜歡看球嗎？   Wáng Péng xǐhuan kàn qiú ma?

You, as a fan, will answer

B: 王朋不但喜歡看球，   Wáng Péng búdàn xǐhuan kàn qiú,
而且喜歡打球。   érqiě xǐhuan dǎ qiú.

1.

A: 高文中高嗎？ 帥   Gāo Wénzhōng gāo ma?   shuài

B:

A: 高文中喜歡
唱歌嗎？

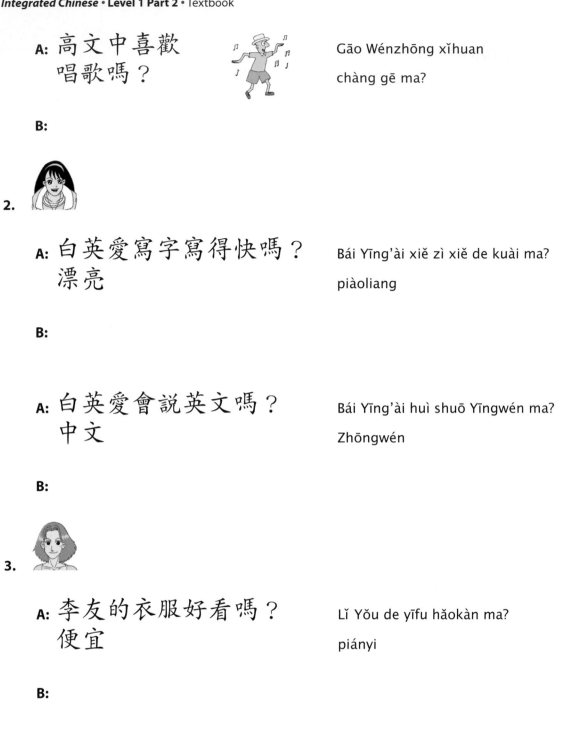

Gāo Wénzhōng xǐhuan

chàng gē ma?

B:

2.

A: 白英愛寫字寫得快嗎？
漂亮

Bái Yīng'ài xiě zì xiě de kuài ma?

piàoliang

B:

A: 白英愛會說英文嗎？
中文

Bái Yīng'ài huì shuō Yīngwén ma?

Zhōngwén

B:

3.

A: 李友的衣服好看嗎？
便宜

Lǐ Yǒu de yīfu hǎokàn ma?

piányi

B:

A: 李友常常復習生詞
語法嗎？
預習

Lǐ Yǒu chángcháng fùxí shēngcí

yǔfǎ ma?

yùxí

B:

D. Giving a Weather Report

Look at the illustrations and give simple descriptions of the weather possibilities for each city tomorrow.

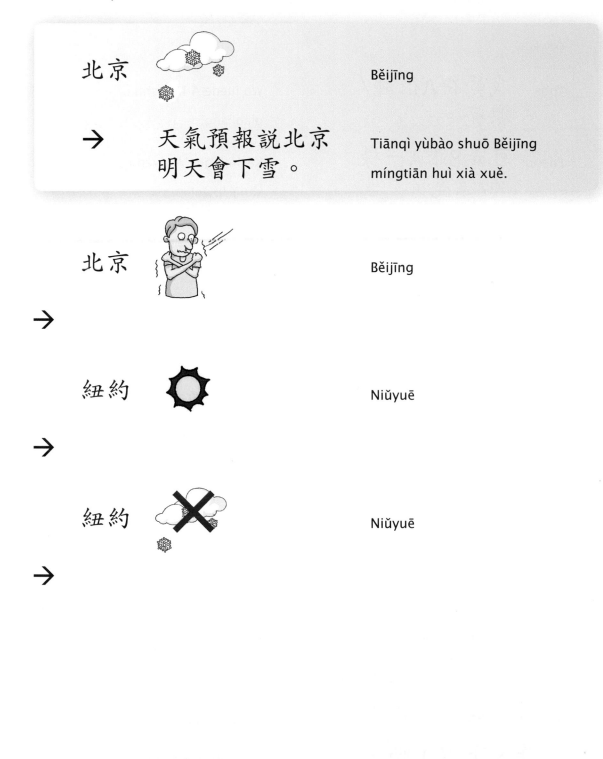

北京　　　　　　　　　　　　　　　Běijīng

→　　天氣預報説北京　　　Tiānqì yùbào shuō Běijīng
　　　明天會下雪。　　　　míngtiān huì xià xuě.

北京　　　　　　　　　　　　　　　Běijīng

→

紐約　　　　　　　　　　　　　　　Niǔyuē

→

紐約　　　　　　　　　　　　　　　Niǔyuē

→

E. Dating Dilemma

You can't make up your mind: "Who should I go out with, A or B?" A has numerous good qualities. Your friend points out that B at least equals A, if not in fact surpasses A. Or your friend reminds you that B trumps A in some other way.

EXAMPLE:

You:	我覺得A很帥/漂亮。	Wǒ juéde A hěn shuài/piàoliang.
Friend:	可是B跟A一樣帥/漂亮。	Kěshì B gēn A yíyàng shuài/piàoliang.
	不，不，不，B比A帥/漂亮多了。	Bù, bù, bù, B bǐ A shuài/piàoliang duō le.

Possible attributes to consider:

1. 高   1. gāo

2. 錢   多   2. qián duō

3. 學習   好   3. xuéxí   hǎo

4. 打球打得好   4. dǎ qiú dǎ de hǎo

All considered:

＿＿＿＿比＿＿＿好。   ＿＿＿ bǐ ＿＿＿ hǎo.

F. Recap and Narrate

Working with a partner, recap the content of Dialogue I:

1. 昨天的天氣好不好？   1. Zuótiān de tiānqì hǎo bù hǎo?

2. 昨天下雪了嗎？   2. Zuótiān xià xuě le ma?

3. 今天的天氣好嗎？
   明天呢？

3. Jīntiān de tiānqì hǎo ma?
   Míngtiān ne?

4. 高文中約了誰去
   公園滑冰？

4. Gāo Wénzhōng yuē le shéi qù
   gōngyuán huá bīng?

5. 白英愛能跟高文中
   去滑冰嗎？為什麼？

5. Bái Yīng'ài néng gēn Gāo
   Wénzhōng qù huá bīng ma?
   Wèishénme?

6. 高小音讓高文中
   明天做什麼？

6. Gāo Xiǎoyīn ràng Gāo
   Wénzhōng   míngtiān zuò
   shénme?

Using the words and phrases in blue as prompts, connect your answers above to form a narrative like this example:

現在是冬天，昨天下雪了，今天的天氣比昨天好，不下雪了。天氣預報說明天的天氣更好，不但不會下雪，而且會暖和一點兒。高文中很高興，因為他約了白英愛去公園滑冰。可是高小音告訴他，白英愛今天早上坐飛機去紐約了。高文中不知道。他問高小音他明天怎麼辦？高小音讓他在家看碟。

Xiànzài shì dōngtiān, zuótiān xià xuě le, jīntiān de tiānqì bǐ zuótiān hǎo, bú xià xuě le. Tiānqì yùbào shuō míngtiān de tiānqì gèng hǎo, búdàn bú huì xià xuě, érqiě huì nuǎnhuo yì diǎnr. Gāo Wénzhōng hěn gāoxìng, yīnwèi tā yuē le Bái Yīng'ài qù gōngyuán huá bīng. Kěshì Gāo Xiǎoyīn gàosù tā, Bái Yīng'ài jīntiān zǎoshang zuò fēijī qù Niǔyuē le. Gāo Wénzhōng bù zhīdào. Tā wèn Gāo Xiǎoyīn tā míngtiān zěnmebàn? Gāo Xiǎoyīn ràng tā zài jiā kàn dié.

Dialogue II: The Weather Here Is Awful!

（高文中在網上找白英愛聊天兒。）

英愛，紐約那麼好玩兒，你怎麼在網上，沒出去？

這兒的天氣非常糟糕。

怎麼了？❶

昨天下大雨，今天又⑤下雨了。

這個週末這兒天氣很好，你快一點兒回來吧。

這個週末紐約也會暖和一點兒。我下個星期有一個面試，還不能回去。

LANGUAGE NOTES

❶ 怎麼了？ (Zěnme le?) is a question that may be asked upon encountering an unusual situation.

我在加州找了一個工作，你也去吧。加州冬天不冷，夏天不熱，春天和秋天更舒服。

 加州好是好⑥，可是我更喜歡紐約。

(Gāo Wénzhōng zài wǎng shang zhǎo Bái Yīng'ài liáo tiānr.)

 Yīng'ài, Niǔyuē nàme hǎowánr, nǐ zěnme zài wǎng shang, méi chū qu?

 Zhèr de tiānqì fēicháng zāogāo.

 Zěnme le?❶

 Zuótiān xià dà yǔ, jīntiān yòu⑤ xià yǔ le.

 Zhè ge zhōumò zhèr tiānqì hěn hǎo, nǐ kuài yì diǎnr huí lai ba.

 Zhè ge zhōumò Niǔyuē yě huì nuǎnhuo yì diǎnr. Wǒ xià ge xīngqī yǒu yí ge miànshì, hái bù néng huí qu.

 Wǒ zài Jiāzhōu zhǎo le yí ge gōngzuò, nǐ yě qù ba. Jiāzhōu dōngtiān bù lěng, xiàtiān bú rè, chūntiān hé qiūtiān gèng shūfu.

 Jiāzhōu hǎo shì hǎo⑥, kěshì wǒ gèng xǐhuan Niǔyuē.

VOCABULARY

1.	那麼	nàme	pr	(indicating degree) so, such
2.	好玩兒	hǎowánr	adj	fun, amusing, interesting
3.	出去	chū qu	vc	to go out
4.	非常	fēicháng	adv	very, extremely, exceedingly
5.	糟糕	zāogāo	adj	in a terrible mess; how terrible
6.	下雨	xià yǔ	vo	to rain
7.	又	yòu	adv	again [See Grammar 5.]

VOCABULARY

8.	面試	miànshì	v/n	to interview; interview
9.	回去	huí qu	vc	to go back; to return
10.	冬天	dōngtiān	n	winter
11.	夏天	xiàtiān	n	summer
12.	熱	rè	adj	hot
13.	春天	chūntiān	n	spring
14.	秋天	qiūtiān	n	autumn; fall
15.	舒服	shūfu	adj	comfortable

Proper Nouns

| 16. | 加州 | Jiāzhōu | | California |

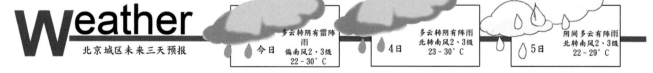

這是哪個城市的天氣預報？
Zhè shì nǎ ge chéngshì de tiānqì yùbào?

Grammar

5. The Adverb 又 (yòu, again)

又 (yòu, again) indicates recurrence of an action.

 昨天早上下雪，今天早上又下雪了。

Zuótiān zǎoshang xià xuě, jīntiān zǎoshang yòu xià xuě le.

(It snowed yesterday morning. It snowed again this morning.)

❷ 媽媽上個星期給我打電話，這個星期又給我打電話了。

Māma shàng ge xīngqī gěi wǒ dǎ diànhuà, zhè ge xīngqī yòu gěi wǒ dǎ
diànhuà le.

(My mom called me last weekend. She called me again this weekend.)

❸ 他昨天復習了第八課的語法，今天又復習了。

Tā zuótiān fùxí le dì bā kè de yǔfǎ, jīntiān yòu fùxí le.

(He reviewed the grammar in Lesson Eight yesterday, and he reviewed it again
today.)

Both 又 (yòu, again) and 再 (zài, again) indicate repetition of an action, but in a
sentence with 又 (yòu, again), usually both the original action and the repetition
occurred in the past, whereas 再 (zài, again) indicates an anticipated repetition of
an action in general.

❹ 我上個週末去跳舞了，昨天我又去跳舞了。

Wǒ shàng ge zhōumò qù tiào wǔ le, zuótiān wǒ yòu qù tiào wǔ le.

(I went dancing last weekend. Yesterday I went dancing again.)

❺ 我昨天去跳舞了，我想明天晚上再去跳舞。

Wǒ zuótiān qù tiào wǔ le, wǒ xiǎng míngtiān wǎnshang zài qù tiào wǔ.

(I went dancing yesterday. I'm thinking of going dancing again tomorrow
night.)

> ## 6. Adj / V + 是 (shì) + Adj / V, + 可是/但是 … (kěshì/dànshì…)

Sentences in this pattern usually imply that the speaker accepts the validity of a certain point of view but wishes to offer an alternative perspective or emphasize a different aspect of the matter.

❶ **A:** 滑冰難不難？

Huá bīng nán bu nán?

(Is ice skating difficult?)

B: 滑冰難是難，可是很有意思。

Huá bīng nán shì nán, kěshì hěn yǒu yìsi.

(It *is* difficult, but it is very interesting.)

❷ **A:** 在高速公路上開車，你緊張嗎？

Zài gāosù gōnglù shang kāi chē, nǐ jǐnzhāng ma?

(Do you get nervous driving on the highway?)

B: 緊張是緊張，可是也很好玩兒。

Jǐnzhāng shì jǐnzhāng, kěshì yě hěn hǎowánr.

(I do get nervous, but I find it a lot of fun, too.)

❸ **A:** 明天學校開會，你去不去？

Míngtiān xuéxiào kāi huì, nǐ qù bu qù?

(There is a meeting at school tomorrow. Will you go?)

B: 我去是去，可是會晚一點兒。

Wǒ qù shì qù, kěshì huì wǎn yì diǎnr.

(I'll go, but I will be a little bit late.)

4 **A:** 你喜歡這張照片嗎？

Nǐ xǐhuan zhè zhāng zhàopiàn ma?

(Do you like this picture?)

B: 喜歡是喜歡，可是這張照片太小了。

Xǐhuan shì xǐhuan, kěshì zhè zhāng zhàopiàn tài xiǎo le.)

(I like it, but this picture is too small.)

This pattern can be used only when the adjective or verb in it has already been mentioned, e.g., 難 (nán) in (1), 緊張 (jǐnzhāng) in (2), 去 (qù) in (3), and 喜歡 (xǐhuan) in (4). In this regard, it is different from the pattern 雖然···可是/但是···(suīrán...kěshì/dànshì...).

Language Practice

G. Plan B

When you plan something and the weather does not cooperate, then what do you do? Ask and answer the following questions with your partner, and see if you can settle on an alternative.

EXAMPLE:

A: 我想出去玩兒，可是下雨了。

Wǒ xiǎng chū qu wánr, kěshì xià yǔ le.

B: 別出去了！還是在家看電視吧。

Bié chū qu le! Háishi zài jiā kàn diànshì ba.

1. **A:** 我想去買點兒東西，可是雪下得很大。

Wǒ xiǎng qù mǎi diǎnr dōngxi, kěshì xuě xià de hěn dà.

B: _____

2. **A:** 我想出去看朋友，可是天氣很糟糕。

Wǒ xiǎng chū qu kàn péngyou, kěshì tiānqì hěn zāogāo.

B: _____

3. A: 我想去公園打球，
但是太熱。

Wǒ xiǎng qù gōngyuán dǎ qiú,

dànshì tài rè.

B: _____

> ## H. Little Zhang's Routine

The following chart shows what Little Zhang did last week. Let's recap by using
又 (yòu).

Monday	Tuesday	Wednesday	Thursday	Friday	Saturday

EXAMPLE:

→ 小張星期一看碟，
星期五又看碟。

Xiǎo Zhāng xīngqīyī kàn dié,

xīngqīwǔ yòu kàn dié.

1.

 →

2.

 →

I. Two Sides to Every Coin

Things are rarely simple. Take turns reminding each other to consider another factor.

EXAMPLE:

| 加州 | 漂亮 | Jiāzhōu | piàoliang |

A: 加州很漂亮。

A: Jiāzhōu hěn piàoliang.

B: 加州漂亮是漂亮，可是東西太貴了。

B: Jiāzhōu piàoliang shì piàoliang, kěshì dōngxi tài guì le.

How about the following

1. 紐約   有意思   Niǔyuē   yǒu yìsi

2. 坐地鐵   便宜   zuò dìtiě   piányi

3. 坐公共汽車   慢   zuò gōnggòng qìchē   màn

4. 北京的冬天   下雪   Běijīng de dōngtiān   xià xuě

J. Beijing Weather

The following is a three-day weather forecast for Beijing. Give a report on which days the weather will be colder/warmer and how the weather will change, and compare it with the weather in your town.

next Monday   next Tuesday   next Wednesday

28°F   37°F   40°F

K. Recap and Narrate

Work with a partner, recap the content of Dialogue II:

1. 高文中説紐約
   好玩兒嗎？

2. 白英愛在紐約為什麼
   在房間裏上網，
   没出去？

3. 高文中為什麼讓
   白英愛週末快
   一點兒回學校？

4. 白英愛這個週末
   能回學校嗎？

5. 高文中在哪兒找了
   一個工作？

6. 高文中説那兒的天氣
   怎麼樣？

7. 白英愛覺得那兒
   怎麼樣？

1. Gāo Wénzhōng shuō Niǔyuē
   hǎowánr ma?

2. Bái Yīng'ài zài Niǔyuē wèishénme
   zài fángjiān li shàng wǎng,
   méi chū qu?

3. Gāo Wénzhōng wèishénme ràng
   Bái Yīng'ài zhōumò kuài
   yì diǎnr huí xuéxiào?

4. Bái Yīng'ài zhè ge zhōumò
   néng huí xuéxiào ma?

5. Gāo Wénzhōng zài nǎr zhǎo le
   yí ge gōngzuò?

6. Gāo Wénzhōng shuō nàr de tiānqì
   zěnmeyàng?

7. Bái Yīng'ài juéde nàr
   zěnmeyàng?

Using the words and phrases in blue as prompts, connect your answers above to form a narrative like this example:

紐約很好玩兒，可是那兒現在的天氣非常糟糕，昨天下大雨，今天又下大雨了。高文中說學校這兒週末的天氣很好，讓白英愛快一點兒回來。可是白英愛說紐約週末的天氣也會好一點兒，而且她下個星期有一個面試，還不能回去。高文中在加州找了一個工作，他告訴英愛加州的天氣很好，冬天不冷，夏天不熱，春天和秋天更舒服，希望白英愛也去加州。英愛說，加州好是好，可是她更喜歡紐約。

Niǔyuē hěn hǎowánr, kěshì nàr xiànzài de tiānqì fēicháng zāogāo, zuótiān xià dà yǔ, jīntiān yòu xià dà yǔ le. Gāo Wénzhōng shuō xuéxiào zhèr zhōumò de tiānqì hěn hǎo, ràng Bái Yīng'ài kuài yì diǎnr huí lai. Kěshì Bái Yīng'ài shuō Niǔyuē zhōumò de tiānqì yě huì hǎo yì diǎnr, érqiě tā xià gè xīngqī yǒu yí ge miànshì, hái bù néng huí qu. Gāo Wénzhōng zài Jiāzhōu zhǎo le yí ge gōngzuò, tā gàosù Yīng'ài Jiāzhōu de tiānqì hěn hǎo, dōngtiān bù lěng, xiàtiān bú rè, chūntiān hé qiūtiān gèng shūfu, xīwàng Bái Yīng'ài yě qù Jiāzhōu. Yīng'ài shuō, Jiāzhōu hǎo shi hǎo, kěshì tā gèng xǐhuan Niǔyuē.

HOW ABOUT YOU?

How's the weather where you are?

1.	潮濕	cháoshī	adj	wet; humid
2.	悶熱	mēnrè	adj	hot and stifling
3.	涼快	liángkuai	adj	pleasantly cool
4.	晴天	qíngtiān	n	sunny day
5.	陰天	yīntiān	n	overcast day
6.	風	fēng	n	wind

If there are other terms that you wish to use to describe the weather, please ask your teacher and make a note here:

Culture Highlights

❶ For measuring temperature, China uses the Celsius rather than the Fahrenheit system. For measuring length and weight, China uses the metric system, even though some people still use the old system. The basic unit of length in the old Chinese system is 里 (lǐ), which equals half a kilometer, or 0.311 mile. The basic unit of weight in the old Chinese system is 斤 (jīn), which equals half a kilogram, or 1.102 pounds.

❷ In China, the climatic conditions differ drastically from one part of the country to another. Generally speaking, just as in America, the north is cold and snowy in winter; the south, hot and wet in summer. Three cities, 重慶 (Chóngqìng), 武漢 (Wǔhàn), and 南京 (Nánjīng), are nicknamed "furnaces" for their notoriously hot temperatures in summer. Some other cities, such as 昆明 (Kūnmíng), are known for their year-round balmy weather. In the lower 長江 (Chángjiāng, the longest river in China, also known as the Yangtze) valley, there is a 黃梅 (huángméi, literally, yellow plum) season in May and June characterized by copious rain and high humidity. But the major rainy season for most of southern China is in July and August, when almost all the rivers swell to flood levels. In winter, the island of 海南 (Hǎinán) provides warmth and appealing resorts for tourists from the north, while many southerners brave the cold and pour into the northern city of 哈爾濱 (Hā'ěrbīn) for its annual exhibition of ice sculptures.

❸ Some Chinese names for Western places were invented by early Chinese immigrants, e.g., 舊金山 (Jiùjīnshān, literally, Old Gold Mountain) for San Francisco. But the vast majority of names for Western places are transliterations. Massachusetts, for instance, is transliterated as 麻薩諸塞 (Másàzhūsài), which is in turn abbreviated to 麻州 (Mázhōu), with the character 州 (zhōu) meaning "state." Similarly, California is transliterated as 加利福尼亞 (Jiālìfúníyà), which is often shortened to 加州 (Jiāzhōu).

❹ China now boasts more internet users than any other country. Many Chinese urbanites have residential internet access, but many youngsters prefer to use the internet at a type of commercial facility called 網吧 (wǎngbā, internet bar). As 網吧 (wǎngbā) provide not only internet access but also snacks and beverages, they are favorite social venues for these young internet users. One can easily locate a 網吧 (wǎngbā) in a commercial area in any Chinese city. In Taiwan, 網吧 (wǎngbā) is commonly known as 網咖 (wǎngkā).

English Text

Dialogue I

Gao Xiaoyin: Today's weather is better than yesterday's. It's not snowing anymore.

Gao Wenzhong: I asked a friend to go ice skating in the park tomorrow. I wonder what the weather is going to be like.

Gao Xiaoyin: I looked up the forecast on the internet. Tomorrow's weather will be even better than today. Not only will it not snow, it'll be a bit warmer, too.

Gao Wenzhong: Really? Fantastic!

Gao Xiaoyin: Whom did you ask to go ice skating?

Gao Wenzhong: Bai Ying'ai.

Gao Xiaoyin: You asked Bai Ying'ai? But she flew to New York this morning.

Gao Wenzhong: Really? Then what do I do tomorrow?

Gao Xiaoyin: Why don't you watch a DVD at home?

Dialogue II

(Gao Wenzhong is chatting with Bai Ying'ai online.)

Gao Wenzhong: Ying'ai, New York is so much fun. How come you're online and not out and about?

Bai Ying'ai: The weather here is awful.

Gao Wenzhong: How come?

Bai Ying'ai: Yesterday it poured. It rained again today.

Gao Wenzhong: The weather here is great this weekend. You'd better come back as soon as you can.

Bai Ying'ai: It's going to be warmer in New York this weekend. Next week I have an interview. I can't come back just yet.

Gao Wenzhong: I found a job in California. Go with me. It's not cold in the winter in California, or hot in the summer. Spring and fall are even more comfortable.

Bai Ying'ai: California is great, but I like New York more.

PROGRESS CHECKLIST

Before proceeding to Lesson 12, be sure you can complete the following tasks in Chinese:

I am able to—

- ☑ Provide a simple description of the weather;
- ☐ Describe the climate in the place where I live;
- ☐ Describe basic weather changes;
- ☐ Compare the weather in two places;
- ☐ Talk about what I may do if the weather is not nice and I cannot go out.

LESSON 12 **Dining**

第十二课 吃飯

Dì shí'èr kè   Chī fàn

LEARNING OBJECTIVES

In this lesson, you will learn to use Chinese to

- Ask if there are seats available in a restaurant;
- Order Chinese dishes;
- Tell the waiter your dietary preferences and restrictions;
- Ask the restaurant to recommend dishes;
- Rush your order;
- Pay for your meal;
- Get the correct change after your payment.

RELATE AND GET READY

In your own culture/community—

1. Do people order and eat their own dishes when dining out, or do they share their dishes with others?
2. Do people order hot or cold beverages to go with their meals?
3. Do people have their soup before or after their main dish?
4. How is being a vegetarian different from being a vegan?
5. How do most people pay for their meal: in cash, with a credit card, or by check?
6. Do people typically get a receipt after paying for a meal?

Dialogue I: Dining Out

（在飯館兒）

請進，請進。

人怎麼這麼❶多？好像一個位
子都① 沒有了。

服務員❷，請問，還有沒有位
子？

有，有，有。那張桌子沒有
人。

＊　＊　＊

兩位想吃點兒什麼？

王朋，你點菜吧。

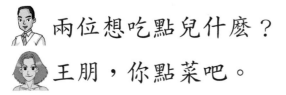

LANGUAGE NOTES

❶ In Beijing, 這麼 (zhème) is commonly pronounced as zème.

❷ In a restaurant, one may address a staff member, either male or female, as 服務員 (fúwùyuán, waiter). In Beijing, however, some customers would address a young waiter as 小夥子 (xiǎohuǒzi, young man) and a young waitress as 小妹 (xiǎomèi, lit., little sister), while some older or middle-aged people would call a young waitress 姑娘 (gūniang, girl; miss). In Taiwan, it is proper to address a waiter as 先生 (xiānsheng) and a waitress as 小姐 (xiǎojiě).

好。先給我們兩盤餃子，要素的。

除了餃子以外，還要什麼？

李友，你說呢？

還要一盤家常豆腐，不要放肉，我吃素。

我們的家常豆腐沒有肉。

還要兩碗酸辣湯③，請別放味精，少② 放點兒鹽。有小白菜嗎？

對不起，小白菜剛③賣完④。

那就不要青菜了。

那喝點兒④ 什麼呢？

我要一杯冰茶。李友，你喝什麼？

我很渴，請給我一杯可樂，多放點兒冰。

好，兩盤餃子，一盤家常豆腐，兩碗酸辣湯，一杯冰茶，一杯可樂，多放冰。還要別的嗎？

不要別的了，這些夠⑤了。服務員，我們都餓了，請上菜快一點兒。

沒問題，菜很快就能做好⑤。

❸ Nouns for containers or vessels such as 碗 (wǎn, bowl), 杯 (bēi, cup/glass), and 盤 (pán, plate/dish) can serve as measure words, e.g., 一碗飯 (yì wǎn fàn, a bowl of rice), 一杯水 (yì bēi shuǐ, a glass of water), and 一盤餃子 (yì pán jiǎozi, a plate of dumplings).

❹ 點兒 (diǎnr) here is the abbreviated form of 一點兒 (yì diǎnr). When used to modify nouns, (一) 點兒 ({yì} diǎnr) can soften the tone and therefore make the sentence more polite.

❺ As an adjective, 夠 (gòu) functions only as a predicate, and never as an attributive before nouns. Thus one says 我的錢不夠 (wǒ de qián bú gòu, my money is not enough), but never *我没有夠錢 (*wǒ méi yǒu gòu qián).

(Zài fànguǎnr)

Qǐng jìn, qǐng jìn.

Rén zěnme zhème❶ duō? Hǎoxiàng yí ge wèizi dōu① méiyǒu le.

Fúwùyuán❷, qǐng wèn, hái yǒu méiyǒu wèizi?

Yǒu, yǒu, yǒu. Nà zhāng zhuōzi méiyǒu rén.

*　*　*

Liǎng wèi xiǎng chī diǎnr shénme?

Wáng Péng, nǐ diǎn cài ba.

Hǎo. Xiān gěi wǒmen liǎng pán jiǎozi, yào sù de.

Chúle jiǎozi yǐwài, hái yào shénme?

Lǐ Yǒu, nǐ shuō ne?

Hái yào yì pán jiācháng dòufu, bú yào fàng ròu, wǒ chī sù.

Wǒmen de jiācháng dòufu méiyǒu ròu.

Hái yào liǎng wǎn suānlàtāng❸, qǐng bié fàng wèijīng, shǎo② fàng diǎnr yán. Yǒu xiǎo báicài ma?

Duìbuqǐ, xiǎo báicài gāng③ mài wán④.

Nà jiù bú yào qīngcài le.

Nà hē diǎnr④ shénme ne?

Wǒ yào yì bēi bīngchá. Lǐ Yǒu, nǐ hē shénme?

Wǒ hěn kě, qǐng gěi wǒ yì bēi kělè, duō fàng diǎnr bīng.

Hǎo, liǎng pán jiǎozi, yì pán jiācháng dòufu, liǎng wǎn suānlàtāng, yì bēi bīngchá, yì bēi kělè, duō fàng bīng. Hái yào bié de ma?

Bú yào bié de le, zhè xiē gòu❺ le. Fúwùyuán, wǒmen dōu è le, qǐng shàng cài kuài yì diǎnr.

Méi wèntí, cài hěn kuài jiù néng zuò hǎo⑤.

VOCABULARY

1.	飯館（兒）	fànguǎn(r)	n	restaurant
2.	好像	hǎoxiàng	v	to seem; to be like
3.	位子	wèizi	n	seat
4.	服務員	fúwùyuán	n	waiter; attendant
	服務	fúwù	v	to serve; to provide service
5.	桌子	zhuōzi	n	table
6.	點菜	diǎn cài	vo	to order food
7.	盤	pán	n	plate; dish
8.	餃子	jiǎozi	n	dumplings (with vegetable and/or meat filling)
9.	素	sù	adj	vegetarian; made from vegetables
10.	家常	jiācháng	n	home-style
11.	豆腐	dòufu	n	tofu; bean curd
12.	放	fàng	v	to put; to place
13.	肉	ròu	n	meat
14.	碗	wǎn	n	bowl
15.	酸辣湯	suānlàtāng	n	hot and sour soup
	酸	suān	adj	sour
	辣	là	adj	spicy; hot
	湯	tāng	n	soup
16.	味精	wèijīng	n	monosodium glutamate (MSG)
17.	鹽	yán	n	salt
18.	白菜	báicài	n	bok choy

VOCABULARY

19.	剛	gāng	adv	just [See Grammar 3.]
20.	賣完	mài wán	vc	to be sold out [See Grammar 4.]
	完	wán	c	finished
21.	青菜	qīngcài	n	green/leafy vegetable
22.	冰茶	bīngchá	n	iced tea
	冰	bīng	n	ice
23.	渴	kě	adj	thirsty
24.	些	xiē	m	(measure word for an indefinite amount); some
25.	夠	gòu	adj	enough
26.	餓	è	adj	hungry
27.	上菜	shàng cài	vo	to serve food

這麼多青菜！
Zhème duō qīngcài!

青菜
qīngcài

牛肉
niúròu
(beef, see
Dialogue II)

餃子
jiǎozi

豆腐
dòufu

Grammar

---

1. 一···也/都···不/没··· (yì...yě/dōu...bù/méi)

These structures are used to form an emphatic negation meaning "not at all" or "not even one."

A. Subject + 一(yī) + Measure Word + Object + 也/都(yě/dōu) + 不/没 (bù/méi) + Verb

    小李一個朋友也沒有。

Xiǎo Lǐ yí ge péngyou yě méiyǒu.

(Little Li does not have a single friend.)

    爸爸今天一杯茶都沒喝。

Bàba jīntiān yì bēi chá dōu méi hē.

(My father didn't have a single cup of tea today.)

B. Topic + Subject + 一 **(yī) + Measure Word +** 也/都**(yě/dōu)**
+ 不/没 **(bù/méi) + Verb**

 這些襯衫我一件也不喜歡。

Zhè xiē chènshān wǒ yí jiàn yě bù xǐhuan.

(I don't like any of these shirts.)

❹ 哥哥的鞋，弟弟一雙都不能穿。

Gēge de xié, dìdi yì shuāng dōu bù néng chuān.

(The younger brother cannot wear any of his older brother's shoes.)

C. Subject + 一點兒 **(yì diǎnr) + Object +** 也/都 **(yě/dōu) +** 不/没 **(bù/méi) +**
Verb

 他去了商店，可是一點兒東西也没買。

Tā qù le shāngdiàn, kěshì yì diǎnr dōngxi yě méi mǎi.

(He went to the store, but he didn't buy anything at all.)

❻ 媽媽做菜一點兒味精都不放。

Māma zuò cài yì diǎnr wèijīng dōu bú fang.

(Mom doesn't use any MSG in her cooking.)

If the noun after 一 (yī) is countable, a proper measure word should be
used between 一 (yī) and the noun, as in (1), (2), (3), and (4). If the noun is
uncountable, the phrase 一點兒 (yì diǎnr) is usually used instead, as in (5) and
(6).

The following sentences are incorrect:

(1a) *小李没有一個朋友。

*Xiǎo Lǐ méiyǒu yí ge péngyou.

(3a) *這些襯衫我不喜歡一件。

*Zhè xiē chènshān wǒ bù xǐhuan yí jiàn.

(5a) *他東西没買一點兒。

*Tā dōngxī méi mǎi yì diǎnr.

The construction 一點兒 (yìdiǎnr) + 也/都 (yě/dōu) + 不 (bù/méi) can also be used before an adjective to express emphatic negation.

 這兒的冬天一點兒也不冷。

Zhèr de dōngtiān yì diǎnr yě bù lěng.

(Winter here is not cold at all.)

 那個學校一點兒也不漂亮。

Nà ge xuéxiào yì diǎn yě bú piàoliang.

(That school is not pretty at all.)

 這杯冰茶一點兒都不好喝。

Zhè bēi bīngchá yì diǎnr dōu bù hǎohē.

(This glass of iced tea doesn't taste good at all.)

2. Adverb 多/少 (duō/shǎo) + V

多 (duō) and 少 (shǎo) are two adjectives whose usage is rather unusual. To express the idea of doing something "more" or "less," one places 多 (duō) or 少 (shǎo) before the verb.

❶ 爸爸告訴媽媽做菜的時候少放鹽，多放點兒糖。

Bàba gàosu māma zuò cài de shíhou shǎo fàng yán, duō fàng diǎnr táng.

(Dad asked Mom to add less salt and more sugar when she cooks.)

❷ 上中文課得多説中文，少説英文。

Shàng Zhōngwén kè děi duō shuō Zhōngwén, shǎo shuō Yīngwén.

(In Chinese class, one should speak more Chinese and less English.)

This "多/少 (duō/shǎo) + verb" construction can sometimes denote a deviation from the correct amount or number.

 你多找了我一塊錢。

Nǐ duō zhǎo le wǒ yí kuài qián.

(You gave me one dollar too many.)

❹ 老師說要寫五十個字，我寫了四十五個，少
寫了五個。

Lǎoshī shuō yào xiě wǔshí ge zì, wǒ xiě le sìshíwǔ ge, shǎo xiě le wǔ ge.

(The teacher told us to write fifty characters. I wrote forty-five. I was five short.)

---

3. 剛 (gāng) vs. 剛才 (gāngcái)

As an adverb, 剛 (gāng) denotes that the action or change in situation took place in the most recent past.

❶ 我哥哥剛從中國來，一個朋友都沒有。

Wǒ gēge gāng cóng Zhōngguó lái, yí ge péngyou dōu méiyǒu.

(My older brother just came from China. He doesn't have a single friend here.)

❷ 我剛洗完澡，舒服極了。

Wǒ gāng xǐ wán zǎo, shūfu jí le.

(I just showered, and feel so great.)

剛才 (gāngcái) is a noun that refers to the time shortly before the act of speaking.

❸ **A:** 你知道王朋在哪兒嗎？

Nǐ zhīdào Wáng Péng zài nǎr ma?

(Do you know where Wang Peng is?)

B: 他剛才在這兒，我不知道他去哪兒了。

Tā gāngcái zài zhèr, wǒ bù zhīdao tā qù nǎr le.

(He was here a moment ago. I don't know where he went.)

❹ 弟弟剛才吃了十五個餃子，喝了兩碗
酸辣湯。

Dìdi gāngcái chī le shíwǔ ge jiǎozi, hē le liǎng wǎn suānlàtāng.

(My younger brother finished fifteen dumplings and two bowls of hot and sour soup a moment ago.)

Although 剛 (gāng) and 剛才 (gāngcái) are similar in meaning, they are classified as different parts of speech and are therefore used differently.

a. 剛 (gāng) can be followed by an expression that indicates the duration of time.

 他剛走了兩天。

Tā gāng zǒu le liǎng tiān.

(He left only two days ago.)

*他剛才走了兩天。

*Tā gāng cái zǒu le liǎng tiān.

Unlike 剛才 (gāngcái), 剛 (gāng) cannot be followed by the negation words 不 (bù) or 没 (méi).

 A: 你剛才為什麼没说？

Nǐ gāngcái wèishénme méi shuō?

(Why didn't you say it a moment ago?)

*你剛為什麼没说？

*Nǐ gāng wèishénme méi shuō?

B: 我剛才不想说。

Wǒ gāngcái bù xiǎng shuō.

(I didn't want to say it a moment ago.)

*我剛不想说。

*Wǒ gāng bù xiǎng shuō.

b. A sentence that includes 剛才 (gāngcái) often ends with 了 (le), but a sentence including 剛 (gāng) cannot have 了 (le) at the end.

❼ A: 你剛才去哪兒了？老師要你去辦公室找他。

Nǐ gāngcái qù nǎr le? Lǎoshī yào nǐ qù bàngōngshì zhǎo tā.

(Where were you a moment ago? The teacher wanted you to go to his office.)

B:　我剛才去圖書館了。

Wǒ gāngcái qù túshūguǎn le.

(I went to the library.)

8 A:　明天的考試你開始準備了嗎？

Míngtiān de kǎo shì nǐ kāishǐ zhǔnbèi le ma?

(Have you started preparing for tomorrow's test?)

B:　剛開始準備。

Gāng kāishǐ zhǔnbèi.

(I just got started.)

*剛開始準備了。

*Gāng kāishǐ zhǔnbèi le.

4. Resultative Complements (I)

Following a verb, an adjective or another verb can be used to denote the result of the action, hence the term resultative complement.

❶　小白菜賣完了。

Xiǎo báicài mài wán le.

(Baby bok choy is sold out.)

❷　你找錯錢了。

Nǐ zhǎo cuò qián le.

(You gave me the incorrect change.)

❸　那個人是誰你看清楚了嗎?

Nà ge rén shì shéi nǐ kàn qīngchu le ma?

(Did you see clearly who that person was?)

[清楚 qīngchu, clear: see Dialogue II]

太好了，這個字你寫對了。

Tài hǎo le, zhè ge zì nǐ xiě duì le.

(Great! You wrote this character correctly.)

Generally, the negative form of a resultative complement is formed by placing 没 (méi, no, not) or 没有 (méiyǒu, have not) before the verb.

 小白菜還没賣完。

Xiǎo báicài hái méi mài wán.

(Baby bok choy is not sold out yet.)

⑥ 那個人我没看清楚。

Nà ge rén wǒ méi kàn qīngchu.

(I didn't see clearly who that person was.)

⑦ 糟糕，這個字你没有寫對。

Zāogāo, zhè ge zì nǐ méiyǒu xiě duì.

(Shoot! You didn't write this character correctly.)

Following certain verbs, the use of an adjective as the resultative complement is not random. In those cases, it is advisable to take the combination of the verb and the complement as a whole unit.

5. 好 (hǎo) as a Resultative Complement

好 (hǎo) can serve as a complement following a verb, indicating the completion of an action. It often indicates readiness to start the next action or event.

 飯做好了，快來吃吧。

Fàn zuò hǎo le, kuài lái chī ba.

(The food is ready. Come and eat.)

 功課做好了，我要睡覺了。

Gōngkè zuò hǎo le, wǒ yào shuì jiào le.

(My homework is done. I want to go to bed.)

❸ 衣服我已經幫你買好了，明天晚會你就可以
穿了。

Yīfu wǒ yǐjīng bāng nǐ mǎi hǎo le, míngtiān wǎnhuì nǐ jiù kěyǐ chuān le.

(I've already bought the dress for you. You can wear it for the party tomorrow night.)

Language Practice

A. Picky Shopper

Your boyfriend/girlfriend is hard to please. You take him/her shopping. As it turns out, he/she doesn't like any of the items in the shopping center. Tell your friends what happened.

EXAMPLE:

→ 那兒的襯衫他/她一件都
不喜歡，一件都没買。 Nàr de chènshān tā yí jiàn dōu bù xǐhuan, yí jiàn dōu méi mǎi.

1.

2.

3.

4.

5.

B. How Was Your Day?

Today is not Wang Peng's lucky day. He rode the wrong bus, wore the wrong clothes, and did the wrong homework. But Li You had a great day today. She understood what the teacher said, finished her homework, and saw her good friend Bai Ying'ai.

Let's recap what happened to Wang Peng and Li You.

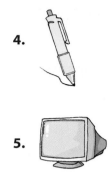

EXAMPLE: (rode the wrong bus)

王朋今天坐錯車了。   Wáng Péng jīntiān zuò cuò chē le.

1. _____

2. _____

1. _____

2. _____

3. _____

C. Ready, Set, Go!

Suppose you have a Chinese test tomorrow. Express your readiness by saying that you have completed all of the following actions.

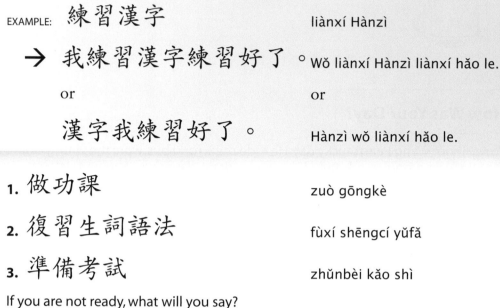

EXAMPLE: 練習漢字   liànxí Hànzì

→ 我練習漢字練習好了。 Wǒ liànxí Hànzì liànxí hǎo le.

or

or

漢字我練習好了。 Hànzì wǒ liànxí hǎo le.

1. 做功課   zuò gōngkè

2. 復習生詞語法   fùxí shēngcí yǔfǎ

3. 準備考試   zhǔnbèi kǎo shì

If you are not ready, what will you say?
Ask the classmate next to you if he/she is ready.

D. Course Evaluation

The following is a wish list of a Chinese language teacher who hopes his students can change some of their habits. As a Chinese language student, powwow with your partner and come up with your own list of what you would like your teacher to do differently.

老師希望學生：   Lǎoshī xīwàng xuésheng:

多來上課   duō lái shàng kè

多預習課文   duō yùxí kèwén

多聽錄音   duō tīng lùyīn

多復習生詞語法   duō fùxí shēngcí yǔfǎ

多練習寫漢字   duō liànxí xiě Hànzì

少說英文   shǎo shuō Yīngwén

少玩兒   shǎo wánr

學生希望老師：

Xuésheng xīwàng lǎoshī:

_____

_____

_____

_____

E. Recap and Narrate

Working with a partner, recap the content of Dialogue I:

1. 王朋和李友到飯館兒的時候，那兒的人多嗎？

1. Wáng Péng hé Lǐ Yǒu dào fànguǎnr de shíhou, nàr de rén duō ma?

2. 李友讓王朋點菜，他點了些什麼？

2. Lǐ Yǒu ràng Wáng Péng diǎn cài, tā diǎn le xiē shénme?

3. 李友點了些什麼？

3. Lǐ Yǒu diǎn le xiē shénme?

4. 服務員説他們的家常豆腐有肉嗎？

4. Fúwùyuán shuō tāmen de jiācháng dòufu yǒu ròu ma?

5. 李友點酸辣湯的時候，跟服務員説了什麼？

5. Lǐ Yǒu diǎn suānlàtāng de shíhou, gēn fúwùyuán shuō le shénme?

6. 王朋和李友點青菜了嗎？

6. Wáng Péng hé Lǐ Yǒu diǎn qīngcài le ma?

7. 王朋和李友要喝什麼？

7. Wáng Péng hé Lǐ Yǒu yào hē shénme?

8. 李友為什麼要服務員上菜快一點兒？

8. Lǐ Yǒu wèishénme yào fúwùyuán shàng cài kuài yì diǎnr?

Using the words and phrases in blue as prompts, connect your answers above to form a narrative like this example:

王朋和李友去一家中國飯館兒吃飯，飯館兒的人很多。王朋先點了兩盤素餃子，李友點了一盤家常豆腐，她告訴服務員家常豆腐不要放肉，因為她吃素。除了餃子和家常豆腐以外，他們還點了兩碗酸辣湯。服務員問他們喝點兒什麼，王朋要了一杯冰茶，李友要了一杯可樂，還告訴服務員多放一點兒冰。因為他們都餓了，所以讓服務員上菜快一點兒。服務員說沒問題，菜很快就能做好。

Wáng Péng hé Lǐ Yǒu qù yì jiā Zhōngguó fànguǎnr chī fàn, fànguǎnr de rén hěn duō. Wáng Péng xiān diǎn le liǎng pán sù jiǎozi, Lǐ Yǒu diǎn le yì pán jiācháng dòufu, tā gàosù fúwùyuán jiācháng dòufu bú yào fàng ròu, yīnwèi tā chī sù. Chúle jiǎozi hé jiācháng dòufu yǐwài, tāmen hái diǎn le liǎng wǎn suānlàtāng. Fúwùyuán wèn tāmen hē diǎnr shénme, Wáng Péng yào le yì bēi bīngchá, Lǐ Yǒu yào le yì bēi kělè, hái gàosù fúwùyuán duō fàng yì diǎnr bīng. Yīnwèi tāmen dōu è le, suǒyǐ ràng fúwùyuán shàng cài kuài yì diǎnr. Fúwùyuán shuō méi wèntí, cài hěn kuài jiù néng zuò hǎo.

一盤餃子
yì pán jiǎozi

Dialogue II: Eating in a Cafeteria

（今天是星期四，學生餐廳有中國菜，師傅是上海人。）

師傅❶，請問今天晚飯有什麼好吃的？

我們今天有糖醋魚，甜甜的⑥、酸酸的，好吃極了❷，你買一個吧。

好。今天有沒有紅燒牛肉？

沒有。你已經要魚了，別吃肉了。來⑦個涼拌黃瓜吧？

好。再來一碗米飯。一共多少錢？

糖醋魚，四塊五，涼拌黃瓜，一塊七；一碗米飯，五毛錢。一共六塊七。

LANGUAGE NOTES

❶ 師傅 (shīfu, master worker) is a common term to address a stranger, especially a blue-collar worker such as a taxi driver or a chef.

❷ When used after an adjective or a verb, 極了 (jí le) usually indicates the superlative degree: 今天熱極了。 (Jīntiān rè jí le, it is extremely hot today.) 他高興極了。 (Tā gāoxìng jí le, he is overjoyed.)

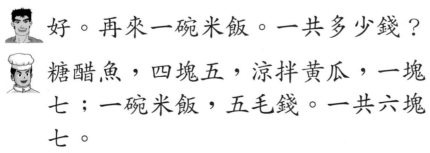

師傅，糟糕，我忘了帶飯卡了。這是十塊錢。

找你三塊三。

師傅，錢你找錯了，多找了我一塊錢。

對不起，我沒有看清楚。

沒關係③。

下個星期四再來。

好，再見。

(Jīntiān shì xīngqīsì, xuéshēng cāntīng yǒu Zhōngguó cài, shīfu shì Shànghǎi rén.)

Shīfu①, qǐng wèn jīntiān wǎnfàn yǒu shénme hàochī de?

Wǒmen jīntiān yǒu tángcùyú, tián tián de⑥, suān suān de, hǎochī jí le②, nǐ mǎi yí ge ba.

Hǎo. Jīntiān yǒu méiyǒu hóngshāo niúròu?

Méiyǒu. Nǐ yǐjīng yào yú le, bié chī ròu le. Lái⑦ ge liángbàn huánggua ba?

Hǎo. Zài lái yì wǎn mǐfàn. Yígòng duōshao qián?

Tángcùyú, sì kuài wǔ, liángbàn huánggua, yí kuài qī; Yì wǎn mǐfàn, wǔ máo qián. Yígòng liù kuài qī.

Shīfu, zāogāo, wǒ wàng le dài fànkǎ le. Zhè shì shí kuài qián.

Zhǎo nǐ sān kuài sān.

Shīfu, qián nǐ zhǎo cuò le, duō zhǎo le wǒ yí kuài qián.

Duìbuqǐ, wǒ méiyǒu kàn qīngchu.

Méi guānxi.③

Xià ge xīngqīsì zài lái.

Hǎo, zàijiàn.

學生在學生餐廳點菜。
Xuésheng zài xuéshēng cāntīng diǎn cài.

VOCABULARY

1.	師傅	shīfu	n	master worker
2.	好吃	hǎochī	adj	delicious
3.	糖醋魚	tángcùyú	n	fish in sweet and sour sauce
	糖	táng	n	sugar
	醋	cù	n	vinegar
4.	甜	tián	adj	sweet
5.	酸	suān	adj	sour
6.	極	jí	adv	extremely
7.	紅燒	hóngshāo	v	to braise in soy sauce

VOCABULARY

8.	牛肉	niúròu	n	beef
	牛	niú	n	cow; ox
9.	魚	yú	n	fish
10.	涼拌	liángbàn	v	(of food) cold "blended"; cold tossed
11.	黄瓜	huánggua	n	cucumber
12.	米飯	mǐfàn	n	cooked rice
13.	忘	wàng	v	to forget
14.	帶	dài	v	to bring; to take; to carry; to come with
15.	飯卡	fànkǎ	n	meal card
16.	錯	cuò	adj	wrong
17.	清楚	qīngchu	adj	clear
18.	没關係	méi guānxi		it doesn't matter

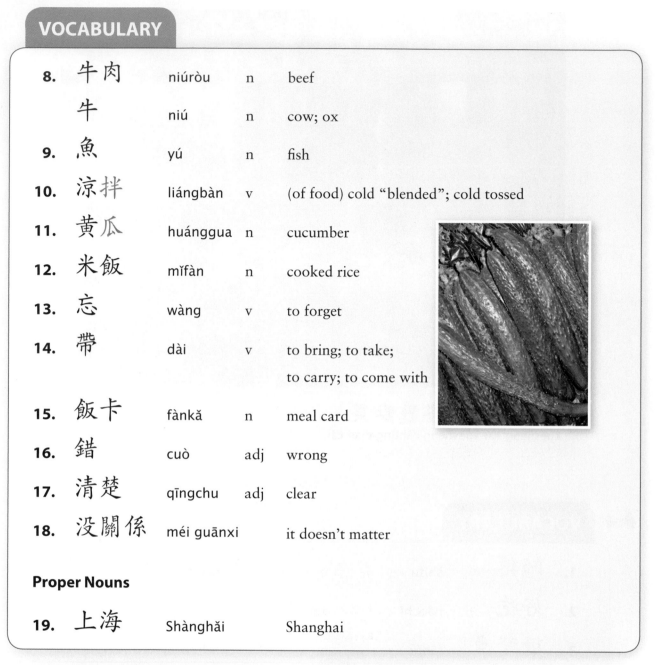

Proper Nouns

19.	上海	Shànghǎi	Shanghai

上海 Shànghǎi

學生食堂就是學生餐廳。
Xuéshēng shítáng jiù shì xuéshēng cāntīng.

Grammar

6. Reduplication of Adjectives

Some Chinese adjectives can be reduplicated. When monosyllabic adjectives are reduplicated, the accent usually falls on the second occurrence. When the reduplicated monosyllabic adjective takes a "r" suffix, like 慢慢兒 (màn mānr, slow), its second occurrence is usually pronounced in the first tone, regardless what the adjective's original tone is. Reduplication of adjectives often suggests an approving and appreciative attitude on the speaker's part.

 王朋高高的，很帥。
Wáng Péng gāo gāo de, hěn shuài.
(Wang Peng is tall and handsome.)

 可樂涼涼的，很好喝。
Kělè liáng liáng de, hěn hǎo hē.
(The cola is nicely chilled and tastes good.)

 酸辣湯酸酸的、辣辣的，非常好喝。
Suānlà tāng suān suān de, là là de, fēicháng hǎo hē.
(The hot and sour soup is a bit sour and a bit hot; it tastes great.)

Reduplication of adjectives usually does not appear in the negative form.

7. The Verb 來 (lái)

In colloquial expressions, the verb 來 (lái) can serve as a substitute for certain verbs, mostly in imperative sentences:

1 ：先生，你們想吃點兒什麼？

Xiānsheng, nǐmen xiǎng chī diǎnr shénme?

(Sir, what would you like?)

：來一盤糖醋魚，一碗酸辣湯，和一碗米飯。

Lái yì pán tángcùyú, yì wǎn suānlàtāng, hé yì wǎn mǐfàn.

(Give me a plate of sweet and sour fish, a bowl of hot and sour soup, and a bowl of rice, please.)

2 (At a party, when someone has sung a song)
再來一個！

Zài lái yí ge!

(Encore!)

The use of 來 (lái) in this sense is rather limited. It is usually used in restaurants and stores, especially when buying small things or coaxing someone to sing a song.

Language Practice

F. Special of the Day

Pretend that you are a waiter in a restaurant; you need to recommend and promote your dishes/drinks to the customers. Let's see how enthusiastic you can be.

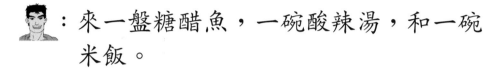

EXAMPLE:

→ 我們的青菜好吃極了。Wǒmen de qīngcài hǎochī jí le.

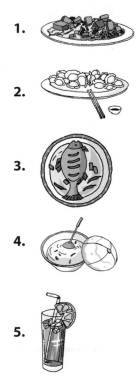

1.
2.
3.
4.
5.

G. Placing Your Order

G. Placing Your Order

Imagine that you are in a restaurant in China, and the waiter is asking you what you want to have. The easiest way to place your order in a Chinese restaurant is by using 來 (lái). Let's practice.

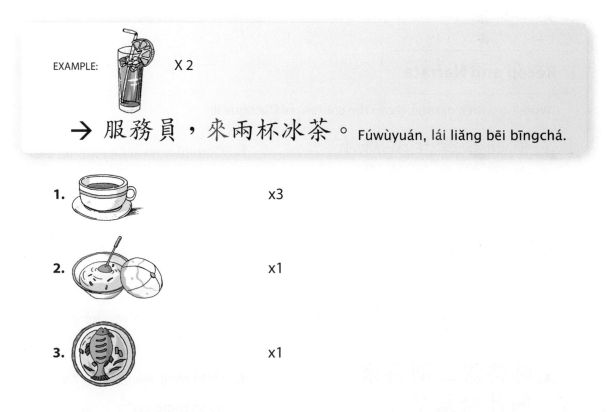

EXAMPLE: X 2

→ 服務員，來兩杯冰茶。Fúwùyuán, lái liǎng bēi bīngchá.

1.   x3

2.   x1

3.   x1

4.   x2

5.   x2

H. Special Requests

Tell the waitperson that you have special dietary requirements and ask that the chef not use certain ingredients. Make sure to use 一···也/都不···(yī...yě/dōu bù...) in your request.

> EXAMPLE: salt
>
> → 我不吃鹽，請師傅   Wǒ bù chī yán, qǐng shīfu
>   一點兒鹽都不要/別放。 yì diǎnr yán dōu bú yào/bié fàng.

1. MSG
2. meat
3. vinegar
4. sugar

I. Recap and Narrate

Working with a partner, recap the content of Dialogue II:

1. 星期幾學生餐廳有中國菜？師傅是哪兒人？

1. Xīngqījǐ xuéshēng cāntīng yǒu Zhōngguó cài? Shīfù shì nǎr rén?

2. 師傅告訴王朋今天有什麼好吃的？

2. Shīfu gàosù Wáng Péng jīntiān yǒu shénme hàochī de?

3. 今天有沒有紅燒牛肉？

3. Jīntiān yǒu méiyǒu hóngshāo niúròu?

4. 師傅讓王朋再來個什麼菜？

4. Shīfu ràng Wáng Péng zài lái ge shénme cài?

5. 王朋要米飯了嗎？

6. 王朋一共花了
多少錢？

7. 王朋忘了帶飯卡，
給了師傅多少錢？

8. 師傅找了他多少錢？

9. 師傅找錢找對了嗎？

10. 師傅說為什麼
他找錢找錯了？

5. Wáng Péng yào mǐfàn le ma?

6. Wáng Péng yígòng huā le
duōshao qián?

7. Wáng Péng wàng le dài fànkǎ,
gěi le shīfu duōshao qián?

8. Shīfu zhǎo le tā duōshao qián?

9. Shīfu zhǎo qián zhǎo duì le ma?

10. Shīfu shuō wèishénme
tā zhǎo qián zhǎo cuò le?

Using the words and phrases in blue as prompts, connect your answers above to form a narrative like this example:

每個星期四學生餐廳都有中國菜，今天是星期四，所以王朋去學生餐廳吃飯。餐廳的師傅是上海人，他告訴王朋今天有糖醋魚，甜甜的、酸酸的，好吃極了。王朋還想吃紅燒牛肉，師傅說今天沒有紅燒牛肉，來個涼拌黃瓜吧。王朋還要了一碗米飯，一共花了六塊七。因為他忘了帶飯卡，就給了師傅十塊錢，師傅多找了他一塊錢。王朋告訴師傅錢找錯了。師傅說對不起，他沒有看清楚。王朋說沒關係。

Měige xīngqīsì xuéshēng cāntīng dōu yǒu Zhōngguó cài, jīntiān shì xīngqīsì, suǒyǐ Wáng Péng qù xuéshēng cāntīng chī fàn. Cāntīng de shīfu shì Shànghǎi rén, tā gàosù Wáng Péng jīntiān yǒu tángcùyú, tiántián de, suānsuān de, hǎochī jí le. Wáng Péng hái xiǎng chī hóngshāo niúròu, shīfu shuō jīntiān méiyǒu hóngshāo niúròu, lái ge liángbàn huánggua ba. Wáng Péng hái yào le yì wǎn mǐfàn, yígòng huā le liù kuài qī. Yīnwèi tā wàng le dài fànkǎ, jiù gěi le shīfu shí kuài qián, shīfu duō zhǎo le tā yí kuài qián. Wáng Péng gàosù shīfu qián zhǎo cuò le. Shīfù shuō duìbuqǐ, tā méiyǒu kàn qīngchu. Wáng Péng shuō méi guānxi.

HOW ABOUT YOU?

What's on your grocery list?

1.	雞	jī	n	chicken
2.	豬肉	zhūròu	n	pork
3.	羊肉	yángròu	n	lamb; mutton
4.	蝦	xiā	n	shrimp
5.	蛋	dàn	n	egg
6.	胡蘿蔔	húluóbo	n	carrot
7.	洋蔥	yángcōng	n	onion

What other grocery items would you like to know? Please ask your teacher and make a note here:

_____

What's your favorite Chinese dish?

1.	宮保雞丁	gōngbǎo jīdīng	n	Kung Pao chicken
2.	麻婆豆腐	mápó dòufu	n	Mapo tofu
3.	蛋花湯	dànhuātāng	n	egg drop soup
4.	炒麵	chǎomiàn	n	stir-fried noodles

What other Chinese dishes do you like? If you don't know their names in Chinese, please ask your teacher and make a note here:

_____

Culture Highlights

❶ The word 中國菜 (Zhōngguó cài) covers all varieties of Chinese food in different styles. There are different ways of delineating Chinese cooking styles. Among the principal regional cuisines in China are the Shandong school, which originated in the northern province of Shandong; the Shanghainese school, favored by people in the lower Yangtze valley; and the Cantonese and Sichuanese schools, based respectively in the southern provinces of Guangdong and Sichuan. A Chinese restaurant usually specializes in only one cooking style, but some are more eclectic.

❷ In a Chinese meal, rice is the 主食 (zhǔshí, staple, or principal food), particularly in the traditional rice-growing region of the country, the south. In the north, 主食 (zhǔshí) often consists of 麵 (miàn, noodles), 餃子 (jiǎozi, dumplings), and 饅頭 (mántou, Chinese bread) instead.

❸ In Chinese food culture, knives (刀 dāo) belong in the kitchen, not at the dining table. The cook preempts the diner's need for a knife by

主食 Rice and Noodle

泰国香米饭 ·· 3元/碗
Thai Flavor Rice

高级知识份子面 ··· 36元
Gao's Noodles with Tomato Sauce

过桥米线 ··· 38元
Cross Bridge Rice Noodle

小锅米线 ··· 16元
Spicy and Sour Rice Noodle in Small Pot

腾冲大救驾 ·· 26元
Stir Fried Rice Pie

贵州炒粉 ··· 26元
Guizhou Fried Rice Noodle

cutting up the food, especially the meat, into small pieces before cooking. As everyone knows, most Chinese people eat not with a fork but with a pair of chopsticks (筷子 kuàizi).

❹ Since the 1990s, American fast food restaurants such as KFC (肯德基, Kěndéjī), McDonald's (麥當勞, Màidāngláo), and Pizza Hut (必勝客, Bìshèngkè) have been popping up in Chinese cities like mushrooms. Many of them have enjoyed flourishing business. The dubious reputation of American fast food as a "fattener" does not scare most Chinese customers away, and it is popular, especially among young people and children, to hang out with friends in an American fast food restaurant. The success of these American restaurants in China has been, at least in part, due to efforts they have made to adapt to local tastes. KFC, for instance, now offers 豆漿 (dòujiāng, soybean milk) and 油條 (yóutiáo, deep-fried dough sticks) for breakfast. McDonald's now sells 雞捲 (jījuǎn, chicken rolls).

油條
yóutiáo

English Text

Dialogue I

(In a restaurant)

Waiter: Come in! Please come in!

Li You: How come there are so many people? It doesn't look like there's a table left.

Wang Peng: Waiter, are there any tables left?

Waiter: Yes, yes. That table is not taken.

*   *   *

Waiter: What would you like to order?

Li You: Wang Peng, why don't you order?

Wang Peng: All right. Give us two plates of dumplings, to start things off. Vegetarian dumplings.

Waiter: What else would you like besides dumplings?

Wang Peng: Li You, what do you say?

Li You: Family-style tofu with no meat in it. I'm a vegetarian.

Waiter: Our family-style tofu has no meat in it.

Li You: Also two bowls of hot and sour soup with no MSG. Not too salty. Do you have baby bok choy?

Waiter: I'm sorry. We've just sold out baby bok choy.

Wang Peng: Then we'll do without green vegetables.

Waiter: What would you like to drink?

Wang Peng: I'd like a glass of iced tea. Li You, what would you like to drink?

Li You: I'm really thirsty. Please give me a cola, with lots of ice.

Waiter: OK. Two plates of dumplings, family-style tofu, two hot and sour soups, a glass of iced tea, a cola with lots of ice. Anything else?

Li You: That'll be all. That's more than enough. Waiter, we're both really hungry. Could you please bring the food as soon as possible?

Waiter: No problem. The dishes will be done in no time.

辣的涼拌黃瓜
là de liángbàn huánggua

不辣的涼拌黃瓜
bú là de liángbàn huánggua

Dialogue II

(It's Thursday. The student cafeteria is serving Chinese food. The chef is from Shanghai.)

Wang Peng: Chef, what's good for dinner today?

Chef: We've got sweet and sour fish. It's a little sweet and a little sour. It's delicious. Why don't you get that?

Wang Peng: Great. Do you have beef braised in soy sauce today?

Chef: No, we don't. You've already got fish, so there's no need to have meat. How about a cucumber salad?

Wang Peng: All right. Give me a bowl of rice. How much all together?

Chef: Sweet and sour fish is $4.50, cucumber salad $1.70; one bowl of rice, 50 cents. All together $6.70.

Wang Peng: Shoot, Chef. I forgot my meal card. Here's $10.

Chef: $3.30 is your change.

Wang Peng: Chef, you've given the wrong change. You gave me one dollar extra.

Chef: I'm sorry. I didn't see it clearly.

Wang Peng: That's all right.

Chef: Come again next Thursday.

Wang Peng: OK. Bye.

PROGRESS CHECKLIST

Before proceeding to Lesson 13, be sure you can complete the following tasks in Chinese:

I am able to—

☑ Ask the restaurant host if there are seats available;

☐ Name some Chinese dishes and place an order;

☐ Tell the waiter my meal preferences and dietary restrictions;

☐ Ask the waiter to recommend dishes and to rush the order if I'm in a hurry;

☐ Pay the bill after my meal;

☐ Get the correct change after my payment.

LESSON 13

Asking Directions

第十三課　問路

Dì shísān kè　Wèn lù

 LEARNING OBJECTIVES

In this lesson, you will learn to use Chinese to

- Ask for and give directions;
- Identify locations by using landmarks as references;
- Describe whether two places are close to or far away from one another;
- State where you are heading and the purpose of going there.

RELATE AND GET READY

In your own culture/community—

1. Besides the basics such as "hello," "how are you," "what's up," and so on, what are some other common greetings?
2. What phrases do people often use when giving directions?
3. What do people usually say to indicate that they don't have a good sense of direction?

Dialogue I: Where Are You Off To?

小白，下課了？上哪兒去❶？

您好，常老師。我想去學校的電腦中心，不知道怎麼走，聽說就在運動場旁邊①。

電腦中心沒有②運動場那麼③遠。你知道學校圖書館在哪裏❷嗎？

知道，離王朋的宿舍不遠。

電腦中心離圖書館很近，就在圖書館和學生活動中心中間。

LANGUAGE NOTES

❶ 上哪兒去 (shàng nǎr qu) is a more casual way of asking 去哪兒 (qù nǎr).

❷ Here 哪裏 (nǎli) is a question word meaning "where." It is interchangeable with 哪兒 (nǎr). People in northern China, especially in Beijing, speak with an "兒 (ér) ending" quite often. For example, some people say 明兒 (míngr) for "tomorrow" instead of 明天 (míngtiān), and 這兒 (zhèr) for "here" instead of 這裏 (zhèli).

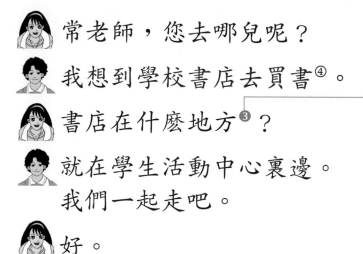 常老師，您去哪兒呢？

我想到學校書店去買書④。

書店在什麼地方❸？

就在學生活動中心裏邊。
我們一起走吧。

好。

❸什麼地方 (shénme dìfang, lit., what place) is generally interchangeable with 哪兒 (nǎr) or 哪裏 (nǎli).

 Xiǎo Bái, xià kè le? Shàng nǎr qu❶?

 Nín hǎo, Cháng lǎoshī. Wǒ xiǎng qù xuéxiào de diànnǎo zhōngxīn, bù zhīdào zěnme zǒu, tīngshuō jiù zài yùndòngchǎng pángbiān①.

 Diànnǎo zhōngxīn méiyǒu② yùndòngchǎng nàme③ yuǎn. Nǐ zhīdào xuéxiào túshūguǎn zài nǎli❷ ma?

Zhīdào, lí Wáng Péng de sùshè bù yuǎn.

Diànnǎo zhōngxīn lí túshūguǎn hěn jìn, jiù zài túshūguǎn hé xuéshēng huódòng zhōngxīn zhōngjiān.

Cháng lǎoshī, nín qù nǎr ne?

Wǒ xiǎng dào xuéxiào shūdiàn qù mǎi shū④.

Shūdiàn zài shénme dìfang❸?

Jiù zài xuéshēng huódòng zhōngxīn lǐbian. Wǒmen yìqǐ zǒu ba.

Hǎo.

VOCABULARY

1.	上	shàng	v	to go [colloq.]
2.	中心	zhōngxīn	n	center
3.	聽說	tīngshuō	v	to be told; to hear of
4.	運動	yùndòng	n	sports
5.	場	chǎng	n	field
6.	旁邊	pángbiān	n	side [See Grammar 1.]
7.	遠	yuǎn	adj	far
8.	離	lí	prep	away from
9.	近	jìn	adj	near
10.	活動	huódòng	n	activity
11.	中間	zhōngjiān	n	middle
12.	書店	shūdiàn	n	bookstore
13.	地方	dìfang	n	place
14.	裏邊	lǐbian	n	inside [See Grammar 1.]

Grammar

1. Direction and Location Words

Direction words 上/下/前/後/左/右/東/南/西/北/裏/外/旁 (shàng/xià/qián/hòu/zuǒ/yòu/dōng/nán/xī/běi/lǐ/wài/páng) often combine with suffixes such as 邊 (biān), 面 (miàn), and 頭 (tóu). As shown below, such compounds become location words. The suffixes 邊 (biān), 面 (miàn), and 頭 (tóu) are all pronounced in the neutral tone, with the exception of the 邊 (biān) in 旁邊 (pángbiān), which remains in the full first tone.

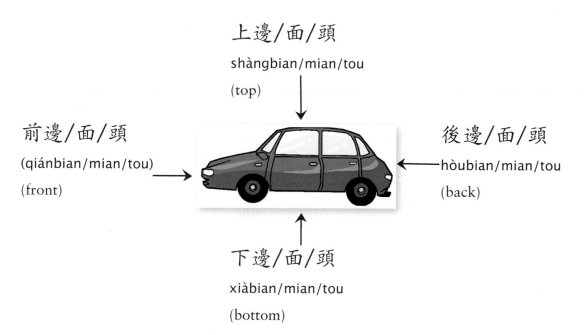

上邊/面/頭
shàngbian/mian/tou
(top)

前邊/面/頭
(qiánbian/mian/tou)
(front)

後邊/面/頭
hòubian/mian/tou
(back)

下邊/面/頭
xiàbian/mian/tou
(bottom)

裏邊/面/頭
lǐbian/mian/tou
(inside)

外邊/面/頭
wàibian/mian/tou
(outside)

中間

zhōngjiān

(middle)

左邊/面   右邊/面

zuǒbian/mian   yòubian/mian

(left side)   (right side)

旁邊

pángbiān

(side)

北邊/面

běibian/mian

(north side)

西邊/面   東邊/面

xībian/mian   dōngbian/mian

(west side)   (east side)

南邊/面

nánbian/mian

(south side)

The direction word 上 (shàng, on) or 裏 (lǐ, in) combines with a noun to form a location expression, e.g., 桌子上 (zhuōzi shang, on the table), 衣服上 (yīfu shang, on the clothes), 書上 (shū shang, in/on the book), 學校裏 (xuéxiào li, in the school), 辦公室裏 (bàngōngshì li, in the office), 教室裏 (jiàoshì li, in the classroom), 電視裏 (diànshì li, on TV). The word 裏 (lǐ) cannot be used after some proper nouns such as the name of a country or a city.

Compare:

學校裏有很多學生。

Xuéxiào li yǒu hěn duō xuésheng.

(There are many students at school.)

北京有很多學生。

Běijīng yǒu hěn duō xuésheng.

(There are many students in Beijing.)

It is incorrect to say:

*北京裏有很多學生。

*Běijīng li yǒu hěn duō xuésheng.

The combination of a direction word plus 邊 (biān) / 面 (miàn) / 頭 (tóu) can follow a noun to indicate a location, e.g., 圖書館(的)旁邊 (túshūguǎn {de} pángbiān, near the library); 學校(的)裏面 (xuéxiào {de} lǐmian, inside the school); 桌子(的)上頭 (zhuōzi {de} shàngtou, on the table); 教室(的)外面 (jiàoshì {de} wàimian, outside the classroom); 城市(的)北邊 (chéngshì {de} běibian, north of the city). In these expressions the particle 的 (de) following the noun is optional.

2. Comparative Sentences with 沒(有) (méi{yǒu})

Besides using 比 (bǐ), another way to make a comparison is to use 沒(有) (méi{yǒu}). In a comparative sentence with 沒有 (méiyǒu), the pronoun 那麼 (nàme) is sometimes added to the sentence. [See more on 那麼 (nàme) below.]

 我弟弟沒有我高。

Wǒ dìdi méiyǒu wǒ gāo.

(My younger brother is not as tall as I am.)

[I am taller than my brother.]

❷   北京沒有上海熱。

Běijīng méiyǒu Shànghǎi rè.

(It is not as hot in Beijing as in Shanghai.)

❸   他姐姐沒有他妹妹那麼喜歡買東西。

Tā jiějie méiyǒu tā mèimei nàme xǐhuan mǎi dōngxi.

(His older sister does not like shopping as much as his younger sister does.)

[His older sister might like shopping too, but not as much as his younger sister.]

❹   我沒有她那麼喜歡刷卡。

Wǒ méiyǒu tā nàme xǐhuan shuā kǎ.

(I don't like to use credit cards as much as she does.)

[I do use credit cards, but she likes to use them more than I do.]

A 沒有 (méiyǒu) B... vs. A 不比 (bù bǐ) B...

While 沒有 (méiyǒu) ... is used to say that one thing is of a lesser degree than another, 不比 (bù bǐ) ... means "no more than..." The two things being compared may be equal, but what is specifically stated is that A is *no more* than B. Compare the following sentences:

❺ **A:**   今天比昨天熱嗎？

Jīntiān bǐ zuótiān rè ma?

(Is today hotter than yesterday?)

B: 今天不比昨天熱。

Jīntiān bù bǐ zuótiān rè.

(Today is not any hotter than yesterday.)

[It could be the same temperature or cooler than yesterday.]

C: 今天沒有昨天熱。

Jīntiān méiyǒu zuótiān rè.

(Today is not as hot as yesterday.)

[Today is cooler.]

❻ A: 這篇課文比那篇課文短嗎？

Zhè piān kèwén bǐ nà piān kèwén duǎn ma?

(Is this text shorter than that one?)

B: 這篇課文不比那篇課文短，兩篇一樣長。

Zhè piān kèwén bù bǐ nà piān kèwén duǎn, liǎng piān yíyàng cháng.)

(This text is not any shorter than that one. They are the same length.)

C: 是嗎？我覺得這篇課文沒有那篇長。

Shì ma? Wǒ juéde zhè piān kèwén méiyǒu nà piān cháng.

(Really? I think this text is not as long as that one.)

[This text is shorter than that one.]

A Quick Summary of Comparative Sentences

A 比 (bǐ)　　　B 大 (dà)　　　　　A>B
A 不比 (bù bǐ)　B 大 (dà)　　　　　A≤B
A 没有 (méiyǒu)　B 大 (dà)　　　　　A<B

3. 那麼 (nàme) Indicating Degree

那麼 (nàme) is often placed before adjectives or verbs such as 想 (xiǎng), 喜歡 (xǐhuan), 會 (huì), 能 (néng), and 希望 (xīwàng), to denote a high degree.

❶ 你那麼不喜歡寫日記，就別寫了吧。

Nǐ nàme bù xǐhuan xiě rìjì, jiù bié xiě le ba.

(Since you dislike writing journals so much, why don't you quit doing it?)

没有…那麼… (méiyǒu... nàme...) means "not reaching the point of."

❷ 弟弟没有哥哥那麼帥，那麼酷。

Dìdi méiyǒu gēge nàme shuài, nàme kù.

(The younger brother is not as handsome and cool as the older brother.)

坐地鐵沒有坐公共汽車那麼麻煩。

Zuò dìtiě méiyǒu zuò gōnggòng qìchē nàme máfan.

(Riding the subway is not as much of a hassle as riding the bus.)

 這個樣子沒有你說的那麼合適。

Zhè ge yàngzi méiyǒu nǐ shuō de nàme héshì.

(This style is not as suitable as you said.)

❺ 這張地圖沒有那張地圖那麼新。

Zhè zhāng dìtú méiyǒu nà zhāng dìtú nàme xīn.

This map is not as new as that one.)

By using 那麼(nàme), the speaker affirms the certain attribute of something or somebody in question. By stating that the younger brother does not reach the same standard of handsomeness and coolness as the older brother, (2), for instance, acknowledges that the older brother is handsome and cool.

---

4. 到 (dào) + Place + 去 (qù) + Action

In this structure, the combination of "到 (dào) + Place + 去 (qù) + Action" denotes the purpose of going somewhere.

❶ 我要到電腦中心去上網。

Wǒ yào dào diànnǎo zhōngxīn qù shàng wǎng.

(I want to go to the computer center to use the internet.)

❷ 他到朋友的宿舍去聊天兒了。

Tā dào péngyou de sùshè qù liáo tiānr le.

(He went to his friend's dorm to chat.)

❸ 我們到飛機場去送李小姐。

Wǒmen dào fēijīchǎng qù sòng Lǐ xiǎojiě.

(We went to the airport to see Miss Li off.)

Language Practice

A. Xiao Peng's Room

The following is Xiao Peng's room. Xiao Peng claims he cannot find his stuff and keeps asking "Where are my things?" Xiao Peng's mother has to tell him where things are. Pair up with a partner and role-play Xiao Peng and his mother.

EXAMPLE:

Xiao Peng: 我的電腦呢？   Wǒ de diànnǎo ne?

Mother: 你的電腦在   Nǐ de diànnǎo zài
桌子上。   zhuōzi shang.

1.

2.

3.

4.

B. Compare and Contrast

Based on the clues given, make comparisons using 没有…（那麼）… (méiyǒu…
{nàme}…, not as…)

EXAMPLE: today   yesterday
              40° F   55° F

→ 今天没有昨天
   （那麼）暖和。

Jīntiān méiyǒu zuótiān

(nàme) nuǎnhuo.

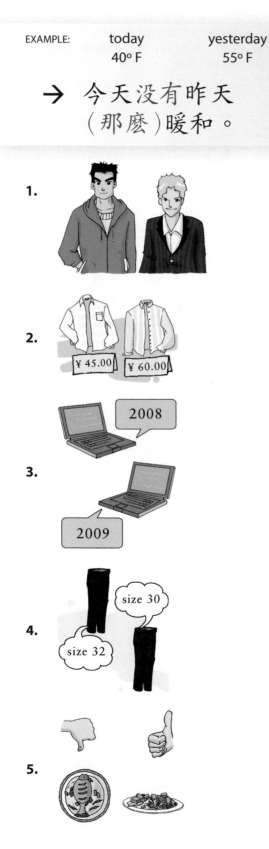

1.

2. ¥ 45.00   ¥ 60.00

2008

3. 2009

size 30

4. size 32

5.

C. Geography Bee

Locate each city on the map and work with your partner to ask and answer whether each city is close to or far away from the place where you are.

EXAMPLE: 紐約   Niǔyuē

→   **A:** 紐約離我們這兒遠嗎？   Niǔyuē lí wǒmen zhèr yuǎn ma?

B: 紐約離我們這兒很遠/不遠/很近。   Niǔyuē lí wǒmen zhèr hěn yuǎn/bù yuǎn/hěn jìn.

1. Boston
2. Chicago
3. Houston
4. Los Angeles
5. Miami
6. San Francisco
7. Honolulu
8. New York

D. Plans for the Weekend

Your friend is coming to visit you at school this weekend, and you want to show him/her around. Your choices of places and activities are shown below. Work with a partner to come up with suggestions.

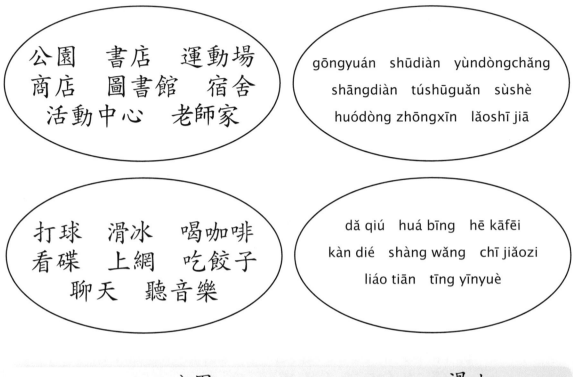

公園　書店　運動場
商店　圖書館　宿舍
活動中心　老師家

gōngyuán　shūdiàn　yùndòngchǎng
shāngdiàn　túshūguǎn　sùshè
huódòng zhōngxīn　lǎoshī jiā

打球　滑冰　喝咖啡
看碟　上網　吃餃子
聊天　聽音樂

dǎ qiú　huá bīng　hē kāfēi
kàn dié　shàng wǎng　chī jiǎozi
liáo tiān　tīng yīnyuè

EXAMPLE: if you choose 公園 (gōngyuán) from the first group and 滑冰 (huá bīng) from the second group, then you will suggest

我們到公園去
滑冰，好嗎？

Wǒmen dào gōngyuán qù

huá bīng, hǎo ma?

or

我們去公園
滑冰，好嗎？

Wǒmen qù gōngyuán

huá bīng, hǎo ma?

1.

2.

3.

4.

5.

E. The Inside Scoop

Your partner always knows where to find the most stylish clothing, delicious food, and fun activities. Ask where he/she goes to buy clothes, to go out to eat, etc.

1. 你喜歡到哪兒去跳舞？

    Nǐ xǐhuan dào nǎr qù tiào wǔ?

2. 你週末晚上常常到哪兒去吃飯？

    Nǐ zhōumò wǎnshang chángcháng dào nǎr qù chī fàn?

3. 你喜歡到哪兒去看電影？

    Nǐ xǐhuan dào nǎr qù kàn diànyǐng?

4. 你常常到哪兒去買衣服？

    Nǐ chángcháng dào nǎr qù mǎi yīfu?

F. Recap and Narrate

Working with a partner, recap the content of Dialogue I:

1. 白英愛要去什麼地方？

    1. Bái Yīng'ài yào qù shénme dìfāng?

2. 白英愛知道學校的電腦中心怎麼走嗎？

    2. Bái Yīng'ài zhīdào xué xiào de diànnǎo zhōngxīn zěnme zǒu ma?

3. 電腦中心有運動場遠嗎？

    3. Diànnǎo zhōngxīn yǒu yùndòngchǎng yuǎn ma?

4. 電腦中心在哪兒？

    4. Diànnǎo zhōngxīn zài nǎr?

5. 常老師去哪兒？

    5. Cháng lǎoshī qù nǎr?

6. 常老師為什麼讓白英愛跟她一起走？

    6. Cháng lǎoshī wèishénme ràng Bái Yīng'ài gēn tā yìqǐ zǒu?

Using the words and phrases in blue as prompts, connect your answers above to form a narrative like this example:

白英愛要去學校的電腦中心，她不知道怎麼走，但是聽說電腦中心就在運動場旁邊。她看見了常老師。常老師告訴她電腦中心沒有運動場那麼遠，離圖書館很近，就在圖書館和學生活動中心中間。白英愛知道圖書館離王朋的宿舍不遠，所以現在知道去電腦中心怎麼走了。常老師要到學校的書店去買書，書店就在學生活動中心裏邊，所以她讓白英愛跟她一起走。

Bái Yīng'ài yào qù xuéxiào de diànnǎo zhōngxīn, tā bù zhīdào zěnme zǒu, dànshì tīngshuō diànnǎo zhōngxīn jiù zài yùndòngchǎng pángbiān. Tā kàn jiàn le Cháng lǎoshī. Cháng lǎoshī gàosù tā diànnǎo zhōngxīn méiyǒu yùndòngchǎng nàme yuǎn, lí túshūguǎn hěn jìn, jiù zài túshūguǎn hé xuéshēng huódòng zhōngxīn zhōngjiān. Bái Yīng'ài zhīdao túshūguǎn lí Wáng Péng de sùshè bù yuǎn, suǒyǐ xiànzài zhīdao qù diànnǎo zhōngxīn zěnme zǒu le. Cháng lǎoshī yào dào xuéxiào de shūdiàn qù mǎi shū, shūdiàn jiù zài xuéshēng huódòng zhōngxīn lǐbian, suǒyǐ tā ràng Bái Yīng'ài gēn tā yìqǐ zǒu.

Dialogue II: Going to Chinatown

我們去中國城吃中國飯吧！

我沒去過⑤中國城，不知道中國城在哪兒。

沒問題❶，你開車，我告訴你怎麼走。

你有地圖嗎？給我看看⑥。

地圖在宿舍裏，我忘了拿來了。

沒有地圖，走錯了怎麼辦？

沒有地圖沒關係，中國城我去過很多次，不用地圖也能找到⑦。

LANGUAGE NOTES

❶ 沒問題 (méi wèntí, no problem) vs. 沒關係 (méi guānxi, it doesn't matter): One uses 沒問題 (méi wèntí) to assure someone that their request will be met or a problem will be solved, e.g. "開車送你去機場？沒問題！" (Kāi chē sòng nǐ qù jīchǎng? Méi wèntí. Drive you to the airport? No problem!) 沒關係 (méi guānxi), on the other hand, downplays the severity or impact of an issue, and is often used in response to someone's apology for a minor mistake.

你從這兒一直往南開，過三個路口，往西一拐②就⑧到了。

哎，我不知道東南西北❸。

那你一直往前開，過三個紅綠燈，往右一拐就到了。

（過了三個路口）

不對，不對。你看，這個路口只能往左拐，不能往右拐。

那就是下一個路口。往右拐，再往前開。到了，到了，你看見了嗎？前面有很多中國字。

那不是中文，那是日文，我們到了小東京了。

是嗎？那我們不吃中國飯了，吃日本飯吧！

❷ 拐 (guǎi), in the sense of "to turn," is used mainly in northern China. In the south, 轉 (zhuǎn) is more commonly used instead, which is also the more formal substitute for 拐 (guǎi) in the north.

❸ Chinese speakers customarily mention the four directions in a set sequence, 東南西北 (dōng nán xī běi) or 東西南北 (dōng xī nán běi). For southeast and northeast, one says 東南 (dōng nán) and 東北 (dōng běi), never *南東 (nán dōng) or *北東 (běi dōng). Similarly, for southwest and northwest, one says 西南 (xī nán) and 西北 (xī běi), never *南西 (nán xī) or *北西 (běi xī).

Wǒmen qù Zhōngguóchéng chī Zhōngguó fàn ba!

Wǒ méi qù guo⑤ Zhōngguóchéng, bù zhīdào Zhōngguóchéng zài nǎr.

Méi wèntí❶, nǐ kāi chē, wǒ gàosù nǐ zěnme zǒu.

Nǐ yǒu dìtú ma? Gěi wǒ kàn kan⑥.

Dìtú zài sùshè li, wǒ wàng le ná lai le.

Méiyǒu dìtú, zǒu cuò le zěnmebàn?

Méiyǒu dìtú méi guānxi, Zhōngguóchéng wǒ qù guo hěn duō cì, bú yòng dìtú yě néng zhǎo dào⑦. Nǐ cóng zhèr yìzhí wǎng nán kāi, guò sān ge lùkǒu, wǎng xī yì guǎi❷ jiù⑧ dào le.

Āi, wǒ bù zhīdào dōng nán xī běi❸.

Nà nǐ yìzhí wǎng qián kāi, guò sān ge hónglǜdēng, wǎng yòu yì guǎi jiù dào le.

(Guò le sān ge lùkǒu)

 Bú duì, bú duì. Nǐ kàn, zhè ge lùkǒu zhǐ néng wǎng zuǒ guǎi, bù néng wǎng yòu guǎi.

 Nà jiù shì xià yí ge lùkǒu. Wǎng yòu guǎi, zài wǎng qián kāi. Dào le, dào le, nǐ kàn jiàn le ma? Qiánmian yǒu hěn duō Zhōngguó zì.

 Nà bú shì Zhōngwén, nà shì Rìwén, wǒmen dào le Xiǎo Dōngjīng le.

 Shì ma? Nà wǒmen bù chī Zhōngguó fàn le, chī Rìběn fàn ba.

VOCABULARY

1.	過	guo	p	(particle used after a verb to indicate a past experience) [See Grammar 5.]
2.	中國城	Zhōngguóchéng	n	Chinatown
	城	chéng	n	town; city
3.	地圖	dìtú	n	map
4.	拿	ná	v	to take; to get
5.	次	cì	m	(measure word for frequency)
6.	從	cóng	prep	from
7.	一直	yìzhí	adv	straight; continuously
8.	往	wǎng	prep	towards
9.	南	nán	n	south
10.	過	guò	v	to pass
11.	路口	lùkǒu	n	intersection

VOCABULARY

12.	西	xī	n	west
13.	拐	guǎi	v	to turn
14.	哎	āi	excl	(exclamatory particle to express surprise or dissatisfaction)
15.	東	dōng	n	east
16.	北	běi	n	north
17.	前	qián	n	forward; ahead
18.	紅綠燈	hónglǜdēng	n	traffic light
	燈	dēng	n	light
19.	右	yòu	n	right
20.	左	zuǒ	n	left
21.	前面	qiánmian	n	ahead; in front of

Proper Nouns

22.	日文	Rìwén		Japanese (language)
23.	東京	Dōngjīng		Tokyo
24.	日本	Rìběn		Japan

北海公園在故宮的哪一邊？
Běihǎi Gōngyuán zài Gùgōng de nǎ yì biān?

Grammar

5. The Dynamic Particle 過 (guo)

The dynamic particle 過 (guo) is used to denote a past experience or occurrence
that did not continue to the present but, typically, had an impact on the present.

 我在中國城工作過一年，所以我知道怎麼走。

Wǒ zài Zhōngguóchéng gōngzuò guo yì nián, suǒyǐ wǒ zhīdào zěnme zǒu.
(I worked in Chinatown for a year, so I know how to get there.)

[The fact that the speaker worked in Chinatown for a year is the reason why
he/she knows how to get there.]

❷   我見過李友，（所以知道）她很高。

Wǒ jiàn guo Lǐ Yǒu, (suǒyǐ zhīdào) tā hěn gāo.

(I've met Li You before, (so I know) she is tall.)

❸ A: 運動場遠不遠，你知道嗎？

Yùndòngchǎng yuǎn bù yuǎn, nǐ zhīdào ma?

(Do you know if the sports field is far from here?)

A: 運動場我去過，(所以我知道)不遠，很近。

Yùndòngchǎng wǒ qù guo, (suǒyǐ wǒ zhīdào) bù yuǎn, hěn jìn.

(I've been to the sports field, (so I know) it is not far away. It's very close.)

In this kind of sentence, expressions of time are often either unspecified or completely absent. If there is no time expression, the implied time for the action or event is 以前 (yǐqián, before; previously). Sometimes 以前 (yǐqián) can appear in the sentence as well.

❹   我以前去過中國城，知道怎麼走。

Wǒ yǐqián qù guo Zhōngguóchéng, zhīdào zěnme zǒu.

(I've been to Chinatown before. I know how to get there.)

❺   以前我們見過面，可是没説過話。

Yǐqián wǒmen jiàn guo miàn, kěshì méi shuō guo huà.

(We've met before, but we've never spoken to each other.)

An expression indicating a specific time can also occasionally appear in a sentence with 過 (guo).

❻ A: 你見過李小姐嗎？

Nǐ jiàn guo Lǐ xiǎojiě ma?

(Have you ever met Miss Li?)

B: 見過，上個月還見過她。

Jiàn guo, shàng ge yuè hái jiàn guo tā.

(Yes. I saw her as recently as last month.)

6. Reduplication of Verbs

Like adjectives [see Grammar 3 in Lesson 12], verbs can also be reduplicated. Reduplication of a verb in this lesson refers to an anticipated or requested action, and it makes the tone of the sentence milder.

❶ 老師，您再說說什麼時候用"了"，好嗎？

Lǎoshī, nín zài shuō shuo shénme shíhou yòng "le", hǎo ma?

(Teacher, would you say a bit more about when to use "le", please?)

❷ 媽，您看看，我這樣寫對不對？

Mā, nín kàn kan, wǒ zhèyàng xiě duì bu duì?

(Mom, take a look—did I write this correctly or not?)

❸ 我用用你的電腦可以嗎？

Wǒ yòng yong nǐ de diànnǎo kěyǐ ma?

(May I use your computer for a minute?)

❹ 你幫我找找我的筆，好嗎？

Nǐ bāng wǒ zhǎo zhao wǒ de bǐ, hǎo ma?

(Could you help me look for my pen for a second?)

❺ 你考完試，我們一起去公園走走，聊聊天兒。

Nǐ kǎo wán shì, wǒmen yìqǐ qù gōngyuán zǒu zou, liáo liao tiānr.

(Let's take a walk in the park and have a chat after your exam.)

If a sentence includes both a modal verb and an action verb, only the action verb can be reduplicated.

❻ 她想看看我的新手機。

Tā xiǎng kàn kan wǒ de xīn shǒujī.

(She wants to take a look at my new cell phone.)

7. Resultative Complements (II)

Let's review all the resultative complements that we have introduced so far, and learn some new ones that can be formed from the verbs and complements you already know.

a. 完 (wán):

看完	(kàn wán)	(finish reading)
吃完	(chī wán)	(finish eating)
喝完	(hē wán)	(finish drinking)
考完	(kǎo wán)	(finish taking a test)
買完	(mǎi wán)	(finish buying)
賣完	(mài wán)	(sell out)

b. 到 (dào):

找到	(zhǎo dào)	(find [something or someone] successfully)
看到	(kàn dào)	(see [something or someone])
聽到	(tīng dào)	(hear [something or someone])
買到	(mǎi dào)	(buy [something] successfully)

c. 見 (jiàn):

看見	(kàn jiàn)	(see [something or someone]) — same as 看到 (kàn dào)
聽見	(tīng jiàn)	(hear [something or someone]) — same as 聽到 (tīng dào)

d. 好 (hǎo):

做好	(zuò hǎo)	(complete doing something, which is now ready)
買好	(mǎi hǎo)	(complete buying something, which is now ready)
準備好	(zhǔnbèi hǎo)	(prepare something, which is ready)

e. 錯 (cuò):

買錯	(mǎi cuò)	(buy the wrong thing)
找錯	(zhǎo cuò)	(give the wrong change; find the wrong person or thing)
寫錯	(xiě cuò)	(write [something] incorrectly)
說錯	(shuō cuò)	(say [something] incorrectly)
走錯	(zǒu cuò)	(go the wrong way)

f. 懂 (dǒng):

聽懂	(tīng dǒng)	(comprehend what one hears)
看懂	(kàn dǒng)	(comprchend what one reads or sees)

g. 清楚 (qīngchu):

看清楚	(kàn qīngchu)	(see [something] clearly)
聽清楚	(tīng qīngchu)	(hear [something] clearly)

h. 會 (huì):

學會	(xué huì)	(acquire the skills [for doing something that one was previously unable to do])

The collocation of a verb with its resultative complement is not random; one has to memorize the whole expression of verb plus resultative complement. Some resultative complements are semantically related to the verb. For instance, in the sentence 我昨天看見她了 (Wǒ zuótiān kàn jiàn tā le, I saw her yesterday), the complement is semantically related to 看 (kàn), the verb of the sentence. Some resultative complements are semantically related to the object. In the sentence 我寫錯了兩個字 (Wǒ xiě cuò le liǎng ge zì, I wrote two characters incorrectly), for instance, it is the object "characters" 字 (zì) that are "wrong" 錯 (cuò). Some resultative complements are related to the subject, e.g., in the sentence 我學會了 (Wǒ xué huì le, I have learned it), the complement 會 (huì) is semantically related to 我 (wǒ), the subject of the sentence.

8. 一···就··· (yī...jiù..., as soon as...then...)

This structure connects two actions. It can be used to combine actions in two different types of situations: habitual situations or one-time situations. In a habitual situation, whenever the first action occurs, the second action immediately follows.

 他一上課就想睡覺。

Tā yí shàng kè jiù xiǎng shuì jiào.

(He feels sleepy every time the class starts.)

 小張平常只吃青菜，一吃肉就不舒服。

Xiǎo Zhāng píngcháng zhǐ chī qīngcài, yì chī ròu jiù bù shūfu.

(Little Zhang normally eats only vegetables. He feels sick whenever he eats meat.)

❸ 李律師一累就喝咖啡。

Lǐ lǜshī yí lèi jiù hē kāfēi.

(Attorney Li drinks coffee whenever he feels tired.)

In a one-time situation, the second action takes place as soon as the first is completed:

❹ 我們一進飯館兒，服務員就告訴我們没位子了。

Wǒmen yí jìn fànguǎnr, fúwùyuán jiù gàosù wǒmen méi wèizi le.

(As soon as we got into the restaurant, the waiter told us there were no seats available.)

 這課的語法很容易，我一看就懂。

Zhè kè de yǔfǎ hěn róngyì, wǒ yí kàn jiù dǒng.

(The grammar in this lesson was very easy. I understood it the moment I read it.)

❻　活動中心離這兒不遠，到第二個路口，往右一拐就到了。

Huódòng zhōngxīn lí zhèr bù yuǎn, dào dì èr ge lùkǒu, wǎng yòu yì guǎi jiù dào le.

(The activity center is not far from here. Turn right at the second intersection, and you'll be there.)

Language Practice

F. Experience Inventory

Ask your partner if he/she has ever tried the activities or tasted the foods shown below. Ask a follow-up question if the answer is affirmative. Ask if he/she wishes to try them if the answer is negative.

EXAMPLE 1:

→　A: 你打過球嗎？

A: Nǐ dǎ guo qiú ma?

　　B: 我打過（球）。

B: Wǒ dǎ guo (qiú).

　　A: 你覺得打球有意思嗎？

A: Nǐ juéde dǎ qiú yǒu yìsi ma?

　　B: 我覺得打球很有意思/没有意思。

B: Wǒ juéde dǎ qiú hěn yǒu yìsi/méi yǒu yìsi.

1.

2.

3.

4.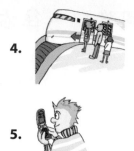

5.

EXAMPLE 2:

A: 你吃過家常豆腐嗎？

B: 我吃過（家常豆腐）。

A: 你覺得家常豆腐好吃嗎？

B: 我覺得家常豆腐很好吃／不好吃。

A: Nǐ chī guo jiācháng dòufu ma?

B: Wǒ chī guo (jiācháng dòufu).

A: Nǐ juéde jiācháng dòufu hàochī ma?

B: Wǒ juéde jiācháng dòufu hěn hàochī/bù hàochī.

1.

2.

3.

G. **One Thing After Another**

Work with your partner and take turns asking each other:

1. **A:** 你平常一吃完早飯
就做什麼？

   Nǐ píngcháng yì chī wán zǎofàn
jiù zuò shénme?

   B: _____ 。

2. **A:** 你平常一下中文
課就做什麼？

   Nǐ píngcháng yí xià Zhōngwén
kè jiù zuò shénme?

   B: _____ 。

3. **A:** 你平常一高興就
做什麼？

   Nǐ píngcháng yì gāoxìng jiù
zuò shénme?

   B: _____ 。

4. **A:** 你昨天早上一
起床就做什麼？

   Nǐ zuótiān zǎoshang yì
qǐ chuáng jiù zuò shénme?

   B: _____ 。

5. **A:** 你昨天一回家就
做什麼？

   Nǐ zuótiān yì huí jiā jiù
zuò shénme?

   B: _____ 。

H. Location, Location, Location

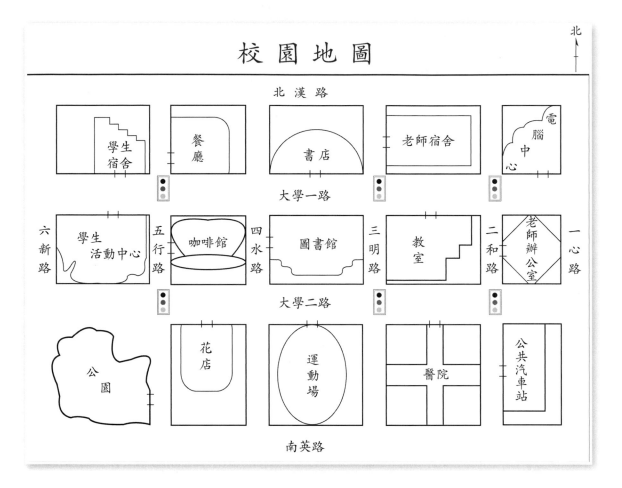

Locate some of the buildings using different landmarks.

EXAMPLE:	圖書館	túshūguǎn
A:	請問圖書館在哪兒？	Qǐng wèn, túshūguǎn zài nǎr?
B:	圖書館在運動場的北邊。	Túshūguǎn zài yùndòngchǎng de běibian.
or		
	圖書館在教室和咖啡館的中間。	Túshūguǎn zài jiàoshì hé kāfēiguǎn de zhōngjiān.

1. 公園   gōngyuán

2. 餐廳   cāntīng

3. 運動場   yùndòngchǎng

4. 公共汽車站   gōnggòng qìchē zhàn

I. How Do I Get There?

Using the map from the previous exercise, practice with your partner how to ask for and give directions.

EXAMPLE: 公園 → 老師辦公室   gōngyuán → lǎoshī bàngōngshì

A: 從公園到老師
辦公室怎麼走？

A: Cóng gōngyuán dào lǎoshī
bàngōngshì zěnme zǒu?

B: 你從公園出來，
上五行路，往北走，
到了第一個路口，
往東拐，過兩個
路口，到了第三個
路口往左一拐，就
到了/老師辦公室就
在你的右邊兒。

B: Nǐ cóng gōngyuán chū lai,
shàng Wǔxínglù, wǎng běi zǒu,
dào le dì yī ge lùkǒu,
wǎng dōng guǎi, guò liǎng ge
lùkǒu, dào le dì sān ge
lùkǒu wǎng zuǒ yì guǎi, jiù
dào le/lǎoshī bàngōngshì jiù
zài nǐ de yòubianr.

1. 電腦中心
→運動場

1. diànnǎo zhōngxīn
→ yùndòngchǎng

2. 學生宿舍
→公共汽車站

2. xuéshēng sùshè
→ gōnggòng qìchē zhàn

3. 書店 → 花店 (florist)

3. shūdiàn → huādiàn

J. Recap and Narrate

Working with a partner, recap the content of Dialogue II:

1. 王朋和高文中
一起去什麼地方？

2. 誰開車？

3. 王朋知道去
中國城
怎麼走嗎？

4. 高文中說他帶
地圖了嗎？

5. 高文中說他知道
去中國城怎麼
走嗎？

6. 高文中說去
中國城怎麼走？

7. 王朋知道東南
西北嗎？

8. 高文中告訴
王朋的路對嗎？

1. Wáng Péng hé Gāo Wénzhōng
yìqǐ qù shénme dìfang?

2. Shéi kāi chē?

3. Wáng Péng zhīdào qù
Zhōngguóchéng
zěnme zǒu ma?

4. Gāo Wénzhōng shuō tā dài
dìtú le ma?

5. Gāo Wénzhōng shuō tā zhīdào
qù Zhōngguóchéng zěnme
zǒu ma?

6. Gāo Wénzhōng shuō qù
Zhōngguóchéng zěnme zǒu?

7. Wáng Péng zhīdào dōng nán
xī běi ma?

8. Gāo Wénzhōng gàosù
Wáng Péng de lù duì ma?

Using the words and phrases in blue as prompts, connect your answers above to form a narrative like this example:

王朋和高文中一起開車去中國城吃中國飯，王朋不知道怎麼走，問高文中帶地圖了沒有。高文中忘了帶地圖，他說他不用地圖也能找到中國城。他說一直往南開，過三個路口，往西一拐就到了。可是王朋說他不知道東南西北。高文中又說一直往前開，過三個紅綠燈，往右一拐就到了。可是，他們最後開到了小東京。

Wáng Péng hé Gāo Wénzhōng yìqǐ kāi chē qù Zhōngguóchéng chī Zhōngguó fàn, Wáng Péng bù zhīdào zěnme zǒu, wèn Gāo Wénzhōng dài dìtú le méiyǒu. Gāo Wénzhōng wàng le dài dìtú, tā shuō tā bú yòng dìtú yě néng zhǎo dào Zhōngguóchéng. Tā shuō yìzhí wǎng nán kāi, guò sān ge lùkǒu, wǎng xī yì guǎi jiù dào le. Kěshì Wáng Péng shuō tā bù zhīdào dōng nán xī běi. Gāo Wénzhōng yòu shuō yìzhí wǎng qián kāi, guò sān ge hónglǜdēng, wǎng yòu yì guǎi jiù dào le. Kěshì, tāmen zuìhòu kāi dào le xiǎo Dōngjīng.

HOW ABOUT YOU?

Where do you walk?

1.	單行道	dānxíngdào	n	one-way street
2.	斑馬線	bānmǎxiàn	n	zebra crossing; pedestrian crosswalk
3.	天橋	tiānqiáo	n	pedestrian overpass
4.	地下（通）道	dìxià (tōng)dào	n	pedestrian underpass

What other traffic-related terms would you like to know how to say? Please ask your teacher and make a note here: _____

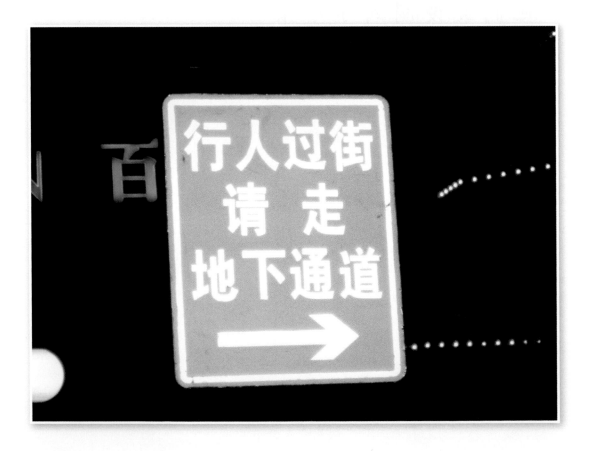

Culture Highlights

1 In Chinese culture, a common and cordial way to greet someone is by asking a casual question about the routine activity that the other person is engaged in at the moment. Thus, upon seeing a friend on her way to a grocery store, one could ask 買菜呀? (Mǎi cài ya? Going grocery shopping, eh?) Running into a fellow student who is leaving a classroom, one could ask 下課了? (Xià kè le? Just had your class?) As the situation is usually very obvious, the speaker does not expect, and is not interested in, an elaborate answer. Nor are these questions considered intrusive or personal.

2 In many cities in China, the array of traffic lights includes an electronic display of the number of seconds before the light turns from green to red, which enables drivers and pedestrians to better manage their time in getting through the intersection.

3 Both 中國話 (Zhōngguó huà) and 中文 (Zhōngwén) refer to the Chinese language. However, while 中文 (Zhōngwén) covers both spoken and written Chinese, 中國話 (Zhōngguó huà) stresses spoken Chinese. 中國字 (Zhōngguó zì) is synonymous with 漢字 (Hànzì). Similarly, both 日語 (Rìyǔ) and 日文 (Rìwén) mean the Japanese language. While 日文 (Rìwén) covers both spoken and written Japanese, 日語 (Rìyǔ) stresses spoken Japanese. 日本話 (Rìběn huà) is synonymous with 日語 (Rìyǔ), but it is more informal.

English Text

Dialogue I

Teacher Chang: Are classes over, Little Bai? Where are you off to?

Bai Ying'ai: Hi, Teacher Chang. I want to go to the school computer center, but I don't know how to get there. I heard it's next to the sports field.

Teacher Chang: The computer center is not as far as the sports field. You know where the school library is?

Bai Ying'ai: Yes, I do. It's not far from Wang Peng's dorm.

Teacher Chang: The computer center is near the library. It's between the library and the student activity center.

Bai Ying'ai: Teacher Chang, where are you headed?

Teacher Chang: I'd like to get some books at the school bookstore.

Bai Ying'ai: Where's the bookstore?

Teacher Chang: It's in the student activity center. We can walk together.

Bai Ying'ai: Wonderful.

Dialogue II

Gao Wenzhong: Let's go to Chinatown to have some Chinese food.

Wang Peng: I've never been to Chinatown. I don't know where Chinatown is.

Gao Wenzhong: No problem. You drive, and I'll tell you how to get there.

Wang Peng: Do you have a map? Let me take a look.

Gao Wenzhong: The map is in the dorm. I forgot to bring it.

Wang Peng: Without the map, what will we do if we go the wrong way?

Gao Wenzhong: It doesn't matter if we don't have the map. I've been to Chinatown many times. I can find it without a map. Go south from here. After three blocks, turn west, and we'll be there.

Wang Peng: Oh, I don't have any sense of direction.

Gao Wenzhong: Then drive straight ahead. After three traffic lights, turn right, and you'll be there.

(After three blocks)

Wang Peng: This isn't right. See, you can only turn left here. You can't turn right.

Gao Wenzhong: Then it'll be the next block. Turn right. Keep going further. We're there, we're there. See, there are lots of Chinese characters in front of us.

Wang Peng: That's not Chinese, that's Japanese. We're in Little Tokyo.

Gao Wenzhong: Really? Then let's not have Chinese food, let's have Japanese food instead.

PROGRESS CHECKLIST

Before proceeding to Lesson 14, be sure you can complete the following tasks in Chinese:

I am able to—

- [x] Ask for directions;
- [ ] Give directions;
- [ ] Locate places using landmark references;
- [ ] Tell someone whether a place is far away from or close to another place;
- [ ] Provide information about where I am going and why.

Birthday Party

第十四課 生日晚會

Dì shísì kè

Shēngrì wǎnhuì

14

LEARNING OBJECTIVES

In this lesson, you will learn to use Chinese to

- Ask a friend to go to a party with you;
- Suggest things to take to a get-together;
- Offer someone a ride and arrange a time and place to meet;
- Thank people for their gifts;
- Describe a duration of time;
- Talk about the year of your birth and your Chinese zodiac sign;
- Give a simple description of someone's facial features.

RELATE AND GET READY

In your own culture/community—

1. How are birthdays usually celebrated?
2. What do people bring to a birthday party?
3. Are there any taboos about gift giving?
4. Are people supposed to open gifts in front of the gift giver?
5. What kinds of facial features are considered attractive?

Dialogue I: Let's Go to a Party!

（李友給王朋打電話。）

🧑 王朋，你做什麼呢①？

👨 我看書呢。

🧑 今天高小音過生日❶，晚上
我們在她家開舞會，你能去
嗎？

👨 能去。幾點？

🧑 七點。我們先吃飯，吃完飯
再唱歌跳舞。

👨 有哪些人？

LANGUAGE NOTES

❶ Apart from 過生日
(guò shēngrì, to celebrate
one's birthday), the verb 過
(guò, to live [a life]; to observe
[a holiday]; to celebrate [a
festival]) appears in many
other expressions such as
過年 (guò nián, to celebrate
the New Year), 過節 (guò jié,
to celebrate a festival), and
過日子 (guò rìzi, to live
one's life; to live from day to
day).

小音和她的男朋友，小音的表姐❷，白英愛，你妹妹王紅，聽說還有小音的中學同學。

你要送給小音什麼生日禮物？

我買了一本書送給她。

那我帶什麼東西？

飲料或者水果都可以。

那我帶一些飲料，再買一把花兒。

小音愛吃水果，我再買一些蘋果、梨和西瓜吧。

你住的地方② 離小音家很遠，水果很重，我開車來接你，我們一起去吧。

好，我六點半在樓下等你。

❷ The kinship term 表姐 (biǎojiě) is more narrowly defined than its translation "older female cousin" would suggest. One's "older female cousin" will be a 表姐 (biǎojiě) if she is a daughter of one's father's sister or one's mother's sister or brother. But if she is one's paternal uncle's daughter, she will then be a 堂姐 (tángjiě) instead of a 表姐 (biǎojiě). For more Chinese kinship terms, see Grammar 4 in Lesson 20.

(Lǐ Yǒu gěi Wáng Péng dǎ diànhuà.)

Wáng Péng, nǐ zuò shénme ne①?

Wǒ kàn shū ne.

Jīntiān Gāo Xiǎoyīn guò shēngrì❶, wǎnshang wǒmen zài tā jiā kāi wǔhuì, nǐ néng qù ma?

Néng qù. Jǐ diǎn?

Qī diǎn. Wǒmen xiān chī fàn, chī wán fàn zài chàng gē tiào wǔ.

Yǒu nǎ xiē rén?

Xiǎoyīn hé tā de nánpéngyou, Xiǎoyīn de biǎojiě❷, Bái Yīng'ài, nǐ mèimei Wáng Hóng, tīngshuō hái yǒu Xiǎoyīn de zhōngxué tóngxué.

Nǐ yào sòng gěi Xiǎoyīn shénme shēngrì lǐwù?

Wǒ mǎi le yì běn shū sòng gěi tā.

Nà wǒ dài shénme dōngxi?

Yǐnliào huòzhě shuǐguǒ dōu kěyǐ.

Nà wǒ dài yì xiē yǐnliào, zài mǎi yì bǎ huār.

Xiǎoyīn ài chī shuǐguǒ, wǒ zài mǎi yì xiē píngguǒ, lí hé xīgua ba.

Nǐ zhù de dìfang[②] lí Xiǎoyīn jiā hěn yuǎn, shuǐguǒ hěn zhòng, wǒ kāi chē lái jiē nǐ, wǒmen yìqǐ qù ba.

Hǎo, wǒ liù diǎn bàn zài lóu xià děng nǐ.

VOCABULARY

1.	舞會	wǔhuì	n	dance party; ball
2.	表姐	biǎojiě	n	older female cousin
3.	中學	zhōngxué	n	middle school; secondary school
4.	送	sòng	v	to give as a gift
5.	禮物	lǐwù	n	gift; present
6.	本	běn	m	(measure word for books)
7.	飲料	yǐnliào	n	beverage
8.	水果	shuǐguǒ	n	fruit
9.	把	bǎ	m	(measure word for bunches of things, and chairs)
10.	花	huā	n	flower
11.	愛	ài	v	to love; to like; to be fond of
12.	蘋果	píngguǒ	n	apple

VOCABULARY

13. 梨	lí	n	pear
14. 西瓜	xīgua	n	watermelon
15. 住	zhù	v	to live (in a certain place)
16. 重	zhòng	adj	heavy; serious
17. 接	jiē	v	to catch; to meet; to welcome
18. 樓	lóu	n	multi-storied building; floor (of a multi-level building)

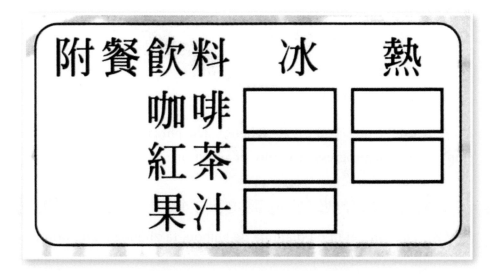

Proper Nouns

19. 王紅	Wáng Hóng	(a personal name)

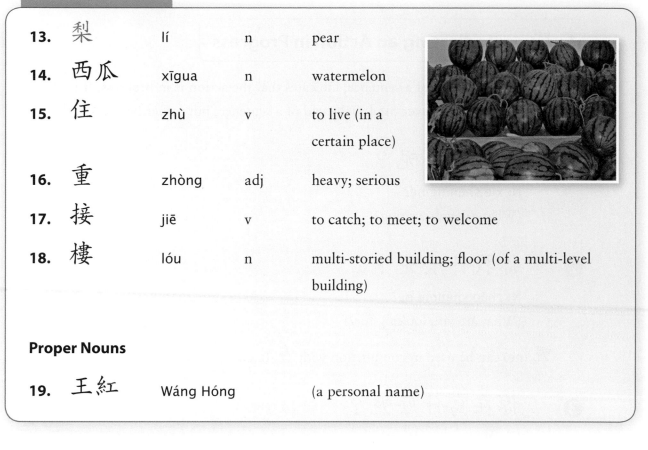

你想喝什麼飲料？熱的還是涼的？
Nǐ xiǎng hē shénme yǐnliào? Rè de háishi liáng de?

Grammar

1. 呢 (ne) Indicating an Action in Progress

呢 (ne), at the end of a sentence, indicates that the action is in progress. It is like 在 (zài), which is never used at the end of a sentence, but rather before a verb.

❶   你寫什麼呢？

Nǐ xiě shénme ne?

(What are you writing?)

❷   你找什麼呢？

Nǐ zhǎo shénme ne?

(What are you looking for?)

呢 (ne) can be used in conjunction with 在 (zài):

❸   你在寫什麼呢？

Nǐ zài xiě shénme ne?

(What are you writing?)

❹   你在找什麼呢？

Nǐ zài zhǎo shénme ne?

(What are you looking for?)

在 (zài) can be preceded by 正 (zhèng). The phrase 正在 (zhèngzài) places extra emphasis on the progressive nature of an action.

❺   我昨天給他打電話的時候，他正在做功課呢。

Wǒ zuótiān gěi tā dǎ diànhuà de shíhou, tā zhèngzài zuò gōngkè ne.

(When I called him yesterday, he was right in the middle of doing his homework.)

❻ 別去找他，他正在睡覺呢。

Bié qù zhǎo tā, tā zhèngzài shuì jiào ne.

(Don't go look for him. He is sleeping.)

在 (zài) alone indicates that an action is in progress; therefore, the 呢 (ne) in (3) and (4) above can be omitted.

2. Verbal Phrases and Subject-Predicate Phrases Used as Attributives

In Chinese, attributives, often followed by the particle 的 (de), always appear before the elements that they modify. Verbs, verbal phrases, and subject-object phrases can all serve as attributives.

❶ 吃的東西

chī de dōngxi

(things to eat)

❷ 穿的衣服

chuān de yīfu

(clothes to wear, or clothes being worn)

❸ 新買的飯卡

xīn mǎi de fànkǎ

(newly-bought meal cards)

❹ 昨天來的同學

zuótiān lái de tóngxué

(the classmate{s} who came yesterday)

❺ 以前認識的朋友

yǐqián rènshi de péngyou

(the friend{s} one got acquainted with in the past)

❻ 我媽媽做的豆腐

wǒ māma zuò de dòufu

(the tofu dish that my mother makes/made)

老師給我們的功課

lǎoshī gěi wǒmen de gōngkè

(the homework the teacher assigned us)

 朋友送的蘋果

péngyou sòng de píngguǒ

(the apples given by a friend)

 請你跳舞的那個人

qǐng nǐ tiào wǔ de nà gè rén

(that person who asked you to dance)

 我妹妹愛的那個很帥的男人

wǒ mèimei ài de nà ge hěn shuài de nánren

(that very handsome man that my sister loves)

Language Practice

> **A. What Are They Doing?**

With a partner, use the pictures to ask and answer what these people are doing.

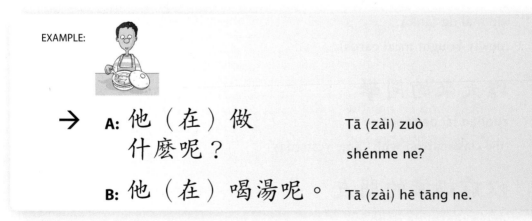

EXAMPLE:

→   A: 他（在）做
什麼呢？   Tā (zài) zuò
                      shénme ne?

B: 他（在）喝湯呢。   Tā (zài) hē tāng ne.

1.

2.

3.

4.

5.

B. Oh, That One!

Combine the two short sentences into one, using the highlighted verb or verb phrase as an attributive:

EXAMPLE:

他買了一件衣服   Tā mǎi le yí jiàn yīfu

那件衣服很貴   nà jiàn yīfu hěn guì

→ 他買的那件衣服很貴。   Tā mǎi de nà jiàn yīfu hěn guì.

1. 他寫了一個字
   那個字很漂亮
2. 她買了一件襯衫
   那件襯衫是紅的
3. 我哥哥給了我一枝筆
   那枝筆是黑的
4. 妹妹帶了一些水果
   那些水果很貴
5. 表姐賣了一些花
   那些花很漂亮

1. Tā xiě le yí ge zì

   nà ge zì hěn piàoliang

2. Tā mǎi le yí jiàn chènshān

   nà jiàn chènshān shì hóng de

3. Wǒ gēge gěi le wǒ yì zhī bǐ

   nà zhī bǐ shì hēi de

4. Mèimei dài le yì xiē shuǐguǒ

   nà xiē shuǐguǒ hěn guì

5. Biǎojiě mài le yì xiē huā

   nà xiē huā hěn piàoliang

C. Who's Who?

Help your new teacher match the names on the class roster with your classmates.

EXAMPLE 1:

A: Jamal 是誰？
B: Jamal 是那個穿黑色
襯衫的學生。

Jamal shì shéi?
Jamal shì nà ge chuān hēisè
chènshān de xuésheng.

EXAMPLE 2:

A: Katy 是誰？
B: Katy 是那個正在看書
的女孩。

Katy shì shéi?
Katy shì nà ge zhèngzài kàn shū
de nǚ hái.

1. Classmate 1
2. Classmate 2
3. Classmate 3
4. Classmate 4
5. Classmate 5

D. Recap and Narrate

Working with a partner, recap the content of Dialogue I:

1. 高小音哪天過
生日？

2. 李友他們晚上要
做什麼？

3. 他們吃晚飯以後還
要做什麼？

4. 哪些人去高小音家？

5. 李友買了什麼送給
小音？

6. 王朋要帶什麼
東西？

7. 李友要帶什麼？

8. 王朋為什麼要
開車接李友？

1. Gāo Xiǎoyīn nǎ tiān guò
shēngrì?

2. Lǐ Yǒu tāmen wǎnshang yào
zuò shénme?

3. Tāmen chī wǎnfàn yǐhòu hái
yào zuò shénme?

4. Nǎ xiē rén qù Gāo Xiǎoyīn jiā?

5. Lǐ Yǒu mǎi le shénme sòng gěi
Xiǎoyīn?

6. Wáng Péng yào dài shénme
dōngxi?

7. Lǐ Yǒu yào dài shénme?

8. Wáng Péng wèishénme yào
kāi chē jiē Lǐ Yǒu?

Using the words and phrases in blue as prompts, connect your answers above to form a narrative like this example:

李友告訴王朋今天是高小音的生日，晚上在小音家開生日舞會。除了小音的男朋友、表姐以外，小音的中學同學和白英愛也會去。她問王朋能不能去，王朋說他能去。他要帶飲料和花，李友買了一本書送給小音，還要帶一些蘋果、梨和西瓜。因為李友住的地方離高小音家很遠，水果很重，所以王朋要開車接李友一起去。李友說她六點半在樓下等王朋。

Lǐ Yǒu gàosù Wáng Péng jīntiān shì Gāo Xiǎoyīn de shēngrì, wǎnshang zài Xiǎoyīn jiā kāi shēngrì wǔhuì. Chúle Xiǎoyīn de nánpéngyou, biǎojiě yǐwài, Xiǎoyīn de zhōngxué tóngxué hé Bái Yīng'ài yě huì qù. Tā wèn Wáng Péng néng bù néng qù, Wáng Péng shuō tā néng qù. Tā yào dài yǐnliào hé huā, Lǐ Yǒu mǎi le yì běn shū sòng gěi Xiǎoyīn, hái yào dài yì xiē píngguǒ, lí hé xīgua. Yīnwèi Lǐ Yǒu zhù de dìfang lí Gāo Xiǎoyīn jiā hěn yuǎn, shuǐguǒ hěn zhòng, suǒyǐ Wáng Péng yào kāi chē jiē Lǐ Yǒu yìqǐ qù. Lǐ Yǒu shuō tā liù diǎn bàn zài lóu xià děng Wáng Péng.

This is a store's name. What do you think the store wants people to buy?

Dialogue II: Attending a Birthday Party

（在高小音家）

王朋，李友，快進來。

小音，祝你生日快樂！
這是送給你的生日禮物。

謝謝！(She opens the gift.) 太好了！
我一直想買這本書。帶這麼
多東西，你們太客氣了。

哥哥，李友，你們來了❶。

啊。小紅，你怎麼樣？

我很好。每天都在學英文。

LANGUAGE NOTES

❶ 你們來了 (Nǐmen lái le, You're here) not only acknowledges the visitors' arrival, but also serves as a casual greeting.

小紅，你每天練習英文練習多長時間③？

三個半鐘頭②。還看兩個鐘頭的英文電視。

哎，你們兩個是什麼時候到的④？

剛到。

白英愛沒跟你們一起來嗎？

她還⑤沒來？我以為③她已經來了。

王朋，李友，來，我給你們介紹一下，這是我表姐海倫，這是她的兒子湯姆。

你好，海倫。

你好，王朋。文中和小音都說你又聰明④又用功⑥。

哪裏，哪裏。你的中文說得真好，是在哪兒學的？

在暑期班⑤學的。

② 鐘頭 (zhōngtóu) is the colloquial equivalent of 小時 (xiǎoshí).

③ 以為 (yǐwéi) is often used to signify an understanding or judgment which has proved to be erroneous. If someone has realized that she was mistaken in assuming someone else to be vegetarian, she could say to that person: 我以為你吃素 (Wǒ yǐwéi nǐ chī sù. I thought you were a vegetarian).

④ About the formation of the adjective 聰明 (cōngming; clever): 聰 (cōng) literally means "able to hear well," and 明 (míng) means "able to see clearly," among other things. Therefore, 聰明 describes someone who is perceptive or bright.

⑤ The Chinese words 班 (bān) and 課 (kè) denote two different concepts that are represented by the same word, "class," in English. While 課 (kè) refers to a course or a meeting time for the course, 班 (bān) is the term for the group of students who take a course together. Thus one says "我今天有電腦課" (Wǒ jīntiān yǒu diànnǎo kè, I have a computer class today), but "我的電腦班有二十個人" (Wǒ de diànnǎo bān yǒu èrshí ge rén, There are twenty people in my computer class).

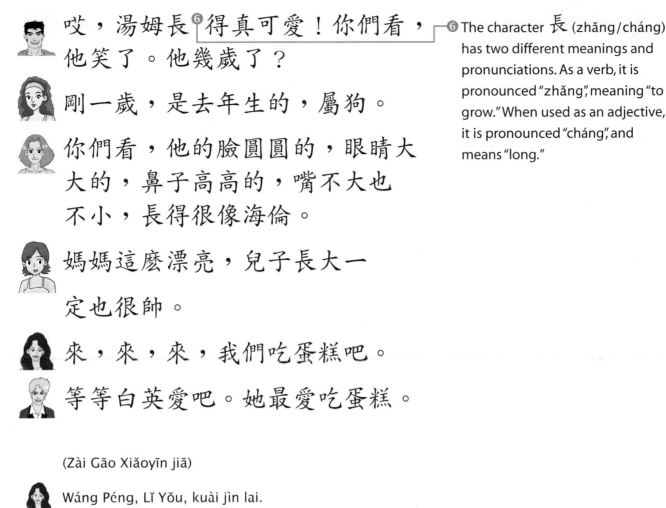

哎，湯姆長得真可愛！你們看，他笑了。他幾歲了？

剛一歲，是去年生的，屬狗。

你們看，他的臉圓圓的，眼睛大大的，鼻子高高的，嘴不大也不小，長得很像海倫。

媽媽這麼漂亮，兒子長大一定也很帥。

來，來，來，我們吃蛋糕吧。

等等白英愛吧。她最愛吃蛋糕。

6 The character 長 (zhǎng/cháng) has two different meanings and pronunciations. As a verb, it is pronounced "zhǎng", meaning "to grow." When used as an adjective, it is pronounced "cháng", and means "long."

(Zài Gāo Xiǎoyīn jiā)

Wáng Péng, Lǐ Yǒu, kuài jìn lai.

Xiǎoyīn, zhù nǐ shēngrì kuàilè! Zhè shì sòng gěi nǐ de shēngrì lǐwù.

Xièxiè! (She opens the gift.) Tài hǎo le! Wǒ yìzhí xiǎng mǎi zhè běn shū. Dài zhème duō dōngxi, nǐmen tài kèqi le.

Gēge, Lǐ Yǒu, nǐmen lái le❶.

À. Xiǎo Hóng, nǐ zěnmeyàng?

Wǒ hěn hǎo. Měitiān dōu zài xué Yīngwén.

Xiǎo Hóng, nǐ měitiān liànxí Yīngwén liànxí duō cháng shíjiān③?

Sān ge bàn zhōngtóu❷. Hái kàn liǎng ge zhōngtóu de Yīngwén diànshì.

Āi, nǐmen liǎng ge shì shénme shíhou dào de④?

Gāng dào.

Bái Yīng'ài méi gēn nǐmen yìqǐ lái ma?

Tā hái⑤ méi lái? Wǒ yǐwéi❸ tā yǐjīng lái le.

Wáng Péng, Lǐ Yǒu, lái, wǒ gěi nǐmen jièshào yí xià, zhè shì wǒ biǎojiě Hǎilún, zhè shì tā de érzi Tāngmǔ.

Nǐ hǎo, Hǎilún.

Nǐ hǎo, Wáng Péng. Wénzhōng hé Xiǎoyīn dōu shuō nǐ yòu cōngming④ yòu yònggōng⑥.

Nǎli, nǎli. Nǐ de Zhōngwén shuō de zhēn hǎo, shì zài nǎr xué de?

Zài shǔqī bān⑤ xué de.

Āi, Tāngmǔ zhǎng⑥ de zhēn kě'ài! Nǐmen kàn, tā xiào le. Tā jǐ suì le?

Gāng yí suì, shì qùnián shēng de, shǔ gǒu.

Nǐmen kàn, tā de liǎn yuán yuán de, yǎnjing dà dà de, bízi gāo gāo de, zuǐ bú dà yě bù xiǎo, zhǎng de hěn xiàng Hǎilún.

Māma zhème piàoliang, érzi zhǎng dà yídìng yě hěn shuài.

Lái, lái, lái, wǒmen chī dàngāo ba.

Děng děng Bái Yīng'ài ba. Tā zuì ài chī dàngāo.

VOCABULARY

1.	鐘頭	zhōngtóu	n	hour
2.	以為	yǐwéi	v	to assume erroneously
3.	聰明	cōngming	adj	smart; bright; clever
4.	用功	yònggōng	adj	hard-working; diligent; studious
5.	暑期	shǔqī	n	summer term
6.	班	bān	n	class
7.	長	zhǎng	v	to grow; to appear
8.	可愛	kě'ài	adj	cute; lovable
9.	去年	qùnián	t	last year
10.	屬	shǔ	v	to belong to

VOCABULARY

11.	狗	gǒu	n	dog
12.	臉	liǎn	n	face
13.	圓	yuán	adj	round
14.	眼睛	yǎnjing	n	eye
15.	鼻子	bízi	n	nose
16.	嘴	zuǐ	n	mouth
17.	像	xiàng	v	to be like; to look like; to take after
18.	長大	zhǎng dà	vc	to grow up
19.	一定	yídìng	adj/adv	certain(ly); definite(ly)
20.	蛋糕	dàngāo	n	cake
21.	最	zuì	adv	most, (of superlative degree) -est

Proper Nouns

22.	海倫	Hǎilún	Helen
23.	湯姆	Tāngmǔ	Tom

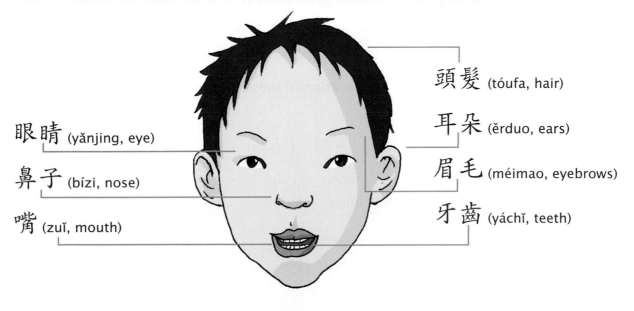

眼睛 (yǎnjing, eye)

鼻子 (bízi, nose)

嘴 (zuǐ, mouth)

頭髮 (tóufa, hair)

耳朵 (ěrduo, ears)

眉毛 (méimao, eyebrows)

牙齒 (yáchǐ, teeth)

Grammar

3. Time Duration

To indicate the duration of an action, the following structure is used:

Subject + Verb + (Object + Verb) + (了) + Duration of time

 老高想在上海住一年。

Lǎo Gāo xiǎng zài Shànghǎi zhù yì nián.)

(Old Gao wishes to live in Shanghai for a year.)

 我每天在書店工作三個鐘頭。

Wǒ měitiān zài shūdiàn gōngzuò sān ge zhōngtóu.

(I work in a bookstore for three hours every day.)

 昨天下雪下了二十分鐘。

Zuótiān xià xuě xià le èrshí fēnzhōng.

(It snowed for twenty minutes yesterday.)

 你上暑期班上了多長時間？

Nǐ shàng shǔqī bān shàng le duō cháng shíjiān?

(How long were you in summer school?)

Sentences in this pattern must be in the affirmative. If the verb takes an object, the verb has to be repeated, as in (3) and (4). If the verb has an object, the following alternative pattern can be used to express the same idea.

Subject + Verb + (了) + Duration of time + (的) + Object

 昨天下了二十分鐘（的）雪。

Zuótiān xià le èrshí fēnzhōng (de) xuě.

(It snowed for twenty minutes yesterday.)

❻   我上了四個星期（的）暑期班。

　　　Wǒ shàng le sì ge xīngqī (de) shǔqī bān.

　　　(I was in summer school for four weeks.)

The phrase for the length of time must not be put before the verb:

(6a)   *我四個星期上了暑期班。

　　　*Wǒ sì ge xīngqī shàng le shǔqī bān.

---

4. Sentences with 是…的 (shì…de)

To describe or inquire about the time, the place, the manner, or the initiator of an action that we know already happened, we need to use the 是…的 (shì…de) structure. The use of 是 (shì), however, is optional.

❶ A: 你去過北京嗎？

　　　Nǐ qù guo Běijīng ma?

　　　(Have you been to Beijing?)

B: 我去過北京。

　　　Wǒ qù guo Běijīng.

　　　(Yes, I've been to Beijing.)

Person A now becomes aware of Person B's action of 去北京 (qù Běijīng, went to Beijing), and wants to find out when, how, and with whom that action was performed:

A: 你是跟誰一起去的？

　　　Nǐ shì gēn shéi yìqǐ qù de?

　　　(With whom did you go?)

B: 我是跟我表姐一起去的。

　　　Wǒ shì gēn wǒ biǎojiě yìqǐ qù de.

　　　(I went with my cousin.)

A: 你們是什麼時候去的？

　　　Nǐmen shì shénme shíhou qù de?

　　　(When did you go?)

B: 我們是寒假去的 。

Wǒmen shì hánjià qù de.

(We went during the winter break.)

A: 你們是怎麼去的？

Nǐmen shì zěnme qù de?

(How did you go?)

B: 我們是坐飛機去的。

Wǒmen shì zuò fēijī qù de.

(We went there by airplane.)

❷ **A:** 你看過這張碟嗎？

Nǐ kàn guo zhè zhāng dié ma?

(Have you watched this DVD?)

B: 看過 。

Kàn guo.

(Yes, I have.)

A: 是什麼時候看的？

Shì shénme shíhou kàn de?

(When did you watch it?)

[A already knows that the action 看 (kàn) was completed.]

B: 上個週末看的 。

Shàng ge zhōumò kàn de.

(I watched it last weekend.)

[It was last weekend that I watched it.]

❸ **A:** 你這條褲子真好看。是在哪兒買的？

Nǐ zhè tiáo kùzi zhēn hǎokàn. Shì zài nǎr mǎi de?

(These pants of yours look great. Where did you get them?)

[It's assumed that one generally buys pants (as opposed to making them at home, etc.), so the action 買 (mǎi) is already known.]

❹ A: 你吃飯了嗎？

Nǐ chī fàn le ma?

(Have you eaten yet?)

B: 吃了。

Chī le.

(Yes, I have.)

[The action 吃 (chī) is now known.]

A: 在哪兒吃的？

Zài nǎr chī de?

(Where did you eat?)

B: 在學生餐廳吃的。

Zài xuéshēng cāntīng chī de.

(In the student cafeteria.)

❺ A: 你學過電腦嗎？

Nǐ xué guo diànnǎo ma?

(Have you ever studied computers?)

B: 學過。

Xué guo.

(Yes, I have.)

A: 是跟誰學的？

Shì gēn shéi xué de?

(With whom did you study?)

B: 是跟王老師學的。

Shì gēn Wáng lǎoshī xué de.

(With Teacher Wang.)

5. 還 (hái, **still**)

還(hái), as an adverb, can mean "still."

 上午十一點了，他還在睡覺。

Shàngwǔ shíyī diǎn le, tā hái zài shuì jiào.

(It's 11 a.m., and he is still sleeping.)

 今天的功課，我還沒寫完。

Jīntiān de gōngkè, wǒ hái méi xiě wán.

(I'm still not done with today's homework.)

 這個語法老師教了，可是我還不懂。

Zhè ge yǔfǎ lǎoshī jiāo le, kěshì wǒ hái bù dǒng.

(The teacher has gone over this grammar point, but I still don't understand it.)

6. 又⋯⋯又⋯⋯ (yòu...yòu..., **both...and...**)

The two adjectives used in this structure are either both positive or both negative in meaning, e.g., 又聰明又用功 (yòu cōngming yòu yònggōng, smart and hardworking) [both adjectives are positive in meaning], 又多又難 (yòu duō yòu nán, too much and difficult) [both adjectives are negative in meaning].

Language Practice

E. Where Did You Get That?

You love your friend's print of an Ansel Adams photograph. You want to find out where and when he or she bought it, how much he or she spent on it, and whether he or she bought it himself or herself. You will start by saying:

這張照片真好看⋯   Zhè zhāng zhàopiàn zhēn hǎokàn...

and then you will ask

（是）在哪兒買的？   (Shì) zài nǎr mǎi de?

（是）什麼時候買的？   (Shì) shénme shíhou mǎi de?

（是）誰買的？   (Shì) shéi mǎi de?

（是）多少錢買的？   (Shì) duōshao qián mǎi de?

Now you are checking out other classmates' shoes, shirts, jeans, pens, cars, etc., and you want to know as much as possible about each of those things.

F. Older or Younger

Go around the class and interview your classmates. Find out everyone's birthplace, birth year, and Chinese zodiac sign. Then report to the class how many classmates are older than you, how many are younger than you, how many were born in the same state/province/city as you were, and which zodiac sign is most common in the class.

1. 你是在哪兒生的？   **1.** Nǐ shì zài nǎr shēng de?

2. 你是哪一年生的？   **2.** Nǐ shì nǎ yì nián shēng de?

3. 你屬什麼？   **3.** Nǐ shǔ shénme?

G. Travel Interview

Work with a partner to discuss where you have traveled. Take turns asking each other:

1. 你去過(a city or a country)嗎？   **1.** Nǐ qù guo (a city or a country) ma?

2. 你（是）什麼時候去的？   **2.** Nǐ (shì) shénme shíhou qù de?

3. 你（是）跟誰一起去的？   **3.** Nǐ (shì) gēn shéi yìqǐ qù de?

4. 你（是）怎麼去的？   **4.** Nǐ (shì) zěnme qù de?

H. Fantasy Trip or Boot Camp?

Imagine that you've signed up to go on a whirlwind tour of China during summer break. You just got your itinerary, and the travel schedule looks very intense. The trip leaders have scheduled each day down to the minute. Answer your classmates' questions on how much time you'll have for each activity.

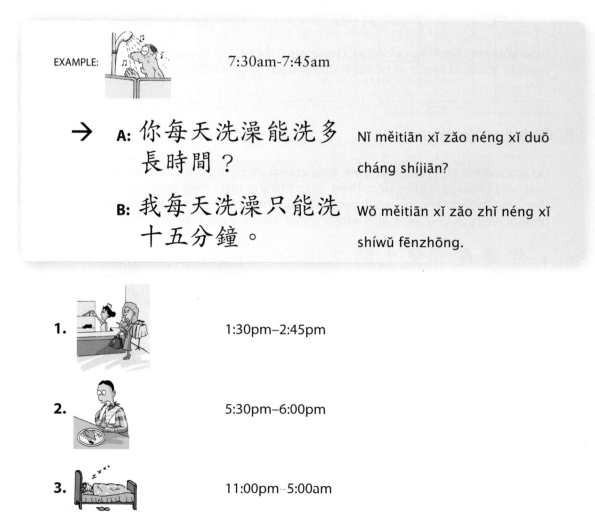

EXAMPLE: 7:30am–7:45am

→ **A:** 你每天洗澡能洗多長時間？   Nǐ měitiān xǐ zǎo néng xǐ duō cháng shíjiān?

B: 我每天洗澡只能洗十五分鐘。   Wǒ měitiān xǐ zǎo zhǐ néng xǐ shíwǔ fēnzhōng.

1.   1:30pm–2:45pm

2.   5:30pm–6:00pm

3.   11:00pm–5:00am

I. Last Night

Move around the class and ask your classmates how they spent their time last night.

EXAMPLE: **Emily**

A: Emily, 你昨天晚上做什麼了？

B: 我昨天晚上看電視了。

A: 你昨天晚上看電視看了多長時間？

B: 我昨天晚上看電視看了半個鐘頭。

A: Emily, nǐ zuótiān wǎnshang zuò shénme le?

B: Wǒ zuótiān wǎnshang kàn diànshì le.

A: Nǐ zuótiān wǎnshang kàn diànshì kàn le duō cháng shíjiān?

B: Wǒ zuótiān wǎnshang kàn diànshì kàn le bàn ge zhōngtóu.

Then record your findings.

Emily 昨天晚上看電視看了半個鐘頭。

Emily zuótiān wǎnshang kàn diànshì kàn le bàn ge zhōngtóu.

1. Classmate 1
2. Classmate 2
3. Classmate 3
4. Classmate 4

J. Is the Baby Cute or What?

Work with your partner to describe the baby's features, and comment on whether the baby is cute.

K. Let's Plan a Party!

Find out among your classmates whose birthday is coming up by asking 誰的生日快到了？(Shéi de shēngrì kuài dào le?) Everyone should take a turn to ask that person what he or she likes to eat, drink, and do. Then work as a class to plan a birthday party together, and decide who will bring what to the party.

L. Recap and Narrate

Working with a partner, recap the content of Dialogue II:

1. 王朋和李友給高小音生日禮物的時候，高小音說什麼了？

   1. Wáng Péng hé Lǐ Yǒu gěi Gāo Xiǎoyīn shēngrì lǐwù de shíhou, Gāo Xiǎoyīn shuō shénme le?

2. 王紅每天練習英文練習多長時間？

   2. Wáng Hóng měitiān liànxí Yīngwén liànxí duō cháng shíjiān?

3. 白英愛來了嗎？

   3. Bái Yīng'ài lái le ma?

4. 高小音的表姐叫什麼名字？表姐的兒子叫什麼名字？

   4. Gāo Xiǎoyīn de biǎojiě jiào shénme míngzi? Biǎojiě de érzi jiào shénme míngzi?

5. 表姐是在哪兒學的中文？

   5. Biǎojiě shì zài nǎr xué de Zhōngwén?

6. 表姐的兒子幾歲了？

   6. Biǎojiě de érzi jǐ suì le?

7. 表姐的兒子長得什麼樣？

   7. Biǎojiě de érzi zhǎng de shénme yàng?

8. 高文中為什麼要等白英愛吃蛋糕？

   8. Gāo Wénzhōng wèishénme yào děng Bái Yīng'ài chī dàngāo?

Using the words and phrases in blue as prompts, connect your answers above to form a narrative like this example:

今天晚上高小音家開生日舞會。王朋和李友是一起去的，他們送給了小音生日禮物，高小音很高興，說王朋和李友太客氣了。王朋的妹妹王紅在高小音家住，每天練習三個半小時的英文，還看兩個小時電視。高小音的表姐叫海倫，她的兒子叫湯姆。海倫在暑期班學過中文，她的中文說得很好。湯姆是去年生的，剛一歲，屬狗。他長得很可愛，臉圓圓的，眼睛大大的，鼻子高高的，嘴不大也不小，很像海倫。高小音讓大家吃蛋糕，可是高文中說要等白英愛，因為白英愛最愛吃蛋糕。真是這樣嗎？還是因為他喜歡白英愛了？

Jīntiān wǎnshang Gāo Xiǎoyīn jiā kāi shēngrì wǔhuì. Wáng Péng hé Lǐ Yǒu shì yìqǐ qù de, tāmen sòng gěi le Xiǎoyīn shēngrì lǐwù, Gāo Xiǎoyīn hěn gāoxìng, shuō Wáng Péng hé Lǐ Yǒu tài kèqi le. Wáng Péng de mèimei Wáng Hóng zài Gāo Xiǎoyīn jiā zhù, měitiān liànxí sān ge bàn xiǎoshí de Yīngwén, hái kàn liǎng ge xiǎoshí diànshì. Gāo Xiǎoyīn de biǎojiě jiào Hǎilún, tā de érzi jiào Tāngmǔ. Hǎilún zài shǔqī bān xué guo Zhōngwén, tā de Zhōngwén shuō de hěn hǎo. Tāngmǔ shì qùnián shēng de, gāng yí suì, shǔ gǒu. Tā zhǎng de hěn kě'ài, liǎn yuán yuán de, yǎnjing dà dà de, bízi gāo gāo de, zuǐ bú dà yě bù xiǎo, hěn xiàng Hǎilún. Gāo Xiǎoyīn ràng dàjiā chī dàngāo, kěshì Gāo Wénzhōng shuō yào děng Bái Yīng'ài, yīnwèi Bái Yīng'ài zuì ài chī dàngāo. Zhēn shì zhèyàng ma? Háishi yīnwèi tā xǐhuan Bái Yīng'ài le?

HOW ABOUT YOU?

What's your favorite fruit?

1.	香蕉	xiāngjiāo	n
2.	草莓	cǎoméi	n
3.	橘子	júzi	n
4.	桃兒	táor	n
5.	葡萄	pútao	n

If your favorite fruit is not listed above, please ask your teacher and make a note here:

_____

What would you bring to a birthday party?

1.	氣球	qìqiú	n	balloons
2.	卡片	kǎpiàn	n	card
3.	汽水（兒）	qìshuǐ(r)	n	soft drink; soda pop
4.	零食	língshí	n	snacks
5.	餅乾	bǐnggān	n	cookies; crackers
6.	糖（果）	táng (guǒ)	n	candy

What other things could one bring to a party? Please ask your teacher and make a note here:

_____

Culture Highlights

❶ Potluck dinner parties are not as popular in China as they are in the United States. The Chinese host or hostess will usually prepare everything for the dinner and not count on the guests for any contributions. But a visitor can still bring something as a token of his or her appreciation, like a fruit basket, a bottle of wine, or a bouquet of flowers.

❷ Nowadays, when Chinese people sing for fun, they usually sing karaoke (卡拉 OK, kǎlā'ōukēi) style. Many people in mainland China and Taiwan regularly go to karaoke bars to have a good time or celebrate someone's birthday. They can order food and beverages and reserve private rooms for their parties. Some people even have karaoke equipment at home.

❸ The Chinese usually express their appreciation of a gift profusely, typically by saying "你太客氣了！" (Nǐ tài kèqi le, You're really too kind!). However, most Chinese people would refrain from opening the present immediately in front of the gift giver lest they appear too greedy. Flowers make good gifts, but for happy occasions one should avoid bouquets of white flowers, which are typically for funerals. Another taboo is giving a clock to an elderly person as a present, because the phrase 送鐘 (sòng zhōng, to give a clock as a present) is ominously homophonous with 送終 (sòng zhōng), which means to attend someone's burial.

❹ There are twelve animal signs in the Chinese zodiac, each representing one year in a twelve-year cycle. According to a popular but unscientific theory, one's personality and temperament have much to do with the animal that represents the year of one's birth. It might be surprising that the twelve-year cycle should start with the year of the rat, the smallest and perhaps the least likable of the twelve animals. At the beginning, as the story goes, there was a bitter quarrel among the animals as to who should represent the first year of the cycle. Finally, they decided to settle the dispute with a race. The robust ox was in the lead all the way, but he did not notice that the tiny rat was taking a ride on his back. As the ox was approaching the end, the rat jumped down and hit the finish line first, while the disappointed ox had to settle for second place. The indolent pig finished last in the race, and accordingly was assigned to the final year of the cycle. The following is a list of the twelve animal signs and the years in recent decades that each of them represents:

1.	鼠	shǔ	rat	1948, 1960, 1972, 1984, 1996, 2008
2.	牛	niú	ox; cow	1949, 1961, 1973, 1985, 1997, 2009
3.	虎	hǔ	tiger	1950, 1962, 1974, 1986, 1998, 2010
4.	兔	tù	rabbit; hare	1951, 1963, 1975, 1987, 1999, 2011
5.	龍	lóng	dragon	1952, 1964, 1976, 1988, 2000, 2012
6.	蛇	shé	snake; serpent	1953, 1965, 1977, 1989, 2001, 2013
7.	馬	mǎ	horse	1954, 1966, 1978, 1990, 2002, 2014
8.	羊	yáng	sheep; goat; ram	1955, 1967, 1979, 1991, 2003, 2015
9.	猴	hóu	monkey	1956, 1968, 1980, 1992, 2004, 2016
10.	雞	jī	rooster; chicken	1957, 1969, 1981, 1993, 2005, 2017
11.	狗	gǒu	dog	1958, 1970, 1982, 1994, 2006, 2018
12.	豬	zhū	pig; boar	1959, 1971, 1983, 1995, 2007, 2019

English Text

Dialogue I

(Li You is on the phone with Wang Peng.)

Li You: Wang Peng, what are you doing?

Wang Peng: I'm reading.

Li You: Today is Gao Xiaoyin's birthday. Tonight we're having a dance party at her place. Can you go?

Wang Peng: Yes. What time?

Li You: Seven o'clock. We'll eat first. After dinner we'll sing and dance.

Wang Peng: Who will be there?

Li You: Xiaoyin and her boyfriend, Xiaoyin's cousin, Bai Ying'ai, your sister Wang Hong, and Xiaoyin's middle school classmates, I hear.

Wang Peng: What birthday gift are you giving Xiaoyin?

Li You: I bought a book to give to her.

Wang Peng: What should I bring?

Li You: Either beverages or fruit would do.

Wang Peng: Then I'll bring some beverages. I'll also get some flowers.

Li You: Xiaoyin loves fruit. I'll get some apples, pears and a watermelon.

Wang Peng: Your place is very far from Xiaoyin's house, and the fruit will be heavy. I'll come to pick you up. Let's go together.

Li You: OK, I'll wait for you downstairs at six-thirty.

Dialogue II

(At Gao Xiaoyin's house)

Gao Xiaoyin: Wang Peng, Li You, come in.

Li You: Happy birthday, Xiaoyin. This is a birthday gift for you.

Gao Xiaoyin: Thank you. (She opens the gift.) I always wanted to buy this book. You brought so many things with you. You're really too kind.

Wang Hong: Hey brother, Li You, you're here.

Li You: Xiao Hong, how are you?

Wang Hong: I'm fine. I'm studying English every day.

Wang Peng: Xiao Hong, how much time do you spend practicing English every day?

Wang Hong: Three and half hours, plus I watch two hours of English-language TV.

Gao Wenzhong: When did you two get here?

Li You: Just now.

Gao Wenzhong: Didn't Bai Ying'ai come with you?

Li You: She's still not here? I thought she'd already gotten here.

Gao Xiaoyin: Wang Peng, Li You, let me introduce you. This is my cousin Helen. This is her son Tom.

Wang Peng: Hello, Helen.

Helen: Hello, Wang Peng. Wenzhong and Xiaoyin say that you're very smart and very hardworking.

Wang Peng: You flatter me. Your Chinese is great. Where did you learn it?

Helen: At summer school.

Wang Peng: Hey, Tom is really cute. Look, he's smiling now. How old is he?

Helen: He just turned one. He was born last year, the year of the dog.

Li You: Look, he's got a round face, big eyes, and a straight nose. His mouth is not too big, and not too small. He looks just like Helen.

Wang Hong: With such a gorgeous mom, the son will definitely be very handsome.

Gao Xiaoyin: Come, let's eat the cake.

Gao Wenzhong: Why don't we wait for Bai Ying'ai? She loves cake.

PROGRESS CHECKLIST

Before proceeding to Lesson 15, be sure you can complete the following tasks in Chinese:

I am able to—

- ☑ Ask a friend to attend a party;
- ☐ Offer a ride and set up a place and time for picking up someone;
- ☐ Talk about the duration of an action;
- ☐ Thank someone for his or her gift;
- ☐ Ask someone about his or her birth year and Chinese zodiac sign, and talk about my own;
- ☐ Give a basic description of someone's facial features.

牛年
Niú nián (the Year of the Ox)

LESSON 15

Seeing a Doctor

15

第十五課 看病

Dì shíwù kè   Kàn bìng

LEARNING OBJECTIVES

In this lesson, you will learn to use Chinese to

- Talk about basic symptoms of a cold;
- Describe common symptoms of allergies;
- Understand and repeat instructions on when and how often to take medications;
- Talk about why you do or don't want to see the doctor;
- Urge others to see a doctor when they are not feeling well.

RELATE AND GET READY

In your own culture/community—

1. Can you see a doctor without an appointment?
2. Do you have to pay an office visit fee before seeing a doctor?
3. Is it common to see the doctor and pay for medication at the same place?
4. Apart from medication, what other kinds of treatment might a doctor recommend?
5. Is everyone covered by health insurance?

Dialogue I: My Stomachache Is Killing Me!

（病人去醫院看病）

醫生，我肚子疼死①了。

你昨天吃什麼東西了？

我姐姐上個星期過生日，蛋糕沒吃完。昨天晚上我吃了幾口②，夜裏肚子就疼起來了③，今天早上上了好幾次②廁所。

你把④蛋糕放在哪兒了？

放在冰箱裏了。

放了幾天了？

五、六❶天了。

發燒嗎？

不發燒。

你躺下。先檢查一下。

* * *

你吃蛋糕把肚子吃壞了。

要不要打針？

不用打針，吃這種藥❷
就可以。一天三次，一次
兩片。

醫生，一天吃幾次？請您
再說一遍。

一天三次，一次兩片。

好！飯前❸吃還是飯後
吃？

飯前飯後都可以。不過，
你最好二十四小時不吃
飯。

那我要餓死了。不行，這
個辦法不好！

LANGUAGE NOTES

❶ A combination of two adjacent numbers can be used to denote an approximate number, e.g., 五十六、七歲 (wǔshí liù, qī suì, fifty-six or fifty-seven years old), 十八、九塊錢 (shí bā, jiǔ kuài qián, eighteen or nineteen dollars), 三、四天 (sān, sì tiān, three or four days), 兩、三枝筆 (liǎng, sān zhī bǐ, two or three pens). However, the numbers nine and ten cannot be used this way since it could lead to ambiguity: it would be difficult to distinguish 九、十天 (jiǔ, shí tiān) from 九十天 (jiǔshí tiān, ninety days) in speech.

❷ "To take medicine" is 吃藥 (chī yào), literally "to eat medicine." A more formal expression is 服藥 (fú yào), which is commonly written on prescriptions and prescription instructions.

❸ 前 (qián, before) in 飯前 (fàn qián, before meals) and 後 (hòu, after) in 飯後 (fàn hòu; after meals) are the shortened forms of 以前 (yǐqián, before) and 以後 (yǐhòu, after) respectively.

(Bìngrén qù yīyuàn kàn bìng)

Yīshēng, wǒ dùzi téng sǐ① le.

Nǐ zuótiān chī shénme dōngxi le?

Wǒ jiějie shàng ge xīngqī guò shēngrì, dàngāo méi chī wán. Zuótiān wǎnshang wǒ chī le jǐ kǒu②, yè li dùzi jiù téng qi lai le③, jīntiān zǎoshang shàng le hǎojǐ cì② cèsuǒ.

Nǐ bǎ④ dàngāo fàng zài nǎr le?

Fàng zài bīngxiāng lǐ le.

Fàng le jǐ tiān le?

Wǔ, liù❶ tiān le.

Fā shāo ma?

Bù fā shāo.

Nǐ tǎng xia. Xiān jiǎnchá yí xià.

* * *

Nǐ chī dàngāo bǎ dùzi chī huài le.

Yào bú yào dǎ zhēn?

Búyòng dǎ zhēn, chī zhè zhǒng yào❷ jiù kěyǐ. Yì tiān sān cì, yí cì liǎng piàn.

Yīshēng, yì tiān chī jǐ cì? Qǐng nín zài shuō yí biàn.

Yì tiān sān cì, yí cì liǎng piàn.

Hǎo! Fàn qián❸ chī háishi fàn hòu chī?

Fàn qián fàn hòu dōu kěyǐ. Búguò, nǐ zuìhǎo èrshí sì xiǎoshí bù chī fàn.

Nà wǒ yào è sǐ le. Bù xíng, zhè ge bànfǎ bù hǎo!

VOCABULARY

1.	病人	bìngrén	n	patient
	病	bìng	n/v	illness; to become ill
2.	醫院	yīyuàn	n	hospital
3.	看病	kàn bìng	vo	to see a doctor; (of a doctor) to see a patient
4.	肚子	dùzi	n	belly; abdomen
5.	疼死	téng sǐ	adj + c	really painful [See Grammar 1.]
	疼	téng	adj	aching
	死	sǐ	v/c	to die; (a complement indicating an extreme degree)
6.	夜裏	yèli	n	at night
7.	好幾	hǎo jǐ		quite a few
8.	廁所	cèsuǒ	n	restroom, toilet
9.	把	bǎ	prep	(indicating a thing is disposed of) [See Grammar 4.]
10.	冰箱	bīngxiāng	n	refrigerator
11.	發燒	fā shāo	vo	to have a fever
12.	躺下	tǎng xia	vc	to lie down
	躺	tǎng	v	to lie
13.	檢查	jiǎnchá	v	to examine
14.	吃壞	chī huài	vc	to get sick because of bad food
	壞	huài	adj	bad
15.	打針	dǎ zhēn	vo	to get an injection
	針	zhēn	n	needle
16.	藥	yào	n	medicine

VOCABULARY

17.	片	piàn	m	(measure word for tablet; slice)
18.	遍	biàn	m	(measure word for complete courses of an action or instances of an action)
19.	最好	zuìhǎo	adv	had better
20.	小時	xiǎoshí	n	hour
21.	辦法	bànfǎ	n	method; way (of doing something)

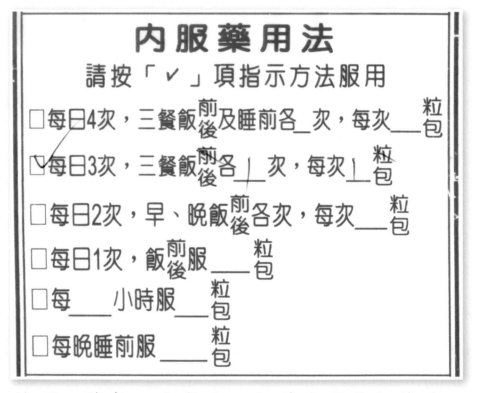

請問，藥每天吃幾次？飯前吃還是飯後吃？
Qǐng wèn, yào měitiān chī jǐ cì? Fàn qián chī háishi fàn hòu chī?

Grammar

1. 死 (sǐ) Indicating an Extreme Degree

Placed after an adjective, 死 (sǐ) can serve as a complement to indicate an extreme degree of the condition named by the adjective.

 打針疼死了。

Dǎ zhēn téng sǐ le.

(It's extremely painful to get a shot.)

② 我餓死了。

Wǒ è sǐ le.

(I'm starving.)

③ 今天熱死了。

Jīntiān rè sǐ le.

(It's awfully hot today.)

死 (sǐ) often follows an adjective with a pejorative meaning and therefore the combination carries a negative connotation, as shown in the examples above. Occasionally, however, it may also be used in a positive context.

④ 知道了這件事，他高興死了。

Zhīdào le zhè jiàn shì, tā gāoxìng sǐ le.

(He was tickled pink when he learned about this.)

Most complimentary adjectives cannot be followed by 死 (sǐ). People therefore seldom say:

 *那件衣服漂亮死了。

*Nà jiàn yīfu piàoliang sǐ le.

 *他跟他女朋友好死了。

*Tā gēn tā de nǚ péngyou hǎo sǐ le.

2. Times of Actions

次 (cì) is the measure word most frequently used to indicate that an action is performed a certain number of times. The "number + 次 (cì)" combination follows the verb.

❶ 上午我打了兩次電話。

Shàngwǔ wǒ dǎ le liǎng cì diànhuà.

(I made two phone calls in the morning.)

❷ 昨天我吃了三次藥。

Zuótiān wǒ chī le sān cì yào.

(I took the medicine three times yesterday.)

If the object is not a person or a place, 次 (cì) should be placed between the verb and the object. If the object represents a person or a place, 次 (cì) can go either between the verb and the object or after the object.

❸ A: 去年我去了一次中國。你呢？

Qùnián wǒ qù le yí cì Zhōngguó. Nǐ ne?

(Last year I went to China once. How about you?)

B: 去年我去了中國兩次。

Qùnián wǒ qù le Zhōngguó liǎng cì.

(Last year I went to China twice.)

❹ A: 昨天我找了三次王醫生。

Zuótiān wǒ zhǎo le sān cì Wáng yīshēng.

(I went looking for Dr. Wang three times yesterday.)

B: 是嗎？昨天我也找了王醫生三次。

Shì ma? Zuótiān wǒ yě zhǎo le Wáng yīshēng sān cì.

(Is that right? I also went looking for Dr. Wang three times yesterday.)

If the object is a personal pronoun, however, 次 (cì) must follow the object.

❺   我昨天找了他兩次，他都不在。

Wǒ zuótiān zhǎo le tā liǎng cì, tā dōu bú zài.

(Yesterday I went looking for him twice, but he was not in either time.)

遍 (biàn) is another measure word for occurrences of actions, but it pertains to the entire course of the action from the beginning to the end.

❻   請你念一遍课文。

Qǐng nǐ niàn yí biàn kèwén.

(Please read the text [from the beginning to the end] once).

Nouns denoting body parts involved in the actions can also sometimes serve as measure words for occurrences of actions. One example is from Dialogue I of the current lesson:

昨天晚上我吃了幾口…

Zuótiān wǎnshang wǒ chī le jǐ kǒu…

(I ate a few mouthfuls last night…)

---

3. 起來 (qi lai) Indicating the Beginning of an Action

起來 (qi lai) indicates the moment when something static becomes dynamic, that is, it signifies the beginning of an action or state.

   我們一見面就聊了起來。

Wǒmen yí jiàn miàn jiù liáo le qi lai

(We began chatting as soon as we met.)

   他一回家就寫起信來。

Tā yì huí jiā jiù xiě qi xìn lai.

(He began to write a letter as soon as he got home.)

❸   下了課以後，學生們打起球來。

Xià le kè yǐhòu, xuésheng men dǎ qi qiú lai.

(The students started to play ball after the class was over.)

Note that the object is placed between 起 (qi) and 來 (lai), rather than after 起來 (qi lai).

---

4. 把 (bǎ) Construction (I)

Sentences with 把 (bǎ) are common in Chinese. The basic construction is as follows:

Subject + 把 (bǎ) + Object + Verb + Other Element (Complement/ 了 {le}, etc.)

In the 把 (bǎ) construction, what follows the position 把 (bǎ) and precedes the verb serves as both the object of 把 (bǎ) and the object of the verb. In general, a sentence in the 把 (bǎ) construction highlights the subject's disposal of or impact upon the object, with the result of the disposal or impact indicated by the element following the verb.

❶   我把你要的書找到了。

Wǒ bǎ nǐ yào de shū zhǎo dào le.

(I have found the books that you wanted.)

[The resultative complement 到 (dào) serves as the "other element."]

In (1), the subject 我 (wǒ) exerts an impact on the book through the action of 找 (zhǎo), of which 到 (dào) is the result.

❷   你把這個字寫錯了。

Nǐ bǎ zhè ge zì xiě cuò le.

(You wrote this character incorrectly.)

[The resultative complement 錯 (cuò) serves as the "other element."]

In (2), the subject 你 (nǐ) exerts an impact on the character through the action of 寫 (xiě), of which 錯 (cuò) is the result.

❸ 請把那條褲子給我。

Qǐng bǎ nà tiáo kùzi gěi wǒ.

(Please pass me that pair of pants.)

[The indirect object 我 (wǒ) serves as the "other element."]

❹ 你把這篇課文看看。

Nǐ bǎ zhè piān kèwén kàn kan.

(Would you take a look at this text?)

[The reduplicated verb 看 (kàn) serves as the "other element."]

 把這杯咖啡喝了！

Bǎ zhè bēi kāfēi hē le!

(Finish up this cup of coffee!)

❻ 你怎麼把女朋友的生日忘了？

Nǐ zěnme bǎ nǚpéngyou de shēngrì wàng le?

(How did you manage to forget your girlfriend's birthday?)

[In (5) and (6), the particle 了 (le) serves as the "other element."]

(3), (4), and (5) suggest what the listener is requested to do to the objects (the pants, the text, and the coffee). The other element could be a complement as in (1) and (2), an indirect object as in (3), a reduplicated verb as in (4), or the particle 了 (le) as in (5) and (6).

In the 把 (bǎ) construction, the object is often something already known to both the speaker and the listener. For example, 你要的書 (nǐ yào de shū) in (1), 這個字 (zhè ge zì) in (2), 那條褲子 (nà tiáo kùzi) in (3), and 女朋友的生日 (nǚpéngyou de shēngrì) in (6) are all things that are already known. Compare the following two sentences:

❼ 老王給了小張一些錢。

Lǎo Wáng gěi le Xiǎo Zhāng yì xiē qián.

(Old Wang gave Little Zhang some money.)

⑧ 老王把錢給小張了。

Lǎo Wáng bǎ qián gěi Xiǎo Zhāng le.

(Old Wang gave the money to Little Zhang.)

The object in (7), "some money," is unspecified. However, in (8), the speaker expects the listener to know what money is being referred to.

If the subject of a sentence is given, the object is something known to both the speaker and listener, and the verb is followed by a complement in the form of a prepositional phrase with 在 (zài) or 到 (dào), that sentence *must* appear in the 把 (bǎ) construction. For example:

你把筆放在桌子上。

Nǐ bǎ bǐ fàng zài zhuōzi shang.

(Put the pen on the desk.)

請你把這封信送到律師的辦公室。

Qǐng nǐ bǎ zhè fēng xìn sòng dào lǜshī de bàngōngshì.

(Please deliver this letter to the attorney's office.)

The following sentences are therefore incorrect:

*你放筆在桌子上。

*Nǐ fàng bǐ zài zhuōzi shang.

*請你送這封信到律師的辦公室。

*Qǐng nǐ sòng zhè fēng xìn dào lǜshī de bàngōngshì.

Language Practice

A. Extreme Cases

EXAMPLE:

→ 他渴死了。   Tā kě sǐ le.

1.   →

2. $250   →

3.   →

B. Study Habits

Work with your partner and find out each other's daily routine for studying Chinese. Then find out what happened yesterday.

EXAMPLE: 聽錄音   tīng lùyīn

→ A: 你每天聽幾遍/次 錄音？   Nǐ měitiān tīng jǐ biàn/cì lùyīn?

B: 我每天聽_____錄音。   Wǒ měitiān tīng _____ lùyīn.

A: 昨天呢？   Zuótiān ne?

B: 我昨天聽了_____ 錄音。   Wǒ zuótiān tīng le _____ lùyīn.

1. 念課文   niàn kèwén

2. 復習生詞語法   fùxí shēngcí yǔfǎ

3. 寫漢字   xiě Hànzì

C. Moving Day

Your friend has offered to help you move into your new apartment, and wants to know where everything should go.

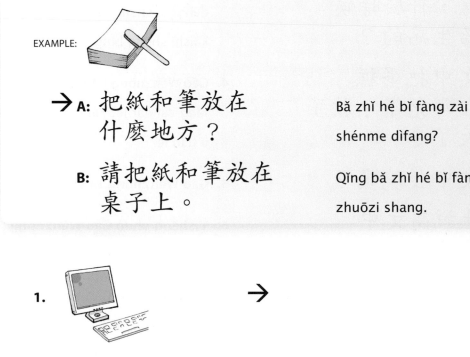

EXAMPLE:

→ **A:** 把紙和筆放在什麼地方？

Bǎ zhǐ hé bǐ fàng zài shénme dìfang?

B: 請把紙和筆放在桌子上。

Qǐng bǎ zhǐ hé bǐ fàng zài zhuōzi shang.

1. →

2. →

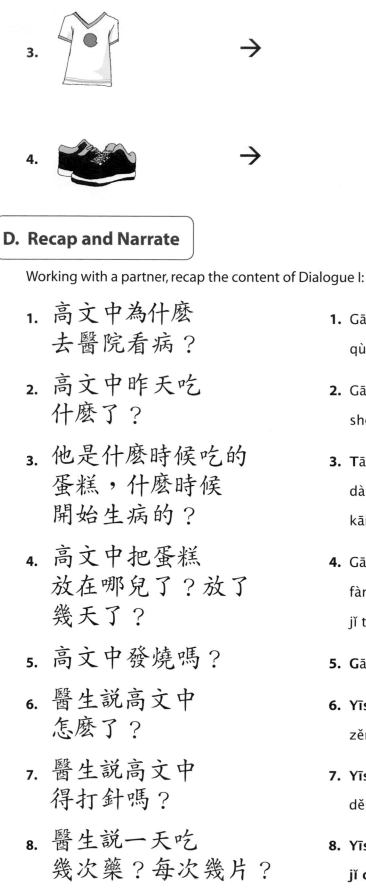

3. →

4. →

D. Recap and Narrate

Working with a partner, recap the content of Dialogue I:

1. 高文中為什麼去醫院看病？

   1. Gāo Wénzhōng wèishénme qù yīyuàn kàn bìng?

2. 高文中昨天吃什麼了？

   2. Gāo Wénzhōng zuótiān chī shénme le?

3. 他是什麼時候吃的蛋糕，什麼時候開始生病的？

   3. Tā shì **shénme shíhou chī de** dàngāo, shénme shíhou kāishǐ shēng bìng de?

4. 高文中把蛋糕放在哪兒了？放了幾天了？

   4. Gāo Wénzhōng bǎ dàngāo fàng zài nǎr le? Fàng le jǐ tiān le?

5. 高文中發燒嗎？

   5. **Gāo Wénzhōng fā shāo ma?**

6. 醫生說高文中怎麼了？

   6. **Yīshēng shuō Gāo Wénzhōng** zěnme le?

7. 醫生說高文中得打針嗎？

   7. **Yīshēng shuō Gāo Wénzhōng** děi dǎ zhēn ma?

8. 醫生說一天吃幾次藥？每次幾片？

   8. **Yīshēng shuō yì tiān chī jǐ cì yào?** Měi cì jǐ piàn?

9. 醫生説高文中
最好怎麼樣？

9. Yīshēng shuō Gāo Wénzhōng

zuìhǎo zěnmeyàng?

10. 高文中覺得這個
辦法好嗎？

10. Gāo Wénzhōng juéde zhè ge

bànfǎ hǎo ma?

Using the words and phrases in blue as prompts, connect your answers above to form a narrative like this example:

高文中的姐姐上個星期
過生日，高文中把沒吃
完的蛋糕放在冰箱裏。
蛋糕放了五六天了，昨
天晚上他吃了幾口，夜
裏肚子就疼起來，今天
早上上了好幾次廁所，
他肚子疼極了，就去醫
院看病。醫生給他檢
查，説他是吃蛋糕把肚
子吃壞了。高文中不希
望打針，醫生説不用打
針，吃藥就可以。那種
藥一天吃三次，一次兩
片，飯前吃飯後吃都可
以。醫生還説最好二十
四小時不吃飯。高文中
覺得這個辦法不好。

Gāo Wénzhōng de jiějie shàng ge xīngqī guò shēngrì, Gāo Wénzhōng bǎ méi chī wán de dàngāo fàng zài bīngxiāng li. Dàngāo fàng le wǔ liù tiān le, zuótiān wǎnshang tā chī le jǐ kǒu, yèli dùzi jiù téng qi lai, jīntiān zǎoshang shàng le hǎo jǐ cì cèsuǒ, tā dùzi téng jí le, jiù qù yīyuàn kàn bìng. Yīshēng gěi tā jiǎnchá, shuō tā shì chī dàngāo bǎ dùzi chī huài le. Gāo Wénzhōng bù xīwàng dǎ zhēn, yīshēng shuō búyòng dǎ zhēn, chī yào jiù kěyǐ. Nà zhǒng yào yì tiān chī sān cì, yí cì liǎng piàn, fàn qián chī fàn hòu chī dōu kěyǐ. Yīshēng hái shuō zuìhǎo èrshí sì xiǎoshí bù chī fàn. Gāo Wénzhōng juéde zhè ge bànfǎ bù hǎo.

Dialogue II: Allergies

 王朋，你怎麼了？眼睛怎麼紅紅的，感冒了嗎？

没感冒。我也不知道怎麼了，最近這幾天身體很不舒服。眼睛又紅又癢。

你一定是對⑤什麼過敏了。

我想也是，所以去藥店買了一些藥。已經吃了四、五種了，花了不少錢，都没有用。

把你買的藥拿出來給我看看。

這些就是。

這些藥没有用。為什麼不去看醫生？你没有健康保險嗎？

我有保險。可是我這個學期功課很多，看醫生太花時間。

那你也得趕快去看醫生❶。
要不然病會越來越⑥重。

我想再吃點兒別的藥試試❷。
我上次生病，没去看醫生，
休息兩天，最後也好了。

不行，不行，你太懶了。
再說⑦，你不能自己亂吃藥。
走，我跟你看病去。

LANGUAGE NOTES

❶ The two phrases 看醫生 (kàn yīshēng) and 看病 (kàn bìng) are interchangeable, although in northern China 看病 (kàn bìng) is much more common than 看醫生 (kàn yīshēng).

❷ When tasting or trying the flavor of a food or drink, one says 我嚐嚐 (Wǒ cháng chang, Let me taste it) instead of 我試試 (Wǒ shì shi, Let me try), although one says 試試 (shì shi) when trying most other things.

Wáng Péng, nǐ zěnme le? Yǎnjing zěnme hóng hóng de, gǎnmào le ma?

Méi gǎnmào. Wǒ yě bù zhīdào zěnme le, zuìjìn zhè jǐ tiān shēntǐ hěn bù shūfu. Yǎnjing yòu hóng yòu yǎng.

Nǐ yídìng shì duì⑤ shénme guòmǐn le.

Wǒ xiǎng yě shì, suǒyǐ qù yàodiàn mǎi le yì xiē yào. Yǐjīng chī le sì, wǔ zhǒng le, huā le bù shǎo qián, dōu méiyǒu yòng.

Bǎ nǐ mǎi de yào ná chu lai gěi wǒ kàn kan.

Zhè xiē jiù shì.

Zhè xiē yào méiyǒu yòng. Wèishénme bú qù kàn yīshēng? Nǐ méiyou jiànkāng bǎoxiǎn ma?

Wǒ yǒu bǎoxiǎn. Kěshì wǒ zhè ge xuéqī gōngkè hěn duō. Kàn yīshēng tài huā shíjiān.

Nà nǐ yě děi gǎnkuài qù kàn yīshēng❹. Yàobùrán bìng huì yuè lái yuè⑥ zhòng.

Wǒ xiǎng zài chī diǎnr bié de yào shì shi. Wǒ shàng cì shēng bìng, méi qù kàn yīshēng, xiūxi liǎng tiān, zuìhòu yě hǎo le.

Bù xíng, bù xíng, nǐ tài lǎn le. Zàishuō⑦, nǐ bù néng zìjǐ luàn chī yào. Zǒu, wǒ gēn nǐ kàn bìng qu.

VOCABULARY

1.	感冒	gǎnmào	v	to have a cold
2.	生病	shēng bìng	vo	to get sick
3.	身體	shēntǐ	n	body; health
4.	癢	yǎng	adj	itchy
5.	過敏	guòmǐn	v	to be allergic to
6.	藥店	yàodiàn	n	pharmacy
7.	健康	jiànkāng	adj/n	healthy; health
8.	保險	bǎoxiǎn	n	insurance
9.	趕快	gǎnkuài	adv	right away; quickly; in a hurry
10.	要不然	yàobùrán	conj	otherwise
11.	越來越	yuè lái yuè	adv	more and more [See Grammar 6.]
12.	上次	shàng cì		last time
13.	休息	xiūxi	v	to take a break; to rest
14.	懶	lǎn	adj	lazy
15.	再説	zàishuō	conj	moreover [See Grammar 7.]
16.	亂	luàn	adv	randomly; arbitrarily; messily

These are signs you may see in clinics and hospitals in China. Can you guess what the rooms are for? Can you read the sign on the right in the correct tones?

Grammar

5. The Preposition 對 (duì)

The preposition 對 (duì) introduces the person or thing that receives a certain effect from someone or something else. Its English translation varies depending on the context.

 這種藥對感冒很有用。

Zhè zhǒng yào duì gǎnmào hěn yǒu yòng.

(This medicine is very effective for colds.)

 他的電腦對他練習發音很有用。

Tā de diànnǎo duì tā liànxí fāyīn hěn yǒu yòng.

(His computer is very useful for his pronunciation practice.)

 你一定對什麼東西過敏了。

Nǐ yídìng duì shénme dōngxi guòmǐn le.

(You must be allergic to something.)

6. 越來越··· (yuè lái yuè...)

The structure 越來越··· (yuè lái yuè...) denotes a progressive change over time.

 李友的中文越來越好。

Lǐ Yǒu de Zhōngwén yuè lái yuè hǎo.

(Li You's Chinese is getting better and better.)

 天氣越來越暖和了。

Tiānqì yuè lái yuè nuǎnhuo le.

(The weather is becoming warmer and warmer.)

❸ 表姐考試考得越來越糟糕。

Biǎojiě kǎo shì kǎo de yuè lái yuè zāogāo.

(My cousin is doing worse and worse on her exams.)

---

7. 再說 (zàishuō)

The expression 再說 (zàishuō) introduces an additional reason for an action that has been taken or decision that has been made. It is different from 再 + 說 (zài + shuō, to say again).

❶ A: 你為什麼不去紐約？

Nǐ wèishénme bú qù Niǔyuē?

(Why aren't you going to New York?)

B: 我沒有時間，再說，也沒有錢。

Wǒ méiyǒu shíjiān, zàishuō, yě méiyǒu qián.

(I don't have the time, and besides, I don't have the money.)

❷ 我不喜歡今天晚上的舞會，音樂不好，再說人也太少。

Wǒ bù xǐhuan jīntiān wǎnshang de wǔhuì, yīnyuè bù hǎo, zàishuō rén yě tài shǎo.

(I didn't like the dance party tonight. The music was lousy. Besides, there were too few people there.)

Like 再說 (zàishuō), 而且 (érqiě, moreover; in addition) also conveys the idea of "furthermore, additionally," etc., but the clause that follows it may or may not be explanatory in nature. Compare the following sentences:

❸ A: 你為什麼不去紐約？

Nǐ wèishénme bú qù Niǔyuē?

(Why aren't you going to New York?)

B: 我沒有時間，而且，也沒有錢。

Wǒ méiyǒu shíjiān, érqiě, yě méiyǒu qián.

(I don't have the time. Besides, I don't have the money.)

Note: In (3), 而且 (érqiě) can be replaced with 再說 (zàishuō).

❹   這是王先生，他不但是我的老師，而且也是
我的朋友。

Zhè shì Wáng xiānsheng, tā búdàn shì wǒ de lǎoshī, érqiě yě shì wǒ de

péngyou.

(This is Mr. Wang. He is not only my teacher but also my friend.)

Note: In (4), 而且 (érqiě) cannot be replaced with 再說 (zàishuō):

4a   *這是王先生，他不但是我的老師，再說也是
我的朋友。

*Zhè shì Wáng xiānsheng, tā búdàn shì wǒ de lǎoshī, zàishuō yě shì wǒ de

péngyou.

Language Practice

E. Allergy! Allergy! Allergy!

Go around the class and ask your classmates if they are allergic to the following items.

EXAMPLE:

→ **A:** Joe, 你對味精   Joe, nǐ duì wèijīng

過敏嗎？   guòmǐn ma?

B: 我對味精過敏。／   Wǒ duì wèijīng guòmǐn./

我對味精不過敏。   Wǒ duì wèijīng bú guòmǐn.

1.      →

2. →

3. →

Then tally who's allergic to what:

Joe, Maya,…, 對味精過敏。

…

Joe, Maya,…, duì wèijīng guòmǐn.

…

F. Role-Play

1. Pretend you are a teacher, and use 要不然 (yàobùrán) to advise your students not to fall into bad study habits.

EXAMPLE:

你得多寫漢字，要不然你的中文不會好。

Nǐ děi duō xiě Hànzì, yàobùrán nǐ de Zhōngwén bú huì hǎo.

1st piece of advice:

2nd piece of advice:

3rd piece of advice:

2. Pretend you are a parent, and use 要不然 (yàobùrán) to advise your child to take care of himself/herself at college.

EXAMPLE:

如果身體不舒服，你得去看醫生，要不然病會越來越重。

Rúguǒ shēntǐ bù shūfu, nǐ děi qù kàn yīshēng, yàobùrán bìng huì yuè lái yuè zhòng.

1st piece of advice:

2nd piece of advice:

3rd piece of advice:

G. Agree or Disagree?

Work with a partner to find out if you both share the same sentiments about how your Chinese study is progressing.

EXAMPLE:　生詞　　多 vs. 少

→ A: 你覺得生詞越來越多還是越來越少？

Nǐ juéde shēngcí yuè lái yuè duō háishi yuè lái yuè shǎo?

B: 我覺得生詞越來越多／少。

Wǒ juéde shēngcí yuè lái yuè duō/shǎo.

1. 功課　　多 vs. 少　　gōngkè　　duō vs. shǎo
2. 課文　　長 vs. 短　　kèwén　　cháng vs. duǎn
3. 考試　　難 vs. 容易　　kǎoshì　　nán vs. róngyì
4. 語法　　難 vs. 容易　　yǔfǎ　　nán vs. róngyì

H. Reasons and Excuses

EXAMPLE:

A: 你為什麼不吃早飯？　Nǐ wèishénme bù chī zǎofàn?

B: 我沒時間，再說我不餓。　Wǒ méi shíjiān, zàishuō wǒ bú è.

1. A: 你為什麼不聽錄音？　A: Nǐ wèishénme bù tīng lùyīn?

B: _____

2. A: 你為什麼不運動？   A: Nǐ wèishénme bú yùndòng?

   B: _____

3. A: 你為什麼寒假沒回
家看爸爸媽媽？   A: Nǐ wèishénme hánjià méi huí jiā kàn bàba māma?

   B: _____

4. A: 你為什麼學中文？   A: Nǐ wèishénme xué Zhōngwén?

   B: _____

5. A: 你為什麼上
這個學校？   A: Nǐ wèishénme shàng zhè ge xuéxiào?

   B: _____

I. Recap and Narrate

Working with a partner, recap the content of Dialogue II:

1. 王朋的眼睛
為什麼紅了？
感冒了嗎？   1. Wáng Péng de yǎnjing wèishénme hóng le? Gǎnmào le ma?

2. 王朋說他怎麼了？   2. Wáng Péng shuō tā zěnme le?

3. 李友說王朋生了
什麼病？   3. Lǐ Yǒu shuō Wáng Péng shēng le shénme bìng?

4. 王朋吃藥了嗎？   4. Wáng Péng chī yào le ma?

5. 李友說王朋得
做什麼？   5. Lǐ Yǒu shuō Wáng Péng děi zuò shénme?

6. 王朋有健康
保險嗎？   6. Wáng Péng yǒu jiànkāng bǎoxiǎn ma?

7. 他為什麼不去看病？

8. 李友說不看醫生
   病會越來越重，
   王朋說什麼？

9. 李友覺得王朋
   的話對嗎？

7. Tā wèishénme bú qù kàn bìng?

8. Lǐ Yǒu shuō bú kàn yīshēng
   bìng huì yuè lái yuè zhòng,
   Wáng Péng shuō shénme?

9. Lǐ Yǒu juéde Wáng Péng
   de huà duì ma?

Using the words and phrases in blue as prompts, connect your answers above to form a narrative like this example:

王朋最近覺得很不舒服，眼睛又紅又癢，不知道生了什麼病。李友說他可能是對什麼過敏。王朋也覺得是對什麼過敏，所以吃了四、五種藥，可是都沒用。李友看了王朋吃的藥，告訴他那些藥沒有用，得去看醫生。王朋說這學期功課太多，看醫生太花時間。李友問王朋是不是沒有健康保險，王朋說他有。李友讓王朋趕快去看病，要不然病會越來越重。王朋說他上次生病，沒看醫生，休息幾天，最後病也好了。李友說王朋太懶，再說也不能自己亂吃藥，所以她要跟王朋一起去看醫生。

Wáng Péng zuìjìn juéde hěn bù shūfu, yǎnjing yòu hóng yòu yǎng, bù zhīdào shēng le shénme bìng. Lǐ Yǒu shuō tā kěnéng shì duì shénme guòmǐn. Wáng Péng yě juéde shì duì shénme guòmǐn, suǒyǐ chī le sì, wǔ zhǒng yào, kěshì dōu méi yòng. Lǐ Yǒu kàn le Wáng Péng chī de yào, gàosù tā nà xiē yào méiyǒu yòng, děi qù kàn yīshēng. Wáng Péng shuō zhè xuéqī gōngkè tài duō, kàn yīshēng tài huā shíjiān. Lǐ Yǒu wèn Wáng Péng shì bú shì méiyǒu jiànkāng bǎoxiǎn, Wáng Péng shuō tā yǒu. Lǐ Yǒu ràng Wáng Péng gǎnkuài qù kàn bìng, yàobùrán bìng huì yuè lái yuè zhòng. Wáng Péng shuō tā shàng cì shēng bìng, méi kàn yīshēng, xiūxi jǐ tiān, zuìhòu bìng yě hǎo le. Lǐ Yǒu shuō Wáng Péng tài lǎn, zàishuō yě bù néng zìjǐ luàn chī yào, suǒyǐ tā yào gēn Wáng Péng yìqǐ qù kàn yīshēng.

HOW ABOUT YOU?

What Are You Allergic To?

1.	花粉	huāfěn	n	pollen
2.	花生	huāshēng	n	peanuts
3.	貓	māo	n	cats
4.	灰塵	huīchén	n	dust

If the source of your allergy is not listed, please ask your teacher and make a note here:

_____

What Allergy Symptoms Do You Have?

1.	頭疼	tóu téng		to have a headache
2.	咳嗽	késòu	v	to cough
3.	打噴嚔	dǎ pēnti	vo	to sneeze
4.	流鼻涕	liú bítì	vo	to have a runny nose

If there are other symptoms you would like to know how to say, please ask your teacher and make a note here:

_____

Culture Highlights

1 Before Western medicine 西醫 (Xīyī) was first introduced to China during the seventeenth century by European missionaries, the Chinese had relied exclusively on traditional Chinese medicine 中醫 (Zhōngyī), a system including acupuncture, herbal medicine, massage, and other therapies. Even now, these indigenous ways of medical treatment remain a well-respected option. Many Chinese people choose to use traditional Chinese medicine for various ailments along with or instead of Western medicine. Although by no means a panacea, traditional Chinese medicine can be surprisingly effective. Many of the reasons for the effectiveness of therapies such as acupuncture and cupping are not fully understood by modern science.

Traditional Chinese herbal medicine being provided at a medical clinic.

To see a doctor, a Chinese outpatient has to pay a registration fee (掛號費 guàhào fèi). The fee is typically equivalent to no more than one US dollar, but could be considerably higher if one wants to consult an esteemed specialist (專家 zhuānjiā). For prescribed tests, outpatients usually have to pay up front.

According to the sign, what do people do here?

 While injections (打針 dǎ zhēn) and intravenous infusion (打點滴 dǎ diǎndī in Taiwan and 輸液 shū yè in mainland China) are seldom used in American hospitals for outpatients, they are much more common treatments for outpatients in Chinese hospitals, clinics and doctors' offices, even for common ailments like a cold.

❹ An outpatient in China would usually pick up his or her prescription from a pharmacy within the hospital itself. One can, however, get medicines from independent pharmacies.

❺ Until the 1980s, employees in all state-owned enterprises and institutions in China were offered free medical care, which became a huge financial burden for the government. That practice was discontinued in the 1990s. The cities in China are currently in a transitional period toward a better-regulated system of medical insurance, while most people in the rural areas are still without any insurance coverage for their health care.

English Text

Dialogue I

(A patient is going to a hospital for treatment)

Gao Wenzhong: Doctor, my stomachache is killing me!

Doctor: What did you have to eat yesterday?

Gao Wenzhong: It was my sister's birthday last week. We didn't finish the cake. Last night I had a few bites. My stomach began to hurt at night, and this morning I went to the bathroom several times.

Doctor: Where did you put the cake?

Gao Wenzhong: In the refrigerator.

Doctor: How long had it been there?

Gao Wenzhong: About five or six days.

Doctor: Do you have a fever?

Gao Wenzhong: No, I don't.

Doctor: Please lie down. Let me check.

* * *

Doctor: You upset your stomach by eating that cake.

Gao Wenzhong: Do I need an injection?

Doctor: No, you don't need an injection. Just take this medicine, three times a day, two pills at a time.

Gao Wenzhong: Doctor, how many times a day? Could you please repeat that?

Doctor: Three times a day, two pills at a time.

Gao Wenzhong: All right. Before or after meals?

Doctor: Either before or after meals is fine, but you'd better not eat anything for twenty-four hours.

Gao Wenzhong: Then I'll be starving. That's not a good idea. That's not a good remedy!

Dialogue II

Li You: Wang Peng, what's the matter? How come your eyes are red? Did you catch a cold?

Wang Peng: No, I didn't catch a cold. I don't know what's wrong with me. I haven't been feeling well the last few days. My eyes are red and itchy.

Li You: You must be allergic to something.

Wang Peng: I think so, too. That's why I went to the pharmacy and got some medicine. I've taken four or five kinds and spent quite a bit of money, but none of them has been effective.

Li You: Take out the medicines you bought. Let me take a look.

Wang Peng: Here you are.

Li You: These medicines are useless. Why didn't you go to the doctor? Don't you have health insurance?

Wang Peng: I do have health insurance. I have too much homework this semester. Going to the doctor takes too much time.

Li You: Even so, you still need to go see a doctor as soon as possible. Otherwise, you'll get sicker and sicker.

Wang Peng: I'd like to try some other medicines first. Last time I was sick I didn't go to the doctor. After a couple days' rest, I was fine.

Li You: No way, no way, you're too lazy. Besides, you can't just randomly take medicine by yourself. Let's go. I'll go to the doctor with you.

This clinic specializes in the seven health problems listed. Do you recognize any of them?

PROGRESS CHECKLIST

Before proceeding to Lesson 16, be sure you can complete the following tasks in Chinese:

I am able to—

- ☑ Tell the doctor about my symptoms;
- ☐ Ask the doctor if a shot or medicine is needed for treatment;
- ☐ Follow and repeat the doctor's instructions on when and how often to take the medicine;
- ☐ Tell people about my allergies and briefly describe my allergy symptoms.

That's How the Chinese Say It!

A Review of Functional Expressions from Lessons 11–15

After gauging your progress and before moving on to the next phase, let's take a break and see how some of the functional expressions that you have encountered in the previous lessons really work!

I. 在 (zài, to exist)

When you think someone else might have something of yours, you should ask "我的…在你那兒嗎？ (Wǒ de…zài nǐ nàr ma?)" instead of "你有我的…嗎？ (Nǐ yǒu wǒ de…ma?)"

❶　A: 老師，我的功課在您那兒嗎？

Lǎoshī, wǒ de gōngkè zài nín nàr ma?

(Teacher, do you have my homework?)

B: 我已經還給你了。

Wǒ yǐjīng huán gěi nǐ le.

(I gave it to you already.)

(還給, huán gěi: to return something [to someone])

A: 是嗎？對不起，我再找找。

Shì ma? Duìbuqǐ, wǒ zài zhǎo zhao.

(Oh, you did? Sorry, I'll look for it again.)

❷　A: 媽媽，我的護照在您那兒嗎？

Māma, wǒ de hùzhào zài nín nàr ma?

(Mom, do you have my passport?)

B: 在我這兒。給你吧。

Zài wǒ zhèr. Gěi nǐ ba.

(Yes, I have it. Here you are.)

❸ A: 我的手機還在你那兒嗎？
昨天你拿去用了。

Wǒ de shǒujī hái zài nǐ nàr ma?

Zuótiān nǐ ná qù yòng le.

(Do you still have my cell phone?
You took it yesterday.)

B: 哦，還在我這兒，
我忘了還給你了。

Gēge: Ò, hái zài wǒ zhèr, wǒ wàng le huán gěi nǐ le.

(Oh yeah, I still have it. I forgot to return it to you.)

II. Complimentary Expressions

Note the different expressions for men, women, and children.

❶ 那個小孩真可愛。

Nà ge xiǎohái zhēn kě'ài.

(That little kid is really cute.)

❷ 她長得真好看！

Tā zhǎng de zhēn hǎokàn!

(She's really beautiful!)

❸ 李友長得很漂亮。

Lǐ Yǒu zhǎng de hěn piàoliang.

(Li You looks very pretty.)

❹ 王朋真帥。

Wáng Péng zhēn shuài.

(Wang Peng is really handsome.)

❺ 那個班的學生都很酷。

Nà ge bān de xuésheng dōu hěn kù.

(The students in that class are all very cool.)

III. 怎麼了? (Zěnme le? What's the matter? What's wrong?)

One can ask "你怎麼了?" (Nǐ zěnme le?) upon finding someone under unusual circumstances or showing signs of concern, anxiety, or pain.

❶ A: 你怎麼了?怎麼這麼不高興?

Nǐ zěnme le? Zěnme zhème bù gāoxìng?

(What's the matter? Why are you so unhappy?)

B: 我的女朋友不愛我了。

Wǒ de nǚpéngyou bú ài wǒ le.

(My girlfriend doesn't love me anymore.)

❷ A: 怎麼了?眼睛怎麼這麼紅?

Zěnme le? Yǎnjing zěnme zhème hóng?

(What's wrong? Why are your eyes so red?)

B: 没什麼。我可能對什麼東西過敏了。

Méi shénme. Wǒ kěnéng duì shénme dōngxi guòmǐn le.

(It's nothing. I may be allergic to something.)

IV. 糟糕 (zāogāo, [It's] awful/What a mess)

This formula is often used when one suddenly realizes that something important has been forgotten or something of consequence has gone wrong.

❶ A: 糟糕,我的信用卡不見了。

Zāogāo, wǒ de xìnyòngkǎ bú jiàn le.

(Shoot! My credit card has disappeared.)

B: 快給你爸爸打電話吧。

Kuài gěi nǐ bàba dǎ diànhuà ba.

(Hurry, call your dad.)

❷ A: 糟糕,快要考試了,我還没準備好。

Zāogāo, kuài yào kǎo shì le, wǒ hái méi zhǔnbèi hǎo.

(Darn it. It's almost time for the test. I am not ready yet.)

B: 你没聽說嗎？老師病了，今天不考試了。

Nǐ méi tīngshuō ma? Lǎoshī bìng le, jīntiān bù kǎo shì le.

(Didn't you hear? The teacher is sick. We don't have the test today!)

A: 是嗎？那太好了！

Shì ma? Nà tài hǎo le!

(Really? That's great!)

Any other useful expressions you would like to learn?

Please ask your teacher and make a note here:

_____

_____

_____

LESSON 16

第十六課

Dì shíliù kè

Dating

約會

Yuēhuì

LEARNING OBJECTIVES

In this lesson, you will learn to use Chinese to

- Describe how long you've known someone;
- Invite someone to go on a date;
- Make the necessary arrangements to go out with friends;
- Accept a date courteously;
- Decline a date politely;
- End a phone conversation without hurting the other person's feelings.

RELATE AND GET READY

In your own culture/community—

1. How can you get tickets for a popular event?
2. Is it socially acceptable to call a person you have only met once and whose phone number you obtained indirectly?
3. Is it impolite to directly say "no" to decline a date?
4. How can you end an unwanted phone conversation without being rude?

Dialogue I: Seeing a Movie

王朋跟李友在同一個學校學
習，他們認識已經快半年了。
王朋常常幫李友練習說中文。
他們也常常一起出去玩兒，每
次都玩兒得①很高興。李友對
王朋的印象❶很好，王朋也很
喜歡李友，他們成了好朋友。

* * *

這個週末學校演❷一個中國電
影，我們一起去看，好嗎？

LANGUAGE NOTES

❶ For the use of the word
印象 (yìnxiàng, impression),
compare these two sentences:
李友對王朋的印
象很好。(Lǐ Yǒu duì
Wáng Péng de yìnxiàng hěn
hǎo, Li You has a very good
impression of Wang Peng.)
李友給王朋的印象
很好。(Lǐ Yǒu gěi Wáng
Péng de yìnxiàng hěn hǎo,
Li You made a very good
impression on Wang Peng.)

❷ The phrase 演電影 (yǎn
diànyǐng, to show a film) in
this lesson is interchangeable
with 放電影 (fàng
diànyǐng), but in addition, 演
電影 (yǎn diànyǐng) can
also mean "to act in a film."

好啊！不過，聽說看電影的人很多，買得到^②票嗎？

票已經買好了，我費了很大的力氣才買到。

好極了！我早^③就想看中國電影了。還有別人跟我們一起去嗎？

沒有，就^③我們倆^④。

好。什麼時候？

後天晚上八點。

看電影以前，我請你吃晚飯。

太好了！一言為定^⑤。

❸ The primary meaning of 早 (zǎo) is "early," but in an extended sense it can also mean "a long time ago," or "early on."

❹ 倆 (liǎ) stands for 兩個 (liǎng ge).

❺ 一言為定 (yì yán wéi dìng), which literally means "achieving certainty with one word," is one of the numerous four-character idioms that have their origins in Classical Chinese but continue to be on the lips of almost every native speaker of the language.

Wáng Péng gēn Lǐ Yǒu zài tóng yí ge xuéxiào xuéxí, tāmen rènshi yǐjīng kuài bàn nián le. Wáng Péng chángcháng bāng Lǐ Yǒu liànxí shuō Zhōngwén. Tāmen yě chángcháng yìqǐ chū qu wánr, měi cì dōu wánr de^① hěn gāoxìng. Lǐ Yǒu duì Wáng Péng de yìnxiàng^❶ hěn hǎo, Wáng Péng yě hěn xǐhuan Lǐ Yǒu, tāmen chéng le hǎo péngyou.

* * *

Zhè ge zhōumò xuéxiào yǎn^❷ yí ge Zhōngguó diànyǐng, wǒmen yìqǐ qù kàn, hǎo ma?

Hǎo a! Búguò, tīngshuō kàn diànyǐng de rén hěn duō, mǎi de dào^② piào ma?

Piào yǐjīng mǎi hǎo le, wǒ fèi le hěn dà de lìqi cái mǎi dào.

Hǎo jí le! Wǒ zǎo^❸ jiù xiǎng kàn Zhōngguó diànyǐng le. Hái yǒu bié rén gēn wǒmen yìqǐ qù ma?

Méiyǒu, jiù^③ wǒmen liǎ^❹.

Hǎo. Shénme shíhou?

Hòutiān wǎnshang bā diǎn.

Kàn diànyǐng yǐqián, wǒ qǐng nǐ chī wǎnfàn.

Tài hǎo le! Yì yán wéi dìng^❺.

VOCABULARY

1.	同	tóng	adj	same; alike
2.	印象	yìnxiàng	n	impression
3.	成	chéng	v	to become
4.	演	yǎn	v	to show (a film); to perform
5.	費	fèi	v	to spend; to take (effort)
6.	力氣	lìqi	n	strength; effort
7.	就	jiù	adv	just; only (indicating a small number)
8.	倆	liǎ	nu+m	(coll.) two
9.	後天	hòutiān	t	the day after tomorrow
10.	一言為定	yì yán wéi dìng		that settles it; that's settled; it's decided

Grammar

1. Descriptive Complements (II)

The subject of a sentence can be described by a complement following 得 (de).

 我們玩兒得很高興。

Wǒmen wánr de hěn gāoxìng.

(We had a happy time playing.)

[We played. We were very happy.]

❷ 孩子笑得很可愛。

Háizi xiào de hěn kě'ài.

(The kid gave a very cute smile.)

[The child smiled, and the child looked cute.]

他打球打得很累。

Tā dǎ qiú dǎ de hěn lèi.

(He was worn out from playing ball.)

[He played ball, and he was worn out.]

❹ 他高興得又唱又跳。

Tā gāoxìng de yòu chàng yòu tiào.

(He was so happy that he ended up singing and dancing.)

[He was happy, and he was singing and dancing.]

In the sentences above, the verbs 玩 (wán), 笑 (xiào), and 打球 (dǎ qiú) and the adjective 高興 (gāoxìng) give the causes, while the complements 高興 (gāoxìng), 可愛 (kě'ài), 累 (lèi) and 又唱又跳 (yòu chàng yòu tiào) describe the effects on the subject.

As shown in (1), (2), and (3), when an adjective serves as a descriptive complement, it is often preceded by the adverb 很 (hěn), just like a predicate adjective.

A complement describing the subject seldom appears in the negative.

(4a) *他高興得沒有又唱又跳。

*Tā gāoxìng de méiyǒu yòu chàng yòu tiào.

2. Potential Complements

得 (de) or 不 (bu) is placed between a verb and a resultative or directional complement to indicate whether a certain result can be realized or not.

❶ 跳舞太難，我學不會。

Tiàowǔ tài nán, wǒ xué bu huì.

(Dancing is too difficult. I can't learn it.)

 A: 你晚上六點半點能回來嗎？我等你吃晚飯。

Nǐ wǎnshang liù diǎn bàn néng huí lai ma? Wǒ děng nǐ chī wǎnfàn.

(Can you be back by 6:30 p.m.? I will wait for you for dinner.)

B: 我得開會，六點半回不來。

Wǒ děi kāi huì, liù diǎn bàn huí bu lái.

(I have a meeting, and can't make it back by 6:30 p.m.)

❸ 這張碟我今天看不完。

Zhè zhāng dié wǒ jīntiān kàn bu wán.

(I can't finish watching this DVD today.)

❹ 那個字怎麼寫，我想不起來了。

Nà ge zì zěnme xiě, wǒ xiǎng bu qǐ lái le.

(I can't remember how to write that character.)

[See Dialogue 2 for 想不起來 (xiǎng bu qǐ lái).]

❺ 健康保險太貴，我買不起。

Jiànkāng bǎoxiǎn tài guì, wǒ mǎi bu qǐ.

(Health insurance is too expensive. I can't afford it.)

❻ A: 這封中文信你看得懂嗎？

Zhè fēng Zhōngwén xìn nǐ kàn de dǒng ma?

(Can you understand this Chinese letter?)

B: 我看得懂。

Wǒ kàn de dǒng.

(Yes, I can understand it.)

Potential complements usually appear in negative sentences. They are used in affirmative sentences much less often, mainly in answering questions that contain a potential complement, as in (6).

The affirmative form and the negative form of a potential complement can be put together to form a question.

❼ 五十個餃子你吃得完吃不完？

Wǔ shí ge jiǎozi nǐ chī de wán chī bu wán?

(Can you eat fifty dumplings or not?)

Potential complements are an important feature of Chinese. They are often the only way to convey the idea that the absence of certain conditions prevents a result from being achieved. Potential complements have a unique function that cannot be fulfilled by the "不能 (bù néng) + verb + resultative/directional complement" construction. For example, 做不完 (zuò bu wán) means "not able to finish," while 不能做完 (bù néng zuò wán) conveys the idea of "not allowed to finish."

8 老師説得太快，我聽不清楚。

Lǎoshī shuō de tài kuài, wǒ tīng bu qīngchu.

(The teacher speaks too fast. I can't hear [him] clearly.)

(8a) *老師説得太快，我不能聽清楚。

*Lǎoshī shuō de tài kuài, wǒ bù néng tīng qīngchu.

9 今天的功課太多，我做不完。

Jīntiān de gōngkè tài duō, wǒ zuò bu wán.

(There is too much homework today. I can't finish it.)

(9a) *今天的功課太多，我不能做完。

*Jīntiān de gōngkè tài duō, wǒ bù néng zuò wán.

A potential complement cannot be used in a 把 (bǎ) sentence, either.

(9b) *我把今天的功課做不完。

*Wǒ bǎ jīntiān de gōngkè zuò bu wán.

3. 就 (jiù)

When used before a noun or pronoun, 就 (jiù) means "only." Often the noun or pronoun is modified by a numeral-measure word combination.

1 我們班人很少，就七個學生。

Wǒmen bān rén hěn shǎo, jiù qī ge xuésheng.

(Our class is small, with just seven students.)

2 今天功課很少，就五個漢字。

Jīntiān gōngkè hěn shǎo, jiù wǔ ge Hànzì.

(There's little homework today. Only five Chinese characters.)

3 我們一家五口，就你對味精過敏。

Wǒmen yì jiā wǔ kǒu, jiù nǐ duì wèijīng guòmǐn.

(There are five people in our family. Only you are allergic to MSG.)

❹ 三個房間我打掃了兩個，就一個房間還沒整理。

Sān ge fángjiān wǒ dǎsǎo le liǎng ge, jiù yí ge fángjiān hái méi zhěnglǐ.

(I have cleaned two of the three rooms. Only one room hasn't been tidied up yet.)

Language Practice

A. Your Comments, Please

Work with your partner and ask each other the following questions:

EXAMPLE:

A: 你昨天晚上寫漢字寫得累不累？

B: 我昨天晚上寫漢字寫得很累/不累。你呢？

A: Nǐ zuótiān wǎnshang xiě Hànzì xiě de lèi bú lèi?

B: Wǒ zuótiān wǎnshang xiě Hànzì xiě de hěn lèi/bú lèi. Nǐ ne?

1. A: 你每天上課上得累不累？

Nǐ měi tiān shàng kè shàng de lèi bú lèi?

2. A: 你昨天晚上睡覺睡得舒服不舒服？

Nǐ zuótiān wǎnshang shuì jiào shuì de shūfu bù shūfu?

3. A: 你上個週末玩兒得高興不高興？

Nǐ shàng ge zhōumò wánr de gāoxìng bù gāoxìng?

B. First Day of School!

Find out about your practice partner's first day of school.

EXAMPLE:

A: 你找得到找不到
你的教室？

A: Nǐ zhǎo de dào zhǎo bu dào
nǐ de jiàoshì?

B: 我找得到我的教室。/
我找不到我的教室。

B: Wǒ zhǎo de dào wǒ de jiàoshì./
Wǒ zhǎo bu dào wǒ de jiàoshì.

1. A: 你買得到買不到
你要的書？

A: Nǐ mǎi de dào mǎi bu dào
nǐ yào de shū?

2. A: 你聽得懂聽不懂
中文老師説的話？

A: Nǐ tīng de dǒng tīng bu dǒng
Zhōngwén lǎoshī shuō de huà?

3. A: 你看得清楚看不
清楚老師寫的字？

A: Nǐ kàn de qīngchu kàn bu
qīngchu lǎoshī xiě de zì?

C. Are You a Competitive Hot Dog Eater?

Do you think you and your partner would be up to the challenge of competing in a hot-dog-eating competition? How about some other competitions? Let's find out.

EXAMPLE:

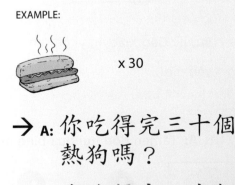

x 30

→ A: 你吃得完三十個
熱狗嗎？

Nǐ chī de wán sānshí ge
règǒu ma?

B: 我吃得完三十個熱狗。/
我吃不完三十個熱狗。

Wǒ chī de wán sānshí ge règǒu.
Wǒ chī bu wán sānshí ge règǒu.

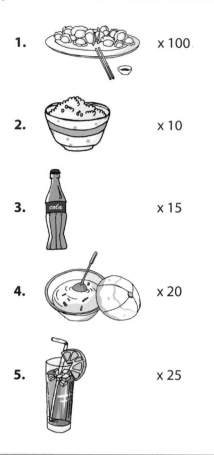

1. x 100

2. x 10

3. x 15

4. x 20

5. x 25

D. How Well Do You Know the *Integrated Chinese* Cast?

EXAMPLE:

A: 他們都有弟弟嗎？

Tāmen dōu yǒu dìdi ma?

B: 不，就高小音一個人
有弟弟。

Bù, jiù Gāo Xiǎoyīn yí ge rén
yǒu dìdi.

1. A: 他們都會滑冰嗎？

1. A: Tāmen dōu huì huá bīng ma?

2. A: 他們都吃素嗎?

2. A: Tāmen dōu chī sù ma?

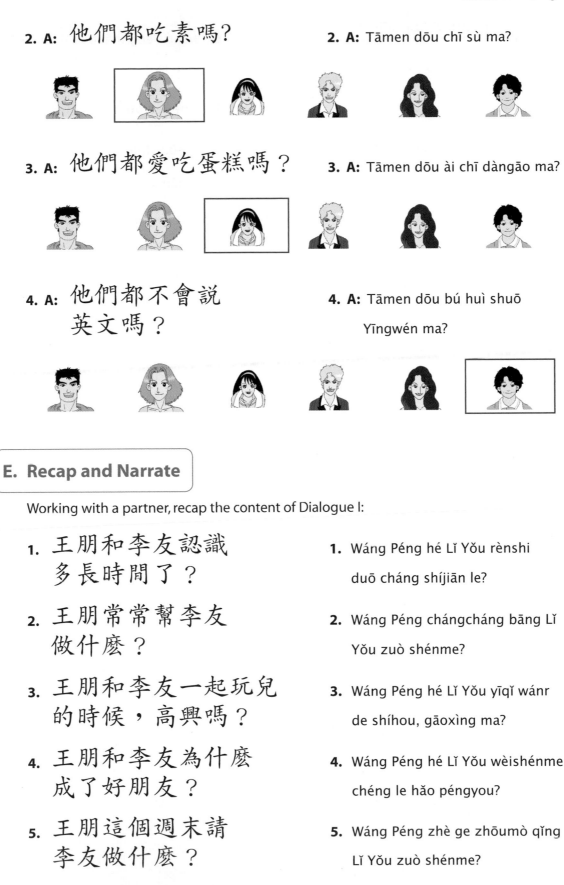

3. A: 他們都愛吃蛋糕嗎?

3. A: Tāmen dōu ài chī dàngāo ma?

4. A: 他們都不會說
英文嗎?

4. A: Tāmen dōu bú huì shuō
Yīngwén ma?

E. Recap and Narrate

Working with a partner, recap the content of Dialogue I:

1. 王朋和李友認識
多長時間了?

1. Wáng Péng hé Lǐ Yǒu rènshi
duō cháng shíjiān le?

2. 王朋常常幫李友
做什麼?

2. Wáng Péng chángcháng bāng Lǐ
Yǒu zuò shénme?

3. 王朋和李友一起玩兒
的時候,高興嗎?

3. Wáng Péng hé Lǐ Yǒu yīqǐ wánr
de shíhou, gāoxìng ma?

4. 王朋和李友為什麼
成了好朋友?

4. Wáng Péng hé Lǐ Yǒu wèishénme
chéng le hǎo péngyou?

5. 王朋這個週末請
李友做什麼?

5. Wáng Péng zhè ge zhōumò qǐng
Lǐ Yǒu zuò shénme?

6. 王朋買到電影
   票了嗎？

7. 幾個人去看電影？

8. 李友説看電影以前要
   做什麼？

6. Wáng Péng mǎi dào diànyǐng piào le ma?

7. Jǐ ge rén qù kàn diànyǐng?

8. Lǐ Yǒu shuō kàn diànyǐng yǐqián yào zuò shénme?

Using the words and phrases in blue as prompts, connect your answers above to form a narrative like this example:

王朋和李友在同一個學校
學習快半年了。王朋常常
幫李友學中文，他們常常
一起玩兒，每次都玩兒得
很高興。李友對王朋的印
象很好，王朋也很喜歡李
友，他們成了好朋友。

這個週末學校演一個中國
電影，看電影的人很多，
王朋費了很大力氣才買到
票。他請李友去看電影，
李友説好極了。她問王朋
還有別人跟他們一起看電
影嗎，王朋説就他們倆。
李友很高興，説看電影以
前她請王朋吃晚飯。

Wáng Péng hé Lǐ Yǒu zài tóng yí ge xuéxiào xuéxí kuài bàn nián le. Wáng Péng chángcháng bāng Lǐ Yǒu xué Zhōngwén, tāmen chángcháng yìqǐ wánr, měi cì dōu wánr de hěn gāoxìng. Lǐ Yǒu duì Wáng Péng de yìnxiàng hěn hǎo, Wáng Péng yě hěn xǐhuan Lǐ Yǒu, tāmen chéng le hǎo péngyou.

Zhè ge zhōumò xuéxiào yǎn yí ge Zhōngguó diànyǐng, kàn diànyǐng de rén hěn duō, Wáng Péng fèi le hěn dà lìqi cái mǎi dào piào. Tā qǐng Lǐ Yǒu qù kàn diànyǐng, Lǐ Yǒu shuō hǎo jí le. Tā wèn Wáng Péng hái yǒu bié rén gēn tāmen yìqǐ kàn diànyǐng ma, Wáng Péng shuō jiù tāmen liǎ. Lǐ Yǒu hěn gāoxìng, shuō kàn diànyǐng yǐqián tā qǐng Wáng Péng chī wǎnfàn.

Dialogue II: Turning Down an Invitation

喂，請問李友小姐在嗎？

我就是。請問你是哪一位？

我姓費，你還記得❶我嗎？

姓費？

你還記得上個月高小音的生日舞會嗎？我就是最後請你跳舞的那個人。你再想想。想起來了嗎？

對不起，我想不起來。

我是高小音的中學同學。

LANGUAGE NOTES

❶ 記得 (jìde, to remember) vs. 想起來 (xiǎng qi lai, to remember; to recall): While 記得 (jìde) pertains to the continuous state of remembering, 想起來 (xiǎng qi lai) refers to the mental act of retrieving information from one's memory. Thus one can say: "我記得他上過我的課，可是我想不起來他叫什麼名字。" (Wǒ jìde tā shàng guo wǒ de kè, kěshì wǒ xiǎng bu qǐ lái tā jiào shénme míngzi, I do remember he took my class, but I can't think of his name at the moment).

是嗎？你是怎麼知道我的電話號碼的？

 是小音告訴我的。

 費先生，你有事嗎？

是這個週末你有空兒嗎？我想請你去跳舞。

這個週末不行，下個星期我有三個考試。

 沒關係，下個週末怎麼樣？你考完試，我們好好兒❷玩兒玩兒。

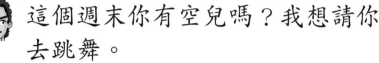

 下個週末也不行，我要從宿舍搬出去④，得打掃、整理房間。

你看下下個週末，好不好？

對不起，下下個週末更不行了，我要跟我的男朋友去紐約旅行。

…那…

費先生，對不起，我的手機沒電了。再見！

喂…喂…

❷ 好好兒 (hǎohāor, all out; to one's heart's content) is a colloquial expression that often precedes a verb to serve as an adverbial, e.g. 考試以後我要去紐約好好兒玩兒玩兒 (Kǎo shì yǐhòu wǒ yào qù Niǔyuē hǎohāor wánr wanr. After the test I want to go to New York and have a great time). Note the different tone for the reduplicated syllable 好. For the rules on the pronunciation of reduplicated monosyllabic adjectives, see Grammar 6 in Lesson 12.

Wéi, qǐng wèn Lǐ Yǒu xiǎojiě zài ma?

Wǒ jiù shì. Qǐng wèn nǐ shì nǎ yí wèi?

Wǒ xìng Fèi, nǐ hái jìde❶ wǒ ma?

Xìng Fèi?

Nǐ hái jìde shàng ge yuè Gāo Xiǎoyīn de shēngrì wǔhuì ma? Wǒ jiù shì zuìhòu qǐng nǐ tiào wǔ de nà ge rén. Nǐ zài xiǎng xiang. Xiǎng qi lai le ma?

Duìbuqǐ, wǒ xiǎng bù qǐ lái.

Wǒ shì Gāo Xiǎoyīn de zhōngxué tóngxué.

Shì ma? Nǐ shì zěnme zhīdào wǒ de diànhuà hàomǎ de?

Shì Xiǎoyīn gàosu wǒ de.

Fèi xiānsheng, nǐ yǒu shì ma?

Zhè ge zhōumò nǐ yǒu kòngr ma? Wǒ xiǎng qǐng nǐ qù tiào wǔ.

Zhè ge zhōumò bù xíng, xià ge xīngqī wǒ yǒu sān ge kǎo shì.

Méi guānxi, xià gè zhōumò zěnmeyàng? Nǐ kǎo wán shì, wǒmen hǎohāor❷ wánr wanr.

Xià ge zhōumò yě bù xíng, wǒ yào cóng sùshè bān chu qu④, děi dǎsǎo, zhěnglǐ fángjiān.

Nǐ kàn xià xià ge zhōumò, hǎo bù hǎo?

Duìbuqǐ, xià xià ge zhōumò gèng bù xíng le, wǒ yào gēn wǒ de nánpéngyou qù Niǔyuē lǚxíng.

…Nà…

Fèi xiānsheng, duìbuqǐ, wǒ de shǒujī méi diàn le. Zàijiàn!

Wéi …wéi …

VOCABULARY

1.	記得	jìde	v	to remember
2.	想起來	xiǎng qi lai	vc	to remember; to recall
3.	號碼	hàomǎ	n	number
4.	搬	bān	v	to move
5.	打掃	dǎsǎo	v	to clean up (a room, apartment or house)
	掃	sǎo	v	to sweep
6.	整理	zhěnglǐ	v	to put in order
7.	房間	fángjiān	n	room
8.	旅行	lǚxíng	v	to travel
9.	電	diàn	n	electricity

There are many parks in Taipei that you could take a date to. Circle four on the map. If you wish to fly out of town for a date, where is the airport?

Grammar

4. Directional Complements (II)

Directional complements indicate the direction in which a person or object moves. A directional verb such as 上 (shàng, to go up), 下 (xià, to go down), 進 (jìn, to go in), 出 (chū, to go out), 回 (huí, to return), 過 (guò, to go over), 起 (qǐ, to rise), 開 (kāi, to part from), 到 (dào, to arrive), 來 (lái, to come) or 去 (qù, to go) can be placed after another verb to become what is known as a "simple directional complement." When a simple directional complement such as 上, 下, 進, 出, 回, 過, 起, 開 or 到 (shang, xia, jin, chu, hui, guo, qi, kai or dao) is combined with 來 or 去 (lai or qu), we have what is called a "compound directional complement."

Simple Directional Complements:

Pattern I:

A. Subject + Verb + Place Word / Noun (Phrase) + 來/去

 她　下　樓　　來。

subject + verb + place word + directional complement

Tā xià lóu lai.

(She is coming downstairs.)

 她上樓去。

Tā shàng lóu qu.

(She is going upstairs.)

❸ 請　你　買　一些水果　來。

subject + verb + noun phrase + directional complement

Qǐng nǐ mǎi yì xiē shuǐguǒ lai.

(Please buy some fruit [and bring it] here.)

❹ 你給他送一點兒吃的東西去。

Nǐ gěi tā sòng yìdiǎnr chī de dōngxi qu.

(Take some food to him.)

When a verb is followed by a location word, that verb can only be a directional verb such as 上 (shàng), 下 (xià), 進 (jìn), 出 (chū), 回 (huí), 過 (guò), or 到 (dào), as shown in (1) and (2).

B. Subject + Verb + 來/去 + Noun

❺ 他買來了一些水果。

Tā mǎi lai le yì xiē shuǐguǒ.

(He bought some fruit and brought it here.)

When the object of the verb is a location word, the sentence can only appear in Pattern A, as in (1) and (2). When the object is a regular noun and the action is not completed, the sentence often appears in Pattern A as well, as in (3) and (4). If the action is completed, the sentence can appear either in Pattern A or in Pattern B. Pattern A should therefore be memorized as the essential form.

Pattern II:

A. Subject + Verb + 上/下··· + Place Word /Noun

❻ 他走上樓。

Tā zǒu shang lóu.

(He walked upstairs.)

[The sentence doesn't indicate whether the speaker is upstairs or downstairs.]

❼ 老師走進教室。

Lǎoshī zǒu jin jiàoshì.

(The teacher walked into the classroom.)

[The sentence doesn't indicate whether the speaker is in the classroom or not.]

❽ 他拿出一張紙。

Tā ná chu yì zhāng zhǐ.

(He took out a piece of paper.)

Compound Directional Complements

A. Subject + Verb + 上/下⋯ + Place Word / Noun+ 來/去

❾ 她走下樓來。

Tā zǒu xia lóu lai.

(She walked downstairs.)

[The speaker is downstairs.]

❿ 老師走進教室去/來。

Lǎoshī zǒu jin jiàoshì qu/lai.

(The teacher walked into the classroom.)

[With 去, the speaker is not in the classroom; with 來, the speaker is in the classroom.]

⓫ 弟弟跳上床來/去。

Dìdi tiào shang chuáng lai/qu.

(My little brother jumped onto the bed.)

[With 來, the speaker is on the bed; with 去, the speaker is not on the bed.]

⓬ 我的同學走進書店來/去。

Wǒ de tóngxué zǒu jin shūdiàn lai/qu.

(My classmate walked into the bookstore.)

[With 來, the speaker was in the bookstore; with 去, the speaker was not in the bookstore.]

⓭ 請你買回一些梨來。

Qǐng nǐ mǎi hui yì xiē lí lai.

(Please buy some pears and bring them back here.)

⓮ 他拿出一張紙來。

Tā ná chu yì zhāng zhǐ lai.

(He took out a piece of paper.)

🄯 請大家都拿起筆來。

Qǐng dàjiā dōu ná qi bǐ lai.

(Please pick up a pen, everyone.)

起 (qi), in the same way as 起來 (qi lai), signifies a movement from a lower point to a higher point.

However, 起 (qi) compounds only with 來 (lai), never with 去 (qu), in forming a directional complement combination.

The difference between 上 (shang) and 起 (qi) is that 上 (shang) is followed by a location word which indicates the end point of the movement, while 起 (qi) never precedes a location word.

🄰 走上樓

zǒu shang lóu

(to go upstairs)

(16a) *走起樓

*zǒu qi lóu

B. Subject + Verb + 上/下··· + 來/去 + Noun

🄱 他買回來了一些水果。

Tā mǎi hui lai le yì xiē shuǐguǒ.

(He bought some fruit and brought it back here.)

As in the case of the simple directional compounds, when the object is a location word, the sentence appears only in Pattern A, as in (11) and (12). If the object is a regular noun and the action is not completed, the sentence often appears in Pattern A as well, as in (13), (14), and (15). If the action is completed, the sentence can appear either in Pattern A or in Pattern B. Again, Pattern A should be memorized as the essential form.

When the 把 (bǎ) construction is used with a directional complement, the sentence can appear in either of these two patterns:

I. Simple Directional Complement

Subject + 把 + Object + Verb + 來/去

🄲 請把你的床搬來。

Qǐng bǎ nǐ de chuáng bān lai.

(Please move your bed here.)

⑲   把這杯冰茶拿去。

Bǎ zhè bēi bīngchá ná qu.

(Take this glass of iced tea [with you].)

II. Compound Directional Complement

Subject + 把 + Object + Verb + 上/下··· (+ place word) + 來/去

⑳   我把書拿起來了。

Wǒ bǎ shū ná qi lai le.

(I picked up the book.)

㉑   快把車開回家去。

Kuài bǎ chē kāi hui jiā qu.

(Drive the car back home right away.)

Language Practice

F. Second Opinion

After you bought or did something, you want to get a second opinion from your friends.

EXAMPLE:

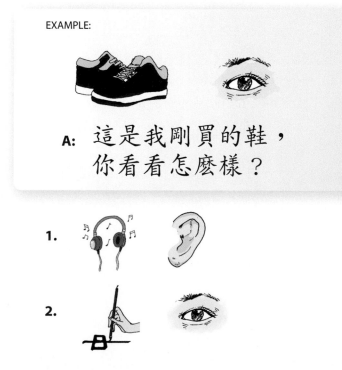

A: 這是我剛買的鞋，
你看看怎麼樣？

Zhè shì wǒ gāng mǎi de xié,

nǐ kàn kan zěnmeyàng?

1.

2.

3. [See Language Note 2 from Dialogue II in Lesson 15.]

4. [See Language Note 2 from Dialogue II in Lesson 15.]

G. Ask Nicely!

Make these requests to your partner, and try to soften the tone by reduplicating the verb:

1. You would like to see your partner's family picture.

2. You want your partner to have a look at the characters you have written.

3. You wish to listen to your partner's MP3.

4. You want to use your partner's cell phone.

5. You want your partner to help you look for your book.

6. You hope your partner will practice Chinese with you.

H. The Big Move

You are moving into the second-floor apartment in the house shown in the picture on the left. You are standing with all your stuff on the first floor, while the previous tenant has left behind some of her stuff upstairs. Tell the movers how to finish the move.

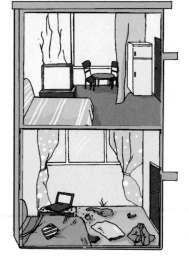

Before   After

Hint: For things to be moved upstairs, you should say 把_____搬/拿上（樓）去 (Bǎ _____ bān/ná shang lóu qu); for things to be placed downstairs, you should say 把_____搬/拿下（樓）來 (Bǎ _____ bān/ná xia lóu lai).

1.

2.

3.

4.

5.

6.

7.

I. Recap and Narrate

Working with a partner, recap the content of Dialogue II:

1. 費先生是誰？

   1. Fèi xiānsheng shì shéi?

2. 費先生是怎麼
   認識李友的？

   2. Fèi xiānsheng shì zěnme
   rènshi Lǐ Yǒu de?

3. 李友還記得
   費先生嗎？

   3. Lǐ Yǒu hái jìde
   Fèi xiānsheng ma?

4. 費先生是怎麼知道
   李友的電話號碼的？

   4. Fèi xiānsheng shì zěnme zhīdào
   Lǐ Yǒu de diànhuà hàomǎ de?

5. 費先生為什麼給
   李友打電話？

   5. Fèi xiānsheng wèishénme gěi
   Lǐ Yǒu dǎ diànhuà?

6. 李友說這個週末她
   為什麼不能去跳舞？

   6. Lǐ Yǒu shuō zhè ge zhōumò tā
   wèishénme bù néng qù tiào wǔ?

7. 下個週末呢？

   7. Xià ge zhōumò ne?

8. 下下個週末呢？

   8. Xià xià ge zhōumò ne?

9. 費先生還想約
   李友嗎？

   9. Fèi xiānsheng hái xiǎng yuē
   Lǐ Yǒu ma?

Using the words and phrases in blue as prompts, connect your answers above to form a narrative like this example:

費先生是高小音的中學同學，在高小音的生日舞會上，他是最後一個請李友跳舞的人。今天他給李友打電話，約李友這個週末去跳舞。李友說下個星期有三個考試，所以這個週末不能去跳舞。費先生問下個週末行不行，李友說她下個週末要從宿舍搬出去，得打掃整理房間。費先生又問下下個週末行不行，李友說更不行，她要跟男朋友去紐約旅行。費先生可能還要約李友別的時間去跳舞，可是李友說她的手機沒電了，費先生就不能再說什麼了。

Fèi xiānsheng shì Gāo Xiǎoyīn de zhōngxué tóngxué, zài Gāo Xiǎoyīn de shēngrì wǔhuì shàng, tā shì zuìhòu yí ge qǐng Lǐ Yǒu tiào wǔ de rén. Jīntiān tā gěi Lǐ Yǒu dǎ diànhuà, yuē Lǐ Yǒu zhè ge zhōumò qù tiào wǔ. Lǐ Yǒu shuō xià ge xīngqī yǒu sān ge kǎo shì, suǒyǐ zhè ge zhōumò bù néng qù tiào wǔ. Fèi xiānsheng wèn xià ge zhōumò xíng bù xíng, Lǐ Yǒu shuō tā xià ge zhōumò yào cóng sùshè bān chu qu, děi dǎsǎo zhěnglǐ fángjiān. Fèi xiānsheng yòu wèn xià xià ge zhōumò xíng bù xíng, Lǐ Yǒu shuō gèng bù xíng, tā yào gēn nánpéngyou qù Niǔyuē lǚxíng. Fèi xiānsheng kěnéng hái yào yuē Lǐ Yǒu bié de shíjiān qù tiào wǔ, kěshì Lǐ Yǒu shuō tā de shǒujī méi diàn le, Fèi xiānsheng jiù bù néng zài shuō shénme le.

HOW ABOUT YOU?

What activity would you enjoy on a date?

1. 聽音樂會   tīng yīnyuèhuì   vo   to go to a concert

2. 唱卡拉OK   chàng kǎlā'ōukēi   vo   to sing karaoke

3. 參觀博物館   cānguān bówùguǎn   vo   to visit a museum

4. 野餐   yěcān   v   to picnic

5. 兜風   dōu fēng   vo   to go for a drive

What other activities do you think would be good ideas for a date?

Please ask your teacher how to say them and make a note here:

_____

Culture Highlights

❶ In premodern China, marriages were almost invariably arranged by the parents. Intimate contact between unmarried young men and women was strictly prohibited. Traditionally, Chinese people shied away from any public display of affection. Even as recently as the 1980s, one seldom saw a couple walking on the street hand-in-hand, but today people do not make much fuss about couples hugging and kissing each other in public.

❷ Valentine's Day, a Western holiday, is becoming popular in China now, especially among young people in the cities. As in the West, it is commercially a big day for retailers and restaurants, and young people spend lavishly on roses, chocolates, and candlelight dinners. Meanwhile, some people have been pushing to make the seventh day of the seventh month on the lunar calendar the Chinese "Valentine's Day," or 情人節 (Qíngrénjié). According to a romantic legend that came into existence nearly two millennia ago, the seventh day of the seventh month is the only day of the year when the Cowherd and the Weaving Girl, a loving couple that was forcibly separated, are allowed to meet each other on a bridge of magpies over the Silver River (銀河, Yínhé), the Chinese name for the Milky Way.

❸ Chinese people are typically very concerned about "saving face," not only for themselves but for other people as well. That is the reason a Chinese person would usually try to find excuses when turning down a request or an offer, instead of rejecting it bluntly.

Seeing movies is part of the nightlife in Chinese cities, especially for people going out on dates. Meanwhile, Peking (Beijing) opera (京劇, jīngjù), a traditional form of entertainment that once flourished in many cities, especially those in the north, has been losing ground in competition with films, TV, karaoke clubs, and internet bars.

A theatrical scene from Beijing Opera

English Text

Dialogue I

Wang Peng and Li You go to the same school. They have known each other for almost six months now. Wang Peng often helps Li You practice speaking Chinese. They also often go out for fun, and they always have a good time. Li You has a very good impression of Wang Peng, and Wang Peng likes Li You very much, too. So they've become good friends.

*   *   *

Wang Peng: This weekend they're showing a Chinese film at school. Shall we go together?

Li You: Yes, but I hear that many people are going to see that film. Will we be able to get tickets?

Wang Peng: I already got the tickets. It took a lot of trying.

Li You: Fantastic. I've wanted to see a Chinese film for a long time. Anyone else going with us?

Wang Peng: No one else. Just the two of us.

Li You: OK. When?

Wang Peng: The day after tomorrow, eight o'clock.

Li You: Before the movie, I'll take you to dinner.

Wang Peng: Great! It's a deal.

Dialogue II

Mr. Fei: Hello, is Miss Li You there?

Li You: This is she. Who is this, please?

Mr. Fei: My name is Fei. Do you remember me?

Li You: Mr. Fei?

Mr. Fei: Do you still remember Gao Xiaoyin's birthday party last month? I was the last person who asked you to dance. Think again. Do you remember now?

Li You: I'm sorry. I can't recall.

Mr. Fei: I was Gao Xiaoyin's high school classmate.

Li You: Is that so? How did you get my number?

Mr. Fei: Xiaoyin gave it to me.

Li You: Mr. Fei, can I help you?

Mr. Fei: Are you free this weekend? I'd like to ask you out to dance.

Li You: This weekend won't do. Next week I have three tests.

Mr. Fei: No problem. What about the following weekend? After your tests are over, we'll go have a good time.

Li You: Next weekend won't work, either. I'm moving out of the dorm. I have to clean and tidy up my room.

Mr. Fei: How about two weeks from now?

Li You: I'm sorry, two weeks from now would be even more impossible. I'm going on a trip to New York with my boyfriend.

Mr. Fei: In that case…

Li You: Mr. Fei, I'm sorry, my cell phone is out of power. Bye.

Mr. Fei: Hello…hello…

PROGRESS CHECKLIST

Before proceeding to Lesson 17, be sure you can complete the following tasks in Chinese:

I am able to—

- ☑ Set up a movie date or another outing with friends;
- ☐ Comment on how much work it takes to make arrangements for a date;
- ☐ Invite someone to go on a date;
- ☐ Accept an invitation to go on a date;
- ☐ Courteously decline a date;
- ☐ End a phone conversation without being rude.

LESSON 17

Renting an Apartment

第十七課 租房子

Dì shíqī kè   Zū fángzi

LEARNING OBJECTIVES

In this lesson, you will learn to use Chinese to

- Describe your current and ideal living quarters;
- Name common pieces of furniture;
- State how long you have been living at your current residence;
- Comment briefly on why a place is or isn't good for someone;
- Discuss and negotiate rent, utilities, and security deposits.

RELATE AND GET READY

In your own culture/community—

1. What is the best way to find an apartment for rent?
2. What defines an "apartment"? What other living arrangements are available?
3. What are the advantages and disadvantages of living in a student dorm? How about living in an apartment?
4. Do people typically sign a lease for an apartment? Do leases include clauses for security deposits and pets? What other issues do leases cover?

Narrative: Finding a Better Place

王朋在學校的宿舍住了兩個學期了①。他覺得宿舍太吵，睡不好覺，房間太小，連電腦都②放不下③，再說也沒有地方可以做飯，很不方便，所以準備下個學期搬出去住。他找房子找了一個多④月了，可是還沒有找到合適的。剛才他在報紙上看到了一個廣告，說學校附近有一套公寓出租，離學校很近，走路只要五分鐘，很方

便。公寓有一個臥
室，一個廚房，一
個衛生間❶，一個客
廳，還帶傢具。王朋
覺得這套公寓可能對
他很合適。

LANGUAGE NOTES

❶ While 洗澡間 (xǐzǎojiān) is often used in Taiwan to refer to a bathroom (with a toilet and shower or bathtub), 衛生間 (wèishēngjiān, lit., hygiene room) is the most frequently used term for bathrooms in mainland China. In public places 衛生間 (wèishēngjiān) simply means "restroom." Other Chinese terms for "bathroom" and "restroom" include:

浴室 (yùshì), bathroom for bathing, usually without a toilet, 廁所 (cèsuǒ), public restroom with no bathing facilities, 洗手間 (xǐshǒujiān), restroom or bathroom, and 化粧室 (huàzhuāngshì), restroom (mainly in Taiwan). Occasionally, some Chinese speakers refer to the restroom euphemistically as 一號 (yī hào), literally, number one.

Wáng Péng zài xuéxiào de sùshè zhù le liǎng ge xuéqī le①. Tā juéde sùshè tài chǎo, shuì bu hǎo jiào. Fángjiān tài xiǎo, lián diànnǎo dōu② fàng bu xià③, zàishuō yě méiyǒu dìfang kěyǐ zuò fàn, hěn bù fāngbiàn, suǒyǐ zhǔnbèi xià ge xuéqī bān chu qu zhù. Tā zhǎo fángzi zhǎo le yí ge duō④ yuè le, kěshì hái méiyǒu zhǎo dào héshì de. Gāngcái tā zài bàozhǐ shang kàn dào le yí ge guǎnggào, shuō xuéxiào fùjìn yǒu yí tào gōngyù chūzū, lí xuéxiào hěn jìn, zǒu lù zhǐ yào wǔ fēnzhōng, hěn fāngbiàn. Gōngyù yǒu yí ge wòshì, yí ge chúfáng, yí ge wèishēngjiān❶, yí ge kètīng, hái dài jiājù. Wáng Péng juéde zhè tào gōngyù kěnéng duì tā hěn héshì.

VOCABULARY

1.	吵	chǎo	v/adj	to quarrel; noisy
2.	連	lián	prep	even
3.	做飯	zuò fàn	vo	to cook; to prepare a meal
4.	報紙	bàozhǐ	n	newspaper
5.	廣告	guǎnggào	n	advertisement
6.	附近	fùjìn	n	vicinity; neighborhood; nearby area
7.	套	tào	m	(measure word for suite or set)
8.	公寓	gōngyù	n	apartment
9.	出租	chūzū	v	to rent out
10.	走路	zǒu lù	vo	to walk
11.	分鐘	fēnzhōng	n	minute
12.	臥室	wòshì	n	bedroom
13.	廚房	chúfáng	n	kitchen
14.	衛生間	wèishēngjiān	n	bathroom
15.	客廳	kètīng	n	living room
16.	傢具	jiājù	n	furniture
17.	可能	kěnéng	adv/adj	maybe; possible

Grammar

1. Verb + 了 (le) + Numeral + Measure Word + Noun + 了 (le)

The sentence 王朋在學校的宿舍住了兩個學期了。(Wáng Péng zài xuéxiào de sùshè zhù le liǎng ge xuéqī le.) means that Wang Peng has been living on campus for two semesters up to this moment. On its own, the sentence usually implies that the action has been continuing for some time and is expected to last into the future.

① A: 你開出租汽車開了幾年了？

Nǐ kāi chūzū qìchē kāi le jǐ nián le?)

(How many years have you been driving a cab?)

B: 一年半了。

Yì nián bàn le.

(For a year and a half now.)

② 弟弟寫電子郵件寫了半個鐘頭了，不知道還要寫多長時間。

Dìdi xiě diànzǐ yóujiàn xiě le bàn ge zhōngtóu le, bù zhīdào hái yào xiě duō cháng shíjiān.

(My younger brother has been writing e-mails for half an hour. Who knows how much longer he will be.)

The following two sentences are different in meaning:

③ 他病了三天了。

Tā bìng le sān tiān le.

(He has been sick for three days.)

[The illness has continued for three days and he currently remains sick.)

④ 他病了三天。

Tā bìng le sān tiān.

(He was sick for three days.)

[He recovered from the illness on the fourth day.]

If, however, a clause in this pattern is followed by another clause, it may suggest that the action may come to an end.

 我打掃房子打掃了一上午了，想休息一下。

Wǒ dǎsǎo fángzi dǎsǎo le yí shàngwǔ le, xiǎng xiūxi yí xià.

(I've been cleaning the house all morning. I'd like to take a break.)

This structure is not limited to temporal expressions. It can also be used to indicate quantity:

 衣服我已經買了三件了，夠了。

Yīfu wǒ yǐjīng mǎi le sān jiàn le, gòu le.

(I have already bought three pieces of clothing. That's plenty.)

 這封信我已經看了兩遍了，不想再看了。

Zhè fēng xìn wǒ yǐjīng kàn le liǎng biàn le, bù xiǎng zài kàn le.

(I've read this letter twice already and don't want to read it again.)

2. 連…都/也 (lián…dōu/yě)

連 (lián) is an intensifier which is always used in conjunction with 都/也 (dōu/yě).

❶ 我姐姐的孩子很聰明，連日本話都會說。

Wǒ jiějie de háizi hěn cōngming, lián Rìběnhuà dōu huì shuō.

(My sister's child is really smart. She can even speak Japanese.)

❷ 我弟弟學中文學了一年了，可是連"天"字都不會寫。

Wǒ dìdi xué Zhōngwén xuéle yì nián le, kěshì lián "tiān" zì dōu bú huì xiě.

(My younger brother has been studying Chinese for a year now, but can't even write the character 天.)

❸ 你怎麼連藥都忘了吃？

Nǐ zěnme lián yào dōu wàng le chī?

(How could you forget even to take your medicine?)

❹   昨天學的生詞我連一個也不記得了。

Zuótiān xué de shēngcí wǒ lián yí ge yě bú jìde le.

(I can't recall even a single word we learned yesterday.)

What follows 連 (lián) usually represents an extreme case: the biggest or smallest, the best or worst, the most difficult or easiest, etc. (1), for instance, implies that Japanese is very difficult. If a child can speak such a difficult language as Japanese, then the child must be very intelligent. Similarly, 天 (tiān) is considered one of the easiest Chinese characters. If the younger brother in (2) does not know how to write 天 (tiān), it goes without saying that he can't write other more difficult characters.

3. Potential complements with Verb + 不下 (bu xià)

The V + 不下 (bu xià) structure suggests that a location or container in question does not have the capacity to hold something.

 這個客廳大是大，不過坐不下二十個人。

Zhè ge kètīng dà shì dà, búguò zuò bu xià èrshí ge rén.

(This living room is pretty spacious, but still not large enough to seat twenty people.)

 這張紙寫不下八百個字。

Zhè zhāng zhǐ xiě bu xià bābǎi ge zì.

(This piece of paper isn't big enough to write 800 characters on.)

 這個冰箱放不下兩個西瓜。

Zhè ge bīngxiāng fàng bu xià liǎng ge xīgua.

(This refrigerator won't fit two watermelons.)

4. 多 (duō) Indicating an Approximate Number

多 (duō) can be placed after a number to indicate an approximate number. The combination indicates not an exact number but a general numeric range, e.g., 十多個 (shí duō ge) means more than ten but fewer than twenty; it could be eleven, twelve, thirteen, etc.

If the concept represented by the noun is not divisible into smaller units, and the number is ten or a multiple of ten, 多 (duō) precedes the measure word, e.g., 二十多個人 (èrshí duō ge rén, more than twenty people), 三十多個學生 (sānshí duō ge xuésheng, more than thirty students), 一百多張紙 (yì bǎi duō zhāng zhǐ, over one hundred sheets of paper).

However, if the concept represented by the noun can be divided into smaller units (e.g., 一塊錢＝十毛, 一個星期＝七天 [yí kuài qián ＝ shí máo, yí ge xīngqī ＝ qī tiān]), there are two possibilities. If the number is not ten or a multiple of ten, 多 (duō) should be used after the measure word, e.g., 七塊多錢 (qī kuài duō qián, more than seven dollars but less than eight), 一個多星期 (yí ge duō xīngqī, more than one week but less than two). If the number is ten or a multiple of ten, 多 (duō) can be used either before the measure word, e.g., 十多塊錢 (shí duō kuài qián, more than ten dollars but less than twenty), or after the measure word, e.g., 十塊多錢 (shí kuài duō qián, more than ten dollars but less than eleven), but these two options represent different numeric ranges.

❶ 這枝筆一塊多錢。

Zhè zhī bǐ yí kuài duō qián.

(This pen is over one dollar.)

[The price is more than one dollar but less than two.]

❷ 我們班有二十多個學生。

Wǒmen bān yǒu èrshí duō ge xuésheng.

(There are over twenty students in our class.)

[There are more than twenty students but fewer than thirty.]

❸ 妹妹感冒十多天了。

Mèimei gǎnmào shí duō tiān le.

(My younger sister has had a cold for more than ten days.)

[The number of days is between ten and twenty.]

❹ 他昨天買了四十多個梨。

Tā zuótiān mǎi le sìshí duō ge lí.

(He bought over forty pears yesterday.)

[The number is between forty and fifty.]

❺   他昨天買禮物花了一百多塊錢。

Tā zuótiān mǎi lǐwù huā le yìbǎi duō kuài qián.

(He bought over one hundred dollars' worth of gifts yesterday.)

[He spent more than one hundred dollars but less than two hundred.]

❻ **A:** 這雙黑鞋十多塊錢。

Zhè shuāng hēi xié shí duō kuài qián.

(This pair of black shoes is over ten dollars.)

[The price is more than ten dollars but less than twenty.]

　　B: 這雙咖啡色的鞋十塊多錢。

Zhè shuāng kāfēi sè de xié shí kuài duō qián.

(This pair of brown shoes is over ten dollars.)

[The price is more than ten dollars but less than eleven.]

❼ **A:** 這家飯館兒的師傅和服務員認識十年多了。

Zhè jiā fànguǎnr de shīfu hé fúwùyuán rènshi shí nián duō le.

(The chef and the waiter in this restaurant have known each other for ten years and some months.)

[The length of time is longer than ten years but shorter than eleven.]

　　B: 我以為他們認識十多年了。

Wǒ yǐwéi tāmen rènshi shí duō nián le.

(I thought they had known each other for more than ten years.)

[The length of time is between ten and twenty years.]

Language Practice

A. Time Flies

Work with your partner and find out the following from each other.

1. 你學中文學了
多長時間了？

Nǐ xué Zhōngwén xué le

duō cháng shíjiān le?

2. 你上(your school's name)上了
多長時間了？

Nǐ shàng (your school's name)

shàng le duō cháng shíjiān le?

3. 你在你現在住的地方
住了多長時間了？

Nǐ zài nǐ xiànzài zhù de dìfang

zhù le duō cháng shíjiān le?

Based on your partner's situation, you may also want to ask how long he/she has been working, involved in his/her hobbies, etc.

B. Can You Believe It?

A. Little Bai is absent-minded and often forgetful.

EXAMPLE:

He even forgot to bring a pen with him when he had to take a test.

→ 考試的時候，
他連筆都/也忘了帶了。

Kǎo shì de shíhòu,

tā lián bǐ dōu/yě wàng le dài le.

In addition:

1. He even forgot his girlfriend's birthday.

2. He didn't even remember his own phone number.

3. He even forgot to bring money when he was treating his friends to dinner.

B. Little Bai just moved into an apartment, and it already has so many problems.

EXAMPLE:

The apartment doesn't even have a kitchen.

→ 公寓連廚房都/
也沒有。

Gōngyù lián chúfáng dōu/

yě méi yǒu.

In addition:

1. His bathroom doesn't even have (running) water.

2. His bedroom is so tiny that even a bed cannot be placed in it.

3. His living room is so small that it cannot even seat five people.

C. Little Bai is also behind the times.

EXAMPLE:

He doesn't even know how to use a computer.

→ 小白連電腦都/
　也不會用。

Xiǎo Bái lián diànnǎo dōu/
yě bú huì yòng.

In addition:

1. He doesn't know how to use a cell phone.

2. He doesn't know how to send email.

3. He doesn't know how to use a credit card.

C. Size-Wise

Take turns with your partner and find out the capacity of your apartment/room, living room, classroom, refrigerator, desk, etc. Use the proper verb for each question.

EXAMPLE:

apartment/room

→ A: 你的公寓/房間
　　住得下多少/幾個人？

Nǐ de gōngyù/fángjiān
zhù de xià duōshao/jǐ ge rén?

B: 我的公寓/房間
　　住得下_____個人。

Wǒ de gōngyù/fángjiān
zhù de xià _____ ge rén.

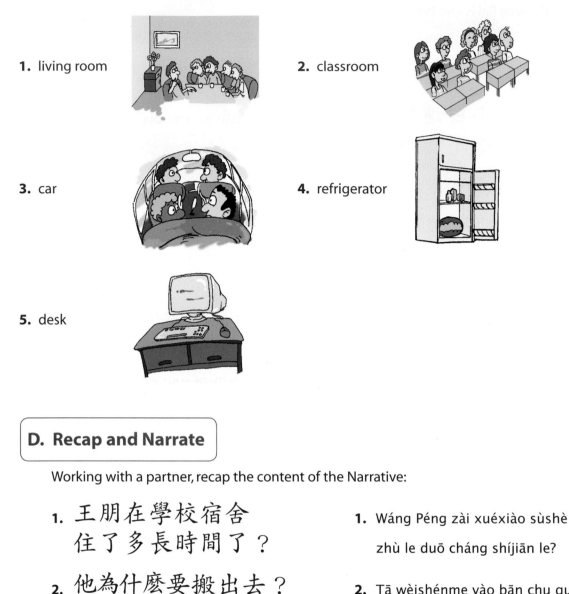

1. living room

2. classroom

3. car

4. refrigerator

5. desk

D. Recap and Narrate

Working with a partner, recap the content of the Narrative:

1. 王朋在學校宿舍住了多長時間了？

   1. Wáng Péng zài xuéxiào sùshè zhù le duō cháng shíjiān le?

2. 他為什麼要搬出去？

   2. Tā wèishénme yào bān chu qu?

3. 他找房子找了多長時間了？

   3. Tā zhǎo fángzi zhǎo le duō cháng shíjiān le?

4. 他找到合適的了嗎？

   4. Tā zhǎo dào héshì de le ma?

5. 報紙的廣告說有一套什麼樣的房子出租？

   5. Bàozhǐ de guǎnggào shuō yǒu yí tào shénme yàng de fángzi chūzū?

6. 王朋覺得這套公寓對他合適嗎？

   6. Wáng Péng juéde zhè tào gōngyù duì tā héshì ma?

Using the words and phrases in blue as prompts, connect your answers above to form a narrative like this example:

王朋在學校的宿舍住了兩個學期了。他覺得宿舍太吵，房間太小，再說也不能做飯，很不方便，所以準備下個學期搬出去。他找房子找了一個多月，也沒有找到合適的。剛才他在報紙上看到了一個廣告，說學校附近有一套公寓出租，那套公寓離學校很近，有一個臥室，一個廚房，一個衛生間，一個客廳，還帶傢具。王朋覺得這套公寓可能對他很合適。

Wáng Péng zài xuéxiào de sùshè zhù le liǎng ge xuéqī le. Tā juéde sùshè tài chǎo, fángjiān tài xiǎo, zàishuō yě bù néng zuò fàn, hěn bù fāngbiàn, suǒyǐ zhǔnbèi xià ge xuéqī bān chu qu. Tā zhǎo fángzi zhǎo le yí ge duō yuè, yě méiyǒu zhǎo dào héshì de. Gāngcái tā zài bàozhǐ shang kàn dào le yí ge guǎnggào, shuō xuéxiào fùjìn yǒu yí tào gōngyù chūzū, nà tào gōngyù lí xuéxiào hěn jìn, yǒu yí ge wòshì, yí ge chúfáng, yí ge wèishēngjiān, yí ge kètīng, hái dài jiājù. Wáng Péng juéde zhè tào gōngyù kěnéng duì tā hěn héshì.

Dialogue: Calling about an Apartment for Rent

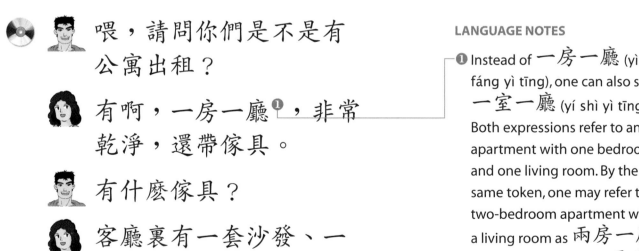

喂，請問你們是不是有公寓出租？

有啊，一房一廳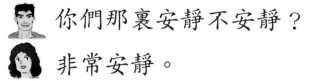，非常乾淨，還帶傢具。

有什麼傢具？

客廳裏有一套沙發、一張飯桌跟四把椅子。臥室裏有一張床、一張書桌和一個書架。

你們那裏安靜不安靜？

非常安靜。

LANGUAGE NOTES

❶ Instead of 一房一廳 (yì fáng yì tīng), one can also say 一室一廳 (yí shì yì tīng). Both expressions refer to an apartment with one bedroom and one living room. By the same token, one may refer to a two-bedroom apartment with a living room as 兩房一廳 (liǎng fáng yì tīng) or 兩室一廳 (liǎng shì yì tīng).

每個月房租多少錢？

八百五十元。

八百五十美元？人民幣差不多是…有一點兒貴，能不能便宜點兒？

那你不用付水電費。

要不要付押金？

要多付一個月的房租當押金，搬出去的時候還給你。另外，我們公寓不准養寵物。

沒關係，我對養寵物沒有興趣❷，什麼寵物都⑤不養。

那太好了。你今天下午來看看吧。

好。

❷ One should not mix up 有興趣 (yǒu xìngqù) with 有意思 (yǒu yìsi). While 有興趣 (yǒu xìngqù) is a verb that pertains to a person who is *interested* (in something), 有意思 (yǒu yìsi) is an adjective describing someone or something that is *interesting*.

Wéi, qǐng wèn nǐmen shì bú shì yǒu gōngyù chūzū?

Yǒu a, yì fáng yì tīng❶, fēicháng gānjìng, hái dài jiājù.

Yǒu shénme jiājù?

Kètīng li yǒu yí tào shāfā, yì zhāng fànzhuō gēn sì bǎ yǐzi. Wòshì li yǒu yì zhāng chuáng, yì zhāng shūzhuō hé yí ge shūjià.

Nǐmen nàli ānjìng bù ānjìng?

Fēicháng ānjìng.

Měi ge yuè fángzū duōshao qián?

Bābǎi wǔshí yuán.

 Bābǎi wǔshí Měiyuán? Rénmínbì chàbuduō shì... Yǒu yì diǎnr guì, néng bù néng piányi diǎnr?

 Nà nǐ búyòng fù shuǐ diàn fèi.

 Yào bú yào fù yājīn?

 Yào duō fù yí ge yuè de fángzū dāng yājīn, bān chu qu de shíhou huán gěi nǐ. Lìngwài, wǒmen gōngyù bù zhǔn yǎng chǒngwù.

 Méi guānxi, wǒ duì yǎng chǒngwù méi yǒu xìngqù❷, shénme chǒngwù dōu⑤ bù yǎng.

 Nà tài hǎo le. Nǐ jīntiān xiàwǔ lái kàn kan ba.

 Hǎo.

 ## VOCABULARY

1.	一房一廳	yì fáng yì tīng	one bedroom and one living room
2.	乾淨	gānjìng	adj	clean
3.	沙發	shāfā	n	sofa
4.	飯桌	fànzhuō	n	dining table
5.	椅子	yǐzi	n	chair
6.	書桌	shūzhuō	n	desk
7.	書架	shūjià	n	bookcase; bookshelf
8.	那裏	nàli	pr	there
9.	安靜	ānjìng	adj	quiet
10.	房租	fángzū	n	rent
11.	元	yuán	m	(measure word for the basic Chinese monetary unit); yuan
12.	美元	Měiyuán	n	U.S. currency

VOCABULARY

13.	人民幣	rénmínbì	n	renminbi (RMB, Chinese currency)
	人民	rénmín	n	the people
	幣	bì	n	currency
14.	差不多	chàbuduō	adv/adj	almost; nearly; similar
15.	費	fèi	n	fee; expenses
16.	押金	yājīn	n	security deposit
17.	當	dāng	v	to serve as; to be
18.	還	huán	v	to return (something)
19.	另外	lìngwài	conj	furthermore; in addition
20.	准	zhǔn	v	to allow; to be allowed
21.	養	yǎng	v	to raise
22.	寵物	chǒngwù	n	pet
23.	興趣	xìngqù	n	interest

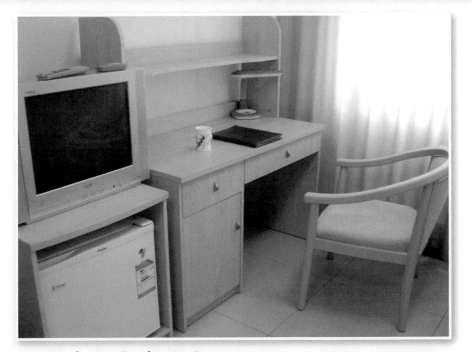

這個房間裏有什麼？
Zhè ge fángjiān li yǒu shénme?

Grammar

5. Question Pronouns with 都/也 (dōu/yě)

A question pronoun can appear in sentences other than questions. When a question pronoun is used in a statement with 都/也 (dōu/yě) appearing after it, it simply means "all" or "none" in the sense of being all-inclusive or all-exclusive.

❶ A: 你想喝點兒什麼飲料？

Nǐ xiǎng hē diǎnr shénme yǐnliào?

(What beverage would you like to drink?)

B: 謝謝，我不渴，什麼都不想喝。

Xièxie, wǒ bù kě, shénme dōu bù xiǎng hē.

(No, thanks. I am not thirsty. I don't feel like drinking anything.)

❷ 這些公寓我哪套都不租。

Zhè xiē gōngyù wǒ nǎ tào dōu bù zū.

(I am not renting any of these apartments.)

❸ 中國我什麼地方都沒去過。

Zhōngguó wǒ shénme dìfang dōu méi qù guo.

(I haven't been to any place in China.)

❹ 我什麼寵物都不養。養寵物太麻煩了！

Wǒ shénme chǒngwù dōu bù yǎng. Yǎng chǒngwù tài máfan le!

(I don't keep any pets. Keeping pets is too much trouble!)

❺ 在這個城市，哪兒也吃不到糖醋魚。

Zài zhè ge chéngshì, nǎr yě chī bu dào tángcùyú.

(You can't find sweet and sour fish anywhere in this city.)

❻ A: 在舞會上你認識了誰？

Zài wǔhuì shang nǐ rènshi le shéi?

(Who did you get to know at the dance party?)

B: 我誰都没認識。

Wǒ shéi dōu méi rènshi.

(I didn't get to know anybody.)

❼ 你明天幾點跟我見面都行。

Nǐ míngtiān jǐ diǎn gēn wǒ jiàn miàn dōu xíng.

(You can meet with me any time tomorrow.)

❽ 這些藥我哪種都試過，對我的過敏都没有用。

Zhè xiē yào wǒ nǎ zhǒng dōu shì quo, duì wǒ de guòmǐn dōu méiyǒu yòng.

(I have tried all these medicines; none of them is effective for my allergies.)

According to the sign, what's not welcome here?

Language Practice

E. The Two Extremes

Aisha and Mona are twin sisters, but they could not be more different: Aisha is easygoing and Mona is difficult.

EXAMPLE 1:

Aisha likes all colors.   vs.   Mona hates all colors.

→ Aisha 什麼顏色都喜歡。   Aisha shénme yánsè dōu xǐhuan.

Mona 什麼顏色都不喜歡。   Mona shénme yánsè dōu bù xǐhuan.

EXAMPLE 2:

Aisha knows everyone.   vs.   Mona knows no one.

→ Aisha 誰都認識。   Aisha shéi dōu rènshi.

Mona 誰都不認識。   Mona shéi dōu bú rènshi.

1. Aisha eats all sorts of fruits and vegetables.   vs.   Mona eats no fruits and vegetables at all.

→

2. Aisha has been to all kinds of places.   vs.   Mona hasn't been anywhere.

→

3. Aisha is happy all the time.   vs.   Mona is unhappy all the time.

→

4. Everyone thinks Aisha is cool.   vs.   Everyone thinks Mona is no fun.

→

F. A Floor Plan

Look at the floor plan of this apartment. Name the rooms and describe what's in each
room.

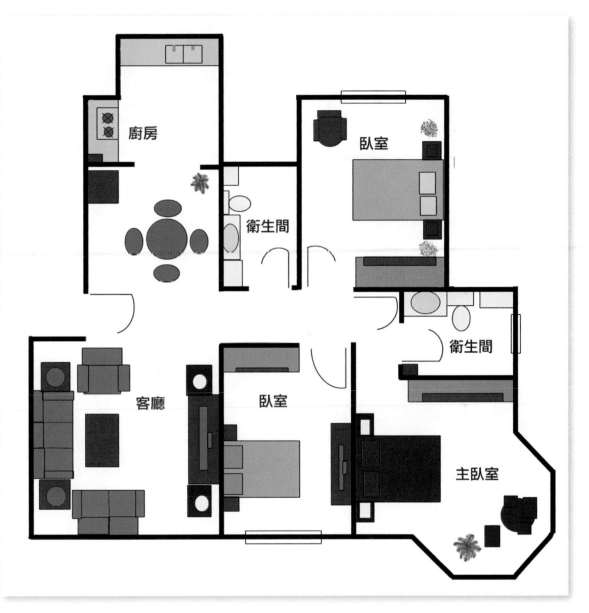

G. Setting the Scene

Look at the picture and work with your partner to describe this room: what's in the room and how things are positioned. Don't forget the person and the dog.

H. To Move or Not to Move

Find out whether your partner likes the place he or she currently lives in. List the pros and cons of the place.

What suits him/her	What doesn't suit him/her
1. _____	1. _____
2. _____	2. _____
3. _____	3. _____
4. _____	4. _____
5. _____	5. _____

Then report to the class why your partner thinks he/she should stay or move out.

Carlos 覺得他的公寓/
宿舍對他很/不合適。
因為 1 _____ , 2 _____ , ···
所以他不想/想搬出去。

Carlos juéde tā de gōngyù/
sùshè duì tā hěn/bù héshì
Yīnwèi 1 _____, 2 _____, ...
suǒyǐ tā bù xiǎng/xiǎng bān chu qu.

I. Recap and Narrate

Working with a partner, recap the content of the Dialogue:

1. 那個要出租的公寓
   租出去了嗎?

2. 那個公寓有什麼
   傢具?

3. 那個公寓安靜嗎?

4. 房租是多少?

1. Nà ge yào chūzū de gōngyù
   zū chu qu le ma?

2. Nà ge gōngyù yǒu shénme
   jiājù?

3. Nà ge gōngyù ānjìng ma?

4. Fángzū shì duōshao?

5. 王朋問出租房子的
   人能不能便宜一點兒，
   那個人説什麼？

6. 要不要付押金？

7. 這個公寓能養
   寵物嗎？

8. 王朋什麼時候會
   去看那個公寓？

5. Wáng Péng wèn chūzū fángzi de rén néng bù néng piányi yì diǎnr, nà ge rén shuō shénme?

6. Yào bú yào fù yājīn?

7. Zhè ge gōngyù néng yǎng chǒngwù ma?

8. Wáng Péng shénme shíhou huì qù kàn nà ge gōngyù?

Using the words and phrases in blue as prompts, connect your answers above to form a narrative like this example:

王朋看了報紙上的出租廣告後，打電話給出租房子的人。出租房子的人説客廳裏有一套沙發、一張飯桌跟四把椅子。臥室裏有一張床、一張書桌和一個書架，還説那裏非常安靜。房租每個月是八百五十元，不用付水電費。那個人還説不准養寵物，得多付一個月的房租當押金，今天下午就可以去看房子。

Wáng Péng kàn le bàozhǐ shang de chūzū guǎnggào hòu, dǎ diànhuà gěi chūzū fángzi de rén. Chūzū fángzi de rén shuō kètīng li yǒu yí tào shāfā, yì zhāng fànzhuō gēn sì bǎ yǐzi. Wòshì li yǒu yì zhāng chuáng, yì zhāng shūzhuō hé yí ge shūjià, hái shuō nàli fēicháng ānjìng. Fángzū měi ge yuè shì bābǎi wǔshí yuán, búyòng fù shuǐ diàn fèi. Nà ge rén hái shuō bù zhǔn yǎng chǒngwù, děi duō fù yí ge yuè de fángzū dāng yājīn, jīntiān xiàwǔ jiù kěyǐ qù kàn fángzi.

HOW ABOUT YOU?

What's in your living quarters?

1.	音響	yīnxiǎng	n	stereo system
2.	燈	dēng	n	lamp; light
3.	櫃子	guìzi	n	cabinet; cupboard
4.	植物	zhíwù	n	plant
5.	海報	hǎibào	n	poster

Any other household items in your room that you want to say in Chinese? Please ask your teacher and make a note here:

_____

房屋出租

三房兩廳
兩個廁所
有冰箱，洗衣機
月租：$1375
有意請電：425-754-
xxxx

房屋出租
$180-$350

電視CABLE，近公車站
有意者請電：206-
682-xxxx

報紙上出租房子的廣告
Bàozhǐ shang chūzū fángzi de guǎnggào

Culture Highlights

1 Until the late 1990s, college students in China were all required to live in dorms on campus, with six or seven of them sharing a room and possibly dozens sharing a bathroom. Because there was no place to cook in the dorms, everyone ate in the students' dining hall (學生 餐廳 xuéshēng cāntīng) on campus. Since the early 1980s, foreign students have generally been segregated into designated dormitories, typically with two to a room. Living conditions for Chinese students, meanwhile, have improved substantially since the late 1990s. At some colleges, students now have the option of renting apartments off campus, if they can afford it.

2 It is becoming increasingly convenient to rent an apartment in a Chinese city. One can look for listings online, in the local newspapers, or simply call or stop by one of the many 仲介公司 (zhòngjiè gōngsī, intermediary companies), agencies that match apartment owners with potential tenants.

3 Traditionally, the Chinese had a special love—many still do—for birds, especially parrots and canaries. Tropical fish also remain popular with many urbanites. Even crickets make good pets for some people. In the countryside, the most popular household pets are cats, at least partly for the practical purpose of keeping rats away. In recent decades, the population of dogs, especially in the cities, has increased dramatically. According to a report by *China News Week* in 2006, there were 550,000 "licensed" dogs in Beijing alone. By receiving the license, these animals became "legal residents" of the city.

English Text

Narrative

Wang Peng has been living in the school dorm for two semesters. He thinks that the dorm is too noisy, and he can't sleep well. His room is too small, and he can't even fit a computer there. Besides, he has nowhere to cook. It's really inconvenient, so he plans to move out next semester. He has been looking for a place for a month now, but he hasn't found anything suitable yet. He just saw an ad in the newspaper saying there's an apartment for rent. It's very close to school, only a five-minute walk—very convenient. The apartment includes a bedroom, a kitchen, a bathroom, and a living room, and it's furnished. Wang Peng thinks this apartment may be just right for him.

Dialogue

Wang Peng: Hi, do you have an apartment for rent?

Landlady: Yes, we do. One bedroom with a living room. It's very clean, and also furnished.

Wang Peng: What kind of furniture does it have?

Landlady: In the living room there is a sofa set, a dining table, and four chairs. The bedroom has a bed, a desk and a bookcase.

Wang Peng: Is it quiet over there?

Landlady: Extremely quiet.

Wang Peng: How much is the monthly rent?

Landlady: $850.

Wang Peng: 850 U.S. dollars? In renminbi that's almost...That's a little bit expensive. Could you come down a little bit?

Landlady: All right. You won't have to pay for the utilities.

Wang Peng: Do I have to pay a deposit?

Landlady: An extra month's rent as a security deposit, which will be returned to you when you move out. And another thing, no pets are allowed in our apartments.

Wang Peng: That doesn't matter. I'm not interested in keeping pets. I don't have pets of any kind.

Landlady: Great. Why don't you come over this afternoon and take a look?

Wang Peng: OK.

PROGRESS CHECKLIST

Before proceeding to Lesson 18, be sure you can complete the following tasks in Chinese:

I am able to—

- [x] Describe my living quarters;
- [ ] Name common pieces of furniture;
- [ ] Discuss the suitability of various living arrangements;
- [ ] Ask about and negotiate rent, utilities, and security deposits.

出租公寓的廣告
chūzū gōngyù de guǎnggào

LESSON 18   Sports

第十八課   運動

Dì shíbā kè   Yùndòng

LEARNING OBJECTIVES

In this lesson, you will learn to use Chinese to

- Name some popular sports;
- Talk about your exercise habits;
- Discuss your feelings about various sports;
- Make a simple comparison between how soccer and American football are played.

RELATE AND GET READY

In your own culture/community—

1. Do people exercise regularly?

2. Are most people sports fans? Which sports are most popular?

3. Are there many sports programs on TV?

4. Which is more popular, American football or soccer?

Dialogue I: My Gut Keeps Getting Bigger and Bigger!

 你看，我的肚子越來越大了。

你平常吃得那麼多，又❶不運動，當然越來越胖了。

那怎麼辦呢？

如果怕胖，你一個星期運動兩、三次，每次半個小時，肚子就會小了。

我兩年沒運動了①，做什麼運動呢？

最簡單的運動是跑步。

冬天那麼冷，夏天那麼熱，跑步太難受②了。

LANGUAGE NOTES

❶ As mentioned before, 又 (yòu) can indicate repetition of an action over the course of time, e.g., 我昨天看了一個電影，今天又看了一個 (Wǒ zuótiān kàn le yí ge diànyǐng, jīntiān yòu kàn le yí ge, I watched a movie yesterday, and watched another one today). 又 (yòu) can also suggest augmentation or exacerbation of certain conditions or circumstances, as in the sentence 你平常吃得那麼多，又不運動，當然越來越胖了。(Nǐ píngcháng chī de nàme duō, yòu bú yùndòng, dāngrán yuè lái yuè pàng le. You usually eat so much, and on top of that you don't exercise. No wonder you're putting on more and more weight).

你打網球吧。

打網球得買網球拍、網球鞋，
你知道，網球拍、網球鞋貴極了！

找幾個人打籃球吧。買個籃球很
便宜。

那每次都得打電話約人，麻煩死了。

你去游泳吧。不用找人，也不用花
很多錢，什麼時候去都可以。

游泳？我怕水，太危險了，淹死了
怎麼辦？

我也沒辦法了。你不願意運動，
那就胖下去③吧。

Nǐ kàn, wǒ de dùzi yuè lái yuè dà le.

Nǐ píngcháng chī de nàme duō, yòu❶ bú yùndòng, dāngrán yuè lái yuè pàng le.

Nà zěnme bàn ne?

Rúguǒ pà pàng, nǐ yí ge xīngqī yùndòng liǎng, sān cì, měi cì bàn ge xiǎoshí, dùzi jiù huì xiǎo le.

Wǒ liǎng nián méi yùndòng le①, zuò shénme yùndòng ne?

Zuì jiǎndān de yùndòng shì pǎo bù.

Dōngtiān nàme lěng, xiàtiān nàme rè, pǎo bù tài nánshòu② le.

Nǐ dǎ wǎngqiú ba.

Dǎ wǎngqiú děi mǎi wǎngqiú pāi, wǎngqiú xié, nǐ zhīdao wǎngqiú pāi, wǎngqiú xié guì jí le!

Zhǎo jǐ ge rén dǎ lánqiú ba. Mǎi ge lánqiú hěn piányi.

Nà měi cì dōu děi dǎ diànhuà yuē rén, máfan sǐ le.

Nǐ qù yóu yǒng ba. Búyòng zhǎo rén, yě búyòng huā hěn duō qián, shénme shíhou qù dōu kěyǐ.

Yóu yǒng? Wǒ pà shuǐ, tài wēixiǎn le, yān sǐ le zěnme bàn?

Wǒ yě méi bànfǎ le. Nǐ bú yuànyì yùndòng, nà jiù pàng xia qu③ ba.

VOCABULARY

1.	當然	dāngrán	adv	of course
2.	胖	pàng	adj	fat
3.	怕	pà	v	to fear; to be afraid of
4.	簡單	jiǎndān	adj	simple
5.	跑步	pǎo bù	vo	to jog
	跑	pǎo	v	to run
6.	難受	nánshòu	adj	hard to bear; uncomfortable [See Grammar 2.]
7.	網球	wǎngqiú	n	tennis
8.	拍	pāi	n	racket
9.	籃球	lánqiú	n	basketball
10.	游泳	yóu yǒng	vo	to swim
11.	危險	wēixiǎn	adj	dangerous
12.	淹死	yān sǐ	vc	to drown
13.	願意	yuànyì	av	to be willing

北京语言大学
网球场

Grammar

1. Duration of Non-Action

Time Expression + 没 (méi) + **V** + (了)

This structure indicates that an action has not been or was not performed for a certain period of time.

 他三天没上網了。

Tā sān tiān méi shàng wǎng le.

(He hasn't gone online for three days.)

 我兩年没檢查身體了。

Wǒ liǎng nián méi jiǎnchá shēntǐ le.

(I haven't had a check-up in two years.)

 我的狗病了，一天没吃東西了。

Wǒ de gǒu bìng le, yì tiān méi chī dōngxi le.

(My dog is sick; she hasn't eaten anything for a day.)

 妹妹上個月特別忙，三個星期没回家。

Mèimei shàng ge yuè tèbié máng, sān ge xīngqī méi huí jiā.

(My younger sister was especially busy last month, and she didn't come home for three weeks.)

❺ 去年寒假我去英國旅行，一個月没吃中國菜。

Qùnián hánjià wǒ qù Yīngguó lǚxíng, yí ge yuè méi chī Zhōngguó cài.

(I went on a trip to Britain during the winter break last year, and didn't eat any Chinese food for a month.)

Please note the difference between this construction and the one that indicates the duration of an action in an affirmative sentence. Compare:

6 **A:** 我學了兩年中文了。

Wǒ xué le liǎng nián Zhōngwén le.

(I have been studying Chinese for two years.)

B: 是嗎？我兩年没學中文了。

Shì ma? Wǒ liǎng nián méi xué Zhōngwén le.

(Really? I haven't studied Chinese for two years.)

---

2. 好/難 (hǎo/nán) **+ V**

Some verbs can be preceded by 好 or 難 (hǎo or nán), and the resulting compounds become adjectives. In this case, 好 (hǎo) usually means "easy" while 難 (nán) means "difficult," e.g.: 好受/難受 (hǎoshòu/nánshòu, easy to bear/hard to bear), 好寫/難寫 (hǎoxiě/nánxiě, easy to write/hard to write), 好走/難走 (hǎozǒu/nánzǒu, easy to walk on/hard to walk on), 好説/難説 (hǎoshuō/nánshuō, easy to say/difficult to say), 好懂/難懂 (hǎodǒng/nándǒng, easy to understand/hard to understand), 好唱/難唱 (hǎochàng/nánchàng, easy to sing/hard to sing). In some other compounds, however, 好 (hǎo) suggests that the action represented by the verb is pleasant, while 難 (nán) means the opposite, e.g., 好吃/難吃 (hǎochī/nánchī, delicious/unappetizing), 好看/難看 (hǎokàn/nánkàn, pretty/ugly), 好聽/難聽 (hǎotīng/nántīng, pleasant to the ear/unpleasant to the ear), etc.

---

3. 下去 (xia qu) **Indicating Continuation**

下去 (xia qu) signifies the continuation of an action that is already in progress.

1 説下去。

Shuō xia qu.

(Go on speaking.)

2 你别念下去了，我一點兒也不喜歡聽。

Nǐ bié niàn xia qu le, wǒ yì diǎnr yě bù xǐhuan tīng.

(Please stop reading. I don't like listening to it at all.)

❸ 中文很有意思，我想學下去。

Zhōngwén hěn yǒu yìsi, wǒ xiǎng xué xia qu.

(Chinese is very interesting. I'd like to continue learning it.)

❹ 你已經跑了一個多小時了，再跑下去，要累
死了。

Nǐ yǐjǐng pǎo le yí ge duō xiǎoshí le, zài pǎo xia qu, yào lèi sǐ le.

(You've already been running for more than an hour; if you keep running, you'll be exhausted.)

Language Practice

A. What's the Matter?

Gao Wenzhong is not feeling well. Please help him describe his condition to his doctor.

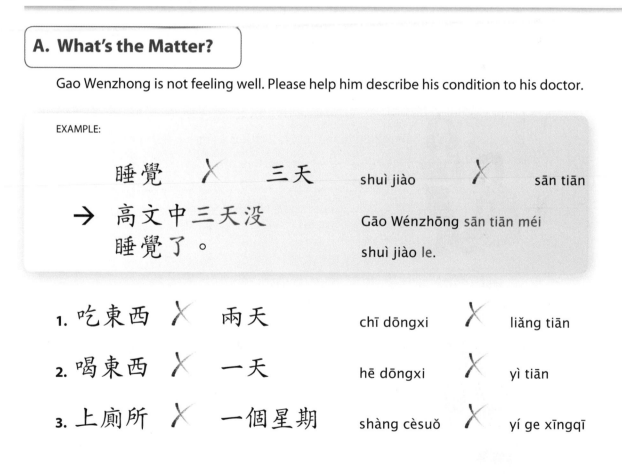

EXAMPLE:

睡覺　✗　三天　　　shuì jiào　✗　sān tiān

→ 高文中三天没
睡覺了。　　　Gāo Wénzhōng sān tiān méi
shuì jiào le.

1. 吃東西　✗　兩天　　chī dōngxi　✗　liǎng tiān

2. 喝東西　✗　一天　　hē dōngxi　✗　yì tiān

3. 上廁所　✗　一個星期　shàng cèsuǒ　✗　yí ge xīngqī

B. Why Hasn't She Called?

Wang Peng and Li You had a fight. They haven't seen each other, called, chatted online, or text-messaged for some time. With your partner, ask and answer questions about their strained relationship based on the visuals.

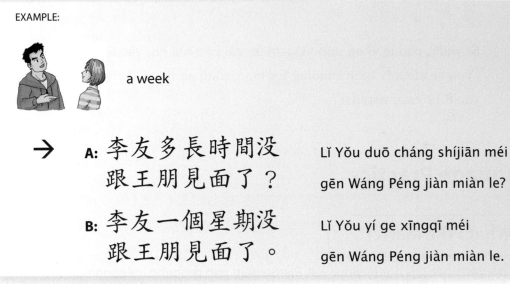

EXAMPLE:

a week

→ A: 李友多長時間沒
跟王朋見面了？

Lǐ Yǒu duō cháng shíjiān méi
gēn Wáng Péng jiàn miàn le?

B: 李友一個星期沒
跟王朋見面了。

Lǐ Yǒu yí ge xīngqī méi
gēn Wáng Péng jiàn miàn le.

1.   5 days

2.   6 days

3.   7 days

C. Opinion Forum

By using the "好/難(hǎo/nán) + V" phrase, have a discussion with your partner and find out whether you have similar or different opinions of the listed items.

EXAMPLE:

A: 你覺得哪種茶好喝，
哪種茶難喝？

Nǐ juéde nǎ zhǒng chá hǎohē,

nǎ zhǒng chá nánhē?

B: 我覺得 (name of the tea)
很好喝。

Wǒ juéde (name of the tea)

hěn hǎohē.

我覺得 (name of the tea)
很難喝。

Wǒ juéde (name of the tea)

hěn nánhē.

1.

2.

3.

4.

Then report your findings to the class.

If you two share the same opinion, you can say:

Anya 跟我一樣，
我們都覺得…

Anya gēn wǒ yíyàng,
wǒmen dōu juéde…

If you don't share the same opinion, then you can say:

Anya 跟我不一樣，
她覺得…我覺得…

Anya gēn wǒ bù yíyàng,
tā juéde… wǒ juéde…

D. Recap and Narrate

Working with a partner, recap the content of Dialogue I:

1. 王朋説高文中
的肚子為什麼越來
越大？

2. 王朋説高文中得
得怎麼辦？

3. 高文中幾年沒
運動了？

4. 王朋説最簡單
的運動是跑步，
高文中説什麼？

5. 高文中想打
網球嗎？為什麼？

1. Wáng Péng shuō Gāo Wénzhōng
de dùzi wèishénme yuè lái
yuè dà?

2. Wáng Péng shuō Gāo Wénzhōng
děi zěnme bàn?

3. Gāo Wénzhōng jǐ nián méi
yùndòng le?

4. Wáng Péng shuō zuì jiǎndān
de yùndòng shì pǎo bù,
Gāo Wénzhōng shuō shénme?

5. Gāo Wénzhōng xiǎng dǎ
wǎngqiú ma? Wèishénme?

6. 高文中想打
籃球嗎？為什麼？

7. 高文中想游泳
嗎？為什麼？

8. 王朋還有別的
辦法嗎？

6. Gāo Wénzhōng xiǎng dǎ
lánqiú ma? Wèishénme?

7. Gāo Wénzhōng xiǎng yóu yǒng
ma? Wèishénme?

8. Wáng Péng hái yǒu bié de
bànfǎ ma?

Using the words and phrases in blue as prompts, connect your answers above to form a narrative like this example:

高文中兩年沒運動了，平常又吃得很多，所以肚子越來越大，他問王朋怎麼辦。王朋説一個星期運動兩、三次，每次半個小時，肚子就會小了。高文中不知道做什麼運動好。王朋跟他説了幾種運動，他都沒有興趣。跑步，他覺得冬天太冷，夏天太熱，太難受；打網球，他覺得買網球拍、網球鞋太貴了；打籃球，他覺得每次約人太麻煩了；游泳，他覺得太危險，怕淹死。王朋也沒有辦法了，他告訴高文中如果不願意運動，那就胖下去吧。

Gāo Wénzhōng liǎng nián méi yùndòng le, píngcháng yòu chī de hěn duō, suǒyǐ dùzi yuè lái yuè dà, tā wèn Wáng Péng zěnme bàn. Wáng Péng shuō yí ge xīngqī yùndòng liǎng, sān cì, měi cì bàn ge xiǎoshí, dùzi jiù huì xiǎo le. Gāo Wénzhōng bù zhīdào zuò shéme yùndòng hǎo. Wáng Péng gēn tā shuō le jǐ zhǒng yùndòng, tā dōu méiyǒu xìngqù. Pǎo bù, tā juéde dōngtiān tài lěng, xiàtiān tài rè, tài nánshòu; dǎ wǎngqiú, tā juéde mǎi wǎngqiú pāi, wǎngqiú xié tài guì le; dǎ lánqiú, tā juéde měi cì yuē rén tài máfan le; yóu yǒng, tā juéde tài wēixiǎn, pà yān sǐ. Wáng Péng yě méiyǒu bànfǎ le, tā gàosù Gāo Wénzhōng rúguǒ bú yuànyì yùndòng, nà jiù pàng xia qu ba.

Dialogue II: Watching American Football

王朋的妹妹王紅剛從北京來，要在美國上大學❶，現在住在高小音家裏學英文。為了❷提高英文水平，她每天都看兩個小時的電視④。

LANGUAGE NOTES

❶ 上 (shàng) is a versatile verb. To board a car or plane is 上車/飛機 (shàng chē/fēijī), and to go to the bathroom is 上廁所 (shàng cèsuǒ). In this lesson, to go to school is 上學 (shàng xué) in colloquial Mandarin. So one can say 上小學/中學/大學 (shàng xiǎoxué/zhōngxué/dàxué) for attending elementary school/middle school/college.

❷ 為了 (wèile) usually appears in the first clause of a complex sentence, e.g., 為了學好中文，他每天聽兩個小時錄音 (Wèile xué hǎo Zhōngwén, tā měitiān tīng liǎng ge xiǎoshí lùyīn. In order to learn Chinese well, he listens to the recording for two hours everyday).

*　*　*

快把電視打開，足球比賽開始了。

是嗎？我也喜歡看足球賽❸。…這是什麼足球❹ 啊？怎麼不是圓的？

❸ 賽 (sài) stands for 比賽 (bǐsài).

❹ Although the term 足球 (zúqiú) literally means "football," it refers to soccer, rather than American football. To avoid confusion, Chinese speakers refer to American football as 美式足球 (Měishì zúqiú, American-style football) or 橄欖球 (gǎnlǎn qiú, lit., "olive ball").

這不是國際足球，這是美式足球。

足球應該用腳踢，為什麼那個人用手抱著③ 跑呢？

美式足球可以用手。

你看，你看，那麼多人都壓在一起，下面的人不是要被⑥ 壓壞了嗎？

別擔心，他們的身體都很棒，而且還穿特別的運動服，沒問題。

❺ 半天 (bàntiān) does not always mean exactly a "half day" as the word literally suggests. Rather, it often metaphorically denotes a comparatively long stretch of time.

我看了半天❺也看不懂。還是看別的吧。

你在美國住半年就會喜歡了。我男朋友看美式足球的時候，常常連飯都忘了吃。

Wáng Péng de mèimei Wáng Hóng gāng cóng Běijīng lái, yào zài Měiguó shàng dàxué①,

xiànzài zhù zài Gāo Xiǎoyīn jiā li xué Yīngwén. Wèile② tígāo Yīngwén shuǐpíng, tā měi tiān

dōu kàn liǎng ge xiǎoshí de diànshì④.

*   *   *

Kuài bǎ diànshì dǎ kāi, zúqiú bǐsài kāishǐ le.

Shì ma? Wǒ yě xǐhuan kàn zúqiú sài③...Zhè shì shénme zúqiú④ a? Zěnme bú shì yuán de?

Zhè bú shì guójì zúqiú, zhè shì Měishì zúqiú.

Zúqiú yīnggāi yòng jiǎo tī, wèishénme nà ge rén yòng shǒu bào zhe⑤ pǎo ne?

Měishì zúqiú kěyǐ yòng shǒu.

Nǐ kàn, nǐ kàn, nàme duō rén dōu yā zài yìqǐ, xiàmian de rén bú shì yào bèi⑥ yā huài le ma?

Bié dān xīn, tāmen de shēntǐ dōu hěn bàng, érqiě hái chuān tèbié de yùndòngfú, méi wèntí.

Wǒ kàn le bàntiān⑤ yě kàn bu dǒng. Háishi kàn bié de ba.

Nǐ zài Měiguó zhù bànnián jiù huì xǐhuan le. Wǒ nánpéngyou kàn Měishì zúqiú de shíhou, chángcháng lián fàn dōu wàng le chī.

VOCABULARY

1.	上大學	shàng dàxué	vo	to attend college/university
2.	為了	wèile	prep	for the sake of
3.	提高	tígāo	v	to improve; to raise; to heighten
4.	水平	shuǐpíng	n	level; standard
5.	足球	zúqiú	n	soccer; football
6.	比賽	bǐsài	n/v	game; match; competition; to compete
7.	國際	guójì	adj	international
8.	美式	Měishì	adj	American-style
9.	應該	yīnggāi	mv	should; ought to
10.	腳	jiǎo	n	foot

VOCABULARY

11.	踢	tī	v	to kick
12.	手	shǒu	n	hand
13.	抱	bào	v	to hold or carry in the arms
14.	壓	yā	v	to press; to hold down; to weigh down
15.	被	bèi	prep	by [See Grammar 6.]
16.	擔心	dān xīn	vo	to worry
17.	棒	bàng	adj	fantastic; super [colloq.]
18.	運動服	yùndòngfú	n	sportswear; athletic clothing
19.	半天	bàntiān		half a day; a long time

东亚足球四强赛

中国女足 0:2 负于韩国队

In this headline, what kind of sport event is reported?

Grammar

4. Duration of Actions

When a sentence contains both a time expression that indicates the duration of an action and an object, it needs to be formed in one of these two patterns:

A. Repetition of the verb

or

B. Time expression placed before the object, often with 的 (de).

 A. 她每天聽錄音聽一個小時。

Tā měitiān tīng lùyīn tīng yí ge xiǎoshí.

B. 她每天聽一個小時(的)錄音。

Tā měitiān tīng yí ge xiǎoshí (de) lùyīn.

(She listens to recordings for an hour every day.)

❷ A. 她每天下午游泳游四十分鐘。

Tā měitiān xiàwǔ yóu yǒng yóu sìshí fēnzhōng.

B. 她每天下午游四十分鐘(的)泳。

Tā měitiān xiàwǔ yóu sìshí fēnzhōng (de) yǒng.

(She swims for forty minutes every afternoon.)

❸ A. 她每天看英文報紙看兩個小時，所以英文越來越好了。

Tā měitiān kàn Yīngwén bàozhǐ kàn liǎng ge xiǎoshí, suǒyǐ Yīngwén yuè lái yuè hǎo le.

B. 她每天看兩個小時(的)英文報紙，所以英文越來越好了。

Tā měitiān kàn liǎng ge xiǎoshí (de) Yīngwén bàozhǐ, suǒyǐ Yīngwén yuè lái yuè hǎo le.

(She reads English newspapers for two hours every day, so her English is getting better and better.)

5. The Particle 著 (zhe)

著 (zhe) signifies the continuation of an action or a state. Its function is descriptive. When 著 (zhe) is used between two verbs, the one that precedes 著 (zhe) signifies the accompanying action, while the second verb signifies the main action.

❶ 老師站著教課，學生坐著聽課。

Lǎoshī zhàn zhe jiāo kè, xuésheng zuò zhe tīng kè.

(While the teacher stood lecturing, the students sat listening.)

❷ 我喜歡躺著聽音樂。

Wǒ xǐhuan tǎng zhe tīng yīnyuè.

(I like to listen to music while lying down.)

❸ 美式足球可以抱著球跑。

Měishì zúqiú kěyǐ bào zhe qiú pǎo.

(In American football, you can run with the ball in your hands.)

著 (zhe) is normally used after a verb to indicate a continuing action or a state. 在 (zài) is normally used before a verb to indicate an ongoing action.

❹ **A:** 學生們在做什麼呢？

Xuésheng men zài zuò shénme ne?

(What are the students doing?)

B: 在運動。

Zài yùndòng.

(They're exercising.)

在 (zài) in (4) above cannot be replaced with 著 (zhe). Likewise, 著 (zhe) in the earlier sentences cannot be replaced with 在 (zài), either.

6. 被／叫／讓 (bèi/jiào/ràng) in Passive-Voice Sentences

A sentence in the passive voice can be constructed with 被 (bèi), 叫 (jiào), or 讓 (ràng). Its structure is as follows:

receiver of the action + 被 (bèi)/ 叫 (jiào)/ 讓 (ràng)
+ agent of the action + verb + other element (complement/ 了 {le}, etc.)

❶ 我的功課被／叫／讓狗吃了。

Wǒ de gōngkè bèi/jiào/ràng gǒu chī le.

(My homework was eaten by my dog.)

❷   你買的那些書被/叫/讓你的女朋友拿去了。

Nǐ mǎi de nà xiē shū bèi/jiào/ràng nǐ de nǚpéngyou ná qù le.

(The books that you bought were taken away by your girlfriend.)

❸   糟糕，你的網球拍被/叫/讓我壓壞了。

Zāogāo, nǐ de wǎngqiú pāi bèi/jiào/ràng wǒ yā huài le.

(Oh gosh, your tennis racket was crushed [by me].)

❹   你看，我的梨被/叫/讓
你的西瓜壓壞了。

Nǐ kàn, wǒ de lí bèi/jiào/ràng nǐ de xīgua yā huài le.

(Take a look. My pears were crushed by your watermelon.)

In Chinese, the passive voice is not used as often as it is in English. It often carries negative connotations and usually appears in situations that are unpleasant for the receiver of the action, or in situations where something is lost. As in the 把 (bǎ) structure (see Lesson 13), the verb is usually followed by another element, such as a complement or 了 (le).

In a passive-voice sentence with 被 (bèi)/叫 (jiào) /讓 (ràng), the agent of the action does not always have to be specified. If the agent of the action is someone that is not identifiable or need not be identified, it can be referred to simply as 人 (rén, someone; people).

❺   我的信用卡被/叫/讓人拿走了。

Wǒ de xìnyòngkǎ bèi/jiào/ràng rén ná zǒu le.)

(My credit card was taken away.)

With 被 (bèi), the agent of the action can be omitted from the sentence:

❻   同學們在教室裏又唱又跳，他快
被吵死了。

Tóngxué men zài jiàoshì li yòu chàng yòu tiào, tā kuài
bèi chǎo sǐ le.

(His classmates are singing and dancing in the classroom.
The noise is driving him to distraction.)

被 (bèi) sometimes can be used in a positive sense, but we will not discuss it in detail here.

Language Practice

E. A Busy Day?

Take a look at the chart and summarize who did what for how long yesterday.

EXAMPLE	1.	2.	3.	4.	5.
8:00pm–11:00pm	7:00am–8:00am	7:30am–8:15am	11:00am–12:00pm	10:00am–12:30pm	4:00pm–6:30pm

EXAMPLE:

→ 費先生昨天跳舞跳
了三個小時。

Fèi xiānsheng zuótiān tiào wǔ tiào le sān ge xiǎoshí.

or 費先生昨天跳了三
個小時（的）舞。

Fèi xiānsheng zuótiān tiào le sān ge xiǎoshí (de) wǔ.

1.

2.

3.

4.

5.

F. Study Strategies

Wang Hong came to the United States to improve her English. To achieve her goal, she watches two hours of English-language TV every day. How can you improve your Chinese? Get together with a group of classmates and get everyone's suggestions by asking 怎麼才能提高中文水平 (Zěnme cái néng tígāo Zhōngwén shuǐpíng?)

EXAMPLE:

→ 為了提高中文水平，你應該每天聽兩個小時（的）錄音。

Wèile tígāo Zhōngwén shuǐpíng, nǐ yīnggāi měitiān tīng liǎng ge xiǎo shí (de) lùyīn.

1. Classmate #1

2. Classmate #2

3. Classmate #3

...

G. **Describing What You See**

Describe the persons in the pictures using "V + 著 (zhe)" structure.

EXAMPLE:

→ 王朋、高文中、
　李友坐著聊天兒。
　高小音站著聊天兒。

Wáng Péng, Gāo Wénzhōng,

Lǐ Yǒu zuò zhe liáo tiānr.

Gāo Xiǎoyīn zhàn zhe liáo tiānr.

1.

2.

3.

4.

H. Not His Lucky Day!

Use the 被 (bèi)/叫 (jiào)/讓 (ràng) structure to describe what happened to Little Gao yesterday.

1. His homework was eaten by his dog.

→

2. His coffee was drunk by his sister.

→

3. His credit card was taken away from him by his mother.

→

4. His car was driven to school by his brother.

→

5. The birthday gift that he was going to give to his friend was crushed by the sofa.

→

Have any of these ever happened to you? Do you have any similar experiences that you could share with your class?

_____

_____

I. Workout Queen/King!

Go around the class and ask one another:

1. Do you exercise?

If so:

2. What sports do you play?

3. Why do you like them?

If not:

2. What sports do you dislike?

3. Why don't you like them?

4. How often do you exercise?

5. How long do you exercise each time?

4. How long have you not been exercising?

5. When do you plan to start exercising?

After gathering everyone's information, then tell the class who the workout king/queen is.

_____ 運動得最多，
是我們的運動天王！

_____ yùndòng de zuì duō,

shì wǒmen de yùndòng tiānwáng!

J. Recap and Narrate

Working with a partner, recap the content of Dialogue II:

1. 王紅看過美式
足球嗎？

1. Wáng Hóng kàn guo Měishì zúqiú ma?

2. 國際足球和美式足球
有什麼不同？

2. Guójì zúqiú hé Měishì zúqiú yǒu shénme bù tóng?

3. 踢美式足球的人
為什麼不會被壓壞？

3. Tī Měishì zúqiú de rén wèishénme bú huì bèi yā huài?

4. 王紅看得懂美式
足球嗎？

4. Wáng Hóng kàn de dǒng Měishì zúqiú ma?

5. 怎麼知道高小音的
男朋友喜歡看美式
足球？

5. Zěnme zhīdào Gāo Xiǎoyīn de nánpéngyou xǐhuan kàn Měishì zúqiú?

Using the words and phrases in blue as prompts, connect your answers above to form a narrative like this example:

王朋的妹妹王紅剛從北京來，要在美國上大學，現在住在高小音裏學英文。為了練習英文，她每天都看兩個小時的電視。這一天剛吃完晚飯，高小音就和王紅看電視裏的足球比賽。正在比賽的是美式足球，王紅沒看過美式足球，不知道球為什麼不是圓的，踢球的人為什麼用手抱著球跑。她看見那麼多人都壓在一起，擔心下面的人會被壓壞了。她看不懂，覺得沒有意思。可是高小音說，在美國住半年就會喜歡了。

Wáng Péng de mèimei Wáng Hóng gāng cóng Běijīng lái, yào zài Měiguó shàng dàxué, xiànzài zhù zài Gāo Xiǎoyīn jiā li xué Yīngwén. Wèile liànxí Yīngwén, tā měi tiān dōu kàn liǎng ge xiǎoshí de diànshì. Zhè yì tiān gāng chī wán wǎnfàn, Gāo Xiǎoyīn jiù hé Wáng Hóng kàn diànshì li de zúqiú bǐsài. Zhèngzài bǐsài de shì Měishì zúqiú, Wáng Hóng méi kàn guo Měishì zúqiú, bù zhīdào qiú wèishénme bú shì yuán de, tī qiú de rén wèishénme yòng shǒu bào zhe qiú pǎo. Tā kàn jiàn nàme duō rén dōu yā zài yìqǐ, dān xīn xiàmian de rén huì bèi yā huài le. Tā kàn bù dǒng, juéde méiyǒu yìsi. Kěshì Gāo Xiǎoyīn shuō, zài Měiguó zhù bànnián jiù huì xǐhuan le.

HOW ABOUT YOU?

What's your favorite or least favorite sport?

1.	慢跑	mànpǎo	v/n	to jog; jogging
2.	打棒球	dǎ bàngqiú	vo	to play baseball
3.	打乒乓球	dǎ pīngpāngqiú	vo	to play table tennis
4.	做瑜伽	zuò yújiā	vo	to do yoga
5.	打太極拳	dǎ tàijíquán	vo	to do Tai Chi (a kind of traditional Chinese shadow boxing)

If the sports that you like and dislike are not listed above, ask your teacher and make a note here:

_____

Culture Highlights

❶ As living standards in China have improved in recent decades, the consumption of calorie-rich foods, especially meat, has been on the rise. Obesity has quietly become a problem for many people in urban areas, especially children. That change is reflected in sociolinguistic effects. Before the 1970s one could say "你胖了" (Nǐ pàng le, You've put on weight) and have it received as a compliment, but now one has to be really careful with that expression.

❷ In recent decades, China has consolidated its status as the leading sports power in Asia. In some sports events, such as table tennis and diving, China has enjoyed a dominant position in the world. By far the most popular sport in China, as in many other countries, is soccer, but ironically, China's national soccer team is second-rate even in Asia. What Chinese speakers call "football" (足球 zúqiú) is actually soccer in American English. American football, called 美式足球 (Měishì zúqiú) or 橄欖球 (gǎnlǎnqiú) in China, is not played there. Actually, not many people in China would understand the frenzy and exhilaration of American fans watching what can seem to be little more than a group scuffling on grass.

❸ One of the most spectacular scenes in a Chinese city is in the early morning, when hundreds or even thousands of men and women, most of them older people and retirees, gather in the parks to do Tai Chi boxing (太極拳 tàijíquán) and other forms of exercise.

4 In China, all television stations are state-owned. Apart from Chinese Central Television (CCTV), each province has its own TV stations. CCTV has a channel, CCTV 5, exclusively devoted to sports, where NBA games are regularly aired. It also offers an English channel, Channel 9, which can be received all over the world through satellite transmission.

●北京电视台—1
11:57 世界你好(午间版)
13:55 20集连续剧:崛起2、3
●北京电视台—2
 7:13 25集连续剧:似水浮生23、24
16:03 东芝动物乐园
●北京电视台—3
16:14 20集连续剧:伴我同行4、5
●北京电视台—4
 7:14 30集连续剧:大马帮12、13
 9:18 28集连续剧:沈香24、25
13:57 40集连续剧:风云争霸37—40
●北京电视台—5
 8:55 北京特快
 9:57 连续剧:倚天屠龙记14、15
●北京电视台—6
11:45 体育新闻
14:00 直播:2004年喜力网球公开赛
●北京电视台—7
12:00 生活面对面
12:35 健康生活
12:48 专家门诊
14:05 魅力前线
15:35 神奇的地球
●北京电视台—8
12:00 开心一刻
12:36 30集连续剧:少年黄飞鸿9、10
●北京电视台—9
 9:06 连续剧:情定爱琴海25—27
14:07 20集连续剧:坐庄16—18
●中央电视台—1
 9:25 20集连续剧:女子监狱20
12:38 今日说法
16:00 天天饮食:干贝云丝豆腐羹
●中央电视台—新闻频道
11:30 法治在线
12:30 共同关注
13:30 体育报道
14:10 面对面
●中央电视台—2
11:00 健康之路:心慌心悸与房颤
11:50 天天饮食:培根奶油蘑菇汤
16:40 全球资讯榜
●中央电视台—3
10:19 曲苑杂坛精编版23

●中央电视台—4
13:05 连续剧:将装修进行到底14
●中央电视台—5
12:00 体坛快讯
●中央电视台—6
 6:19 故事片:黑花杀手
 8:04 故事片:乱世英雄乱世情
10:12 故事片:傅抱石
12:54 蓝天情感剧场:金色黄昏(美国)
14:47 故事片:约会阳光
16:38 故事片:走出硝烟的女神
●中央电视台—8
 6:04 每日佳艺:你是我爸爸27(葡萄牙)
 6:53 20集连续剧:大案追踪19
 7:45 影视同期声
 8:05 影视金曲
 8:24 大剧场:神探狄仁杰7—10
12:01 快乐剧场:室内剧:闲人马大姐245、246
13:22 魅力100分:澡堂老板家的男人们(第一部)1—4(韩国)
●中央电视台—10
 9:50 探索·发现:清宫秘档22:光绪之死
16:43 探索·发现:清宫秘档案18:皇帝的一天(上)
●中央电视台—11
14:35 九州大戏台(京剧版)①京剧:初出茅庐②京剧:杨门女将·探谷选段
●中央电视台—12
14:15 动感剧场:过把瘾7、8
●中国教育台—1
12:15 20集连续剧:嫂子19、20
●上海东方卫视节目
12:40 律师视点
14:10 连续剧:半生缘28、29
●天津电视台
15:20 警方报道
●天津电视台—1
12:10 连续剧:五月槐花香31
●河北电视台—2
 8:15 天下无双13、14
●山西电视台
10:00 剧场:一个医生的故事1、2
13:10 剧场:悲情红与黑16—18

●内蒙古卫视节目
 8:22 连续剧:国家公诉20、21
13:27 法制专线
14:23 连续剧:危险旅程5、6
●辽宁电视台
12:26 法制时空
●吉林电视台
16:18 警界纵横:家庭与社会
●江苏电视台
14:00 剧场:秋香1—3
●浙江电视台
 8:00 连续剧:追捕18—20
●安徽电视台
12:50 连续剧:中国神探4、5
●福建东南电视台
 8:38 剧场:城市女人心17—19
●江西电视台
 7:41 连续剧:孝庄秘史20
 9:09 剧场:玉蜻蜓2—4
●河南电视台
 8:50 好剧回旋:当家的女人17、18
●湖北电视台
13:20 快乐森林
●湖南电视台
 7:40 剧场:封神榜13—16
13:30 剧场:春去春又回38—40
●广东电视台
16:08 连续剧:情满珠江5、6
●旅游卫视节目
12:04 英达剧场:旅行社的故事86
12:34 现在
16:00 玩转地球:旅游探险精选
●四川电视台
 8:58 剧场:法网伊人1—3
●贵州电视台
 9:49 剧场:热血忠魂之独行侍卫29—34
●云南电视台
13:10 连续剧:爱情宝典11—13
●西藏电视台
13:07 连续剧:林则徐9
●陕西电视台
 8:10 连续剧:孝庄秘史21—23
●甘肃电视台
 8:00 连续剧:说出你的爱5、6
14:35 连续剧:十三格格30
●青海电视台
 8:38 连续剧:保卫爱情19、20
13:00 连续剧:保卫爱情21、22
●宁夏电视台
13:42 影院:紧急迫降
●新疆台卫星节目
 9:23 剧场:西厢记1—3

(本版预告为各台昨日11:00公布的节目安排,临时调整请以当日电视台预告为准)

Is CCTV's Channel 9 listed? What other cities' TV listings can you recognize here?

English Text

Dialogue I

Gao Wenzhong: Look, my gut is getting bigger and bigger.

Wang Peng: You usually overeat, and on top of that you don't exercise; of course you're putting on more and more weight.

Gao Wenzhong: What should I do?

Wang Peng: If you're afraid of being overweight, you should exercise two or three times a week, for half an hour each time. Then your belly will get smaller.

Gao Wenzhong: I haven't exercised for two years. What kind of exercise should I do?

Wang Peng: The simplest exercise is jogging.

Gao Wenzhong: It's so cold in winter, and so hot in summer. Jogging is too uncomfortable.

Wang Peng: How about playing tennis?

Gao Wenzhong: Then I'd have to get a tennis racket and tennis shoes. You know tennis rackets and tennis shoes are very expensive!

Wang Peng: How about getting a few people together to play basketball? Buying a basketball is very inexpensive.

Gao Wenzhong: Then every time I'd have to call people and arrange to meet. That's way too much hassle.

Wang Peng: Then why don't you swim? There's no need to look for people, it wouldn't cost much money, and you could go any time.

Gao Wenzhong: Swimming? I'm afraid of water. That's too dangerous. What if I drown?

Wang Peng: There's nothing I can do [to help]. If you're not willing to exercise, then keep packing on the pounds.

Dialogue II

Wang Peng's younger sister, Wang Hong, just came from Beijing. She will be going to college in the United States. Right now she is staying at Gao Xiaoyin's place, studying English. To improve her English, she watches two hours of TV every day.

*   *   *

Gao Xiaoyin: Hurry, turn the TV on. The football game is starting.

Wang Hong: Really? I like watching football games too…What kind of football is this? How come it's not round?

Gao Xiaoyin: This is not international football, this is American football.

Wang Hong: To play football you should kick (the ball) with your feet. Why is that guy running with the ball in his hands?

Gao Xiaoyin: In American football you can use your hands.

Wang Hong: Look! All those people are piling on top of each other. Wouldn't the people underneath be crushed to pieces?

Gao Xiaoyin: Don't worry, they're really strong. Besides, they wear special sports clothing, so everything's fine.

Wang Hong: I've been watching for a while and I still don't get it. Let's watch something else.

Gao Xiaoyin: You only have to live in America for half a year before you will begin to like American football. When my boyfriend is watching a football game, often he will even forget to eat.

PROGRESS CHECKLIST

Before proceeding to Lesson 19, be sure you can complete the following tasks in Chinese:

I am able to—

☑ Explain briefly why certain sports are or are not appealing to me;

☐ Describe the frequency and duration of my exercise routine, or how long I haven't exercised;

☐ Make a simple comparison between how soccer and American football are played.

練好了嗎？約個球場打球吧！

What do you say?

LESSON 19 **Travel**

第十九課 旅行

Dì shíjiǔ kè Lǚxíng

◈ LEARNING OBJECTIVES

In this lesson, you will learn to use Chinese to

* Talk about your plans for summer vacation;
* Describe what kind of city Beijing is;
* Describe your travel itinerary;
* Ask for discounts, compare airfares and routes, and book an airplane ticket;
* Ask about seat assignments and request meal accommodations based on your dietary restrictions or preferences.

◈ RELATE AND GET READY

In your own culture/community—

1. How do students normally spend the summer?
2. What town or city is the nearest cultural or political center? What are its special attractions?
3. Where can people get good deals on airline tickets?
4. What's a common expression for a commercial discount?

Dialogue I: Traveling to Beijing

李友，時間過得真快，馬上就要放假了，我們的同學，有的去暑期班學習，有的去公司實習，有的回家打工，你有什麼計劃？

我還沒有想好。你呢，王朋？

我暑假打算❶回北京去看父母。

是嗎？我聽說北京這個城市很有意思。

當然。北京是中國的首都，也是中國的政治、文化中心，有很多名勝古蹟。

LANGUAGE NOTES

❶ While the verbs 打算 (dǎsuàn) and 計劃 (jìhuà) are synonyms, the former is more colloquial and the latter more formal.

對啊，長城很有名。

還有，北京的好飯館多得
不得了①。

真的？我去過香港、台北，還沒
去過北京，要是能去北京就好了。

那你跟我一起回去吧，我當你
的導遊。

真的嗎？那太好了！護照我已經
有了，我得趕快辦簽證②。

那我馬上給旅行社打電話訂
飛機票。

❷ To apply for a certificate or official documentation, one usually uses the verb 辦 (bàn), especially in spoken Chinese, as in 辦護照 (bàn hùzhào, to apply for a passport) and 辦簽證 (bàn qiānzhèng, to apply for a visa). More examples: 辦學生證 (bàn xuéshēngzhèng, to apply for a student ID), 辦手續 (bàn shǒuxù, to do the paperwork), and 辦結婚證 (bàn jiéhūnzhèng, to apply for a marriage license).

Lǐ Yǒu, shíjiān guò de zhēn kuài, mǎshàng jiù yào fàng jià le, wǒmen de tóngxué, yǒude qù shǔqī bān xuéxí, yǒude qù gōngsī shíxí, yǒude huí jiā dǎ gōng, nǐ yǒu shénme jìhuà?

Wǒ hái méiyǒu xiǎng hǎo. Nǐ ne, Wáng Péng?

Wǒ shǔjià❶ dǎsuàn huí Běijīng qù kàn fùmǔ.

Shì ma? Wǒ tīngshuō Běijīng zhè ge chéngshì hěn yǒuyìsi.

Dāngrán. Běijīng shì Zhōngguó de shǒudū, yě shì Zhōngguó de zhèngzhì, wénhuà zhōngxīn, yǒu hěn duō míngshèng gǔjì.

Duì a, Chángchéng hěn yǒumíng.

Hái yǒu, Běijīng de hǎo fànguǎn duō de bù déliǎo①.

Zhēn de? Wǒ qù guo Xiānggǎng, Táiběi, hái méi qù guo Běijīng, yàoshi néng qù Běijīng jiù hǎo le.

Nà nǐ gēn wǒ yìqǐ huí qu ba, wǒ dāng nǐ de dǎoyóu.

Zhēn de ma? Nà tài hǎo le! Hùzhào wǒ yǐjīng yǒu le. Wǒ děi gǎnkuài bàn qiānzhèng❷.

Nà wǒ mǎshàng gěi lǚxíngshè dǎ diànhuà dìng fēijī piào.

VOCABULARY

1.	馬上	mǎshàng	adv	immediately; right away
2.	放假	fàng jià	vo	go on vacation; have time off
	放	fàng	v	to let go; to set free
	假	jià	n	vacation; holiday
3.	公司	gōngsī	n	company
4.	實習	shíxí	v	to intern
5.	打工	dǎ gōng	vo	to work at a temporary job (often part time)
6.	計劃	jìhuà	n/v	plan; to plan
7.	暑假	shǔjià	n	summer vacation
8.	打算	dǎsuàn	v/n	to plan; plan
9.	父母	fùmǔ	n	parents; father and mother
10.	首都	shǒudū	n	capital city
11.	政治	zhèngzhì	n	politics
12.	文化	wénhuà	n	culture
13.	名勝古蹟	míngshèng gǔjì		famous scenic spots and historic sites
14.	有名	yǒumíng	adj	famous; well-known
15.	導遊	dǎoyóu	n	tour guide
16.	護照	hùzhào	n	passport
17.	訂	dìng	v	to reserve; to book (a ticket, a hotel room, etc.)
18.	簽證	qiānzhèng	n	visa
19.	旅行社	lǚxíngshè	n	travel agency

VOCABULARY

Proper Nouns

20.	長城	Chángchéng	the Great Wall
21.	香港	Xiānggǎng	Hong Kong
22.	台北	Táiběi	Taipei

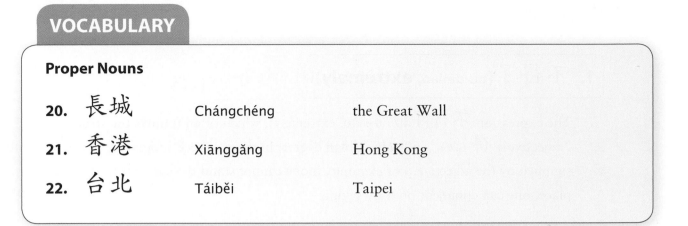

兩張長城的照片
liǎng zhāng Chángchéng de zhàopiàn

你想去香港還是上海？
Nǐ xiǎng qù Xiānggǎng háishi Shànghǎi?

Grammar

1. 不得了 (bù déliǎo, **extremely**)

The expression 不得了 (bù déliǎo, extremely), which often follows the structure "adjective + 得 (de)," indicates a high degree, in the speaker's judgment, of the attribute signified by the adjective. For example, if one cannot stand the summer heat in a certain place, one can comment on it by saying:

❶   那個地方夏天熱得不得了。

　　　Nà ge dìfang xiàtiān rè de bù déliǎo.

　　　(Summer is unbearably hot in that place.)

If the Great Wall is extremely crowded, one can describe the scene by saying:

❷   長城上的人多得不得了。

　　　Chángchéng shàng de rén duō de bù déliǎo.

　　　(There was an incredible number of people on the Great Wall.)

Language Practice

A. Planning Ahead

Ask your partner about his/her plans for tonight, 1) for the coming weekend, 2) for the summer break, 3) for next semester, and 4) for next year.

EXAMPLE:

你今天晚上打算做什麼？

Nǐ jīntiān wǎnshang dǎsuàn zuò shénme?

1.

2.

3.

4.

B. Survey Your Class

Move around the classroom and interview your classmates to find out more about their opinions and experiences. Then report the results of your survey to the class by using "我的同學有的人···有的人··· (Wǒ de tóngxué yǒude rén..., yǒude rén...)." Possible topics include: your classmates' favorite beverages, cuisines, fruits, colors, or sports; their thoughts on Chinese pronunciation, Chinese grammar, or Chinese characters; their allergies, living arrangements, travel plans, etc. Each student should choose a different topic to ask about.

EXAMPLE: beverages

我的同學有的人喜歡
喝可樂，有的人喜歡
喝咖啡。

Wǒ de tóngxué yǒude rén xǐhuan
hē kělè, yǒude rén xǐhuan
hē kāfēi.

C. Name That Capital!

You have learned how to say "the capital of China is Beijing":

中國的首都是北京。 Zhōngguó de shǒudū shì Běijīng.

Now can you name the capitals of the following countries?

1.	美國	Měiguó	
2.	英國	Yīngguó	
3.	日本	Rìběn	
4.	韓國	Hánguó	South Korea
5.	加拿大	Jiā'nádà	Canada
6.	墨西哥	Mòxīgē	Mexico
7.	澳大利亞	Àodàlìyà	Australia

...

D. World Cities

With your partner, recap what you know about Beijing, and then find one or two other cities in the world that are similar to Beijing in some ways. What do they have in common? If you could travel to any city in the world during your next vacation, where would you go? Why? What attractions would you especially want to see?

E. Name That Person! Name That Place!

You must know celebrities that you adore and ones that you dislike; you may have been to attractive places and repulsive ones. Share with the class your sentiments about those people and places by using the "adj + 得不得了 (de bù déliǎo)" formation.

Celebrities

EXAMPLE: 可愛   kě'ài

→   (name of the celebrity)   (name of the celebrity)
     可愛得不得了。   kě'ài de bù déliǎo.

1. 帥   shuài

2. 聰明   cōngming

3. 漂亮   piàoliang

4. 用功   yònggōng

5. 酷   kù

6. 壞   huài

7. 懶   lǎn

. . .

Places

1.	漂亮	piàoliang
2.	有意思	yǒu yìsi
3.	安靜	ānjìng
4.	乾淨	gānjìng
5.	人多	rén duō
6.	熱	rè
7.	冷	lěng
8.	危險	wēixiǎn
9.	吵	chǎo

. . .

F. What Do You Want to Be?

Survey your classmates to find out their aspirations for the future:

你以後想當什麼？   Nǐ yǐhòu xiǎng dāng shénme?

老師、律師，還是醫生？   Lǎoshī, lǜshī, háishi yīshēng?

G. Recap and Narrate

Working with a partner, recap the content of Dialogue I:

1. 快放暑假了，王朋的同學們想做什麼？

1. Kuài fàng shǔjià le, Wáng Péng de tóngxué men xiǎng zuò shénme?

2. 李友暑假打算做
什麼？

3. 王朋暑假打算做
什麼？

4. 李友聽說過北京嗎？

5. 王朋說北京是一
個什麼樣的城市？

6. 李友想去北京嗎？

7. 王朋為什麼說去
北京他可以當李友的
導遊？

8. 王朋和李友去
中國以前，得先
做什麼？

2. Lǐ Yǒu shǔjià dǎsuàn zuò
shénme?

3. Wáng Péng shǔjià dǎsuàn zuò
shénme?

4. Lǐ Yǒu tīngshuō guo Běijīng ma?

5. Wáng Péng shuō Běijīng shì yí
ge shénme yàng de chéngshì?

6. Lǐ Yǒu xiǎng qù Běijīng ma?

7. Wáng Péng wèishénme shuō qù
Běijīng tā kěyǐ dāng Lǐ Yǒu de
dǎoyóu?

8. Wáng Péng hé Lǐ Yǒu qù
Zhōngguó yǐqián, děi xiān
zuò shénme?

Using the words and phrases in blue as prompts, connect your answers above to form a narrative like this example:

快放暑假了，王朋的同學有的去暑期班學習，有的去公司實習，有的回家去打工。李友還沒想好暑假的計劃。王朋要回北京看父母，他給李友介紹說北京是中國的首都，也是中國的政治、文化中心，有很多名勝古蹟，北京的好飯館兒多得不得了。李友去過台北和香港，但是沒去過北京，聽了王朋的介紹很想去北京。王朋讓李友跟他一起回北京，他當李友的導遊。李友聽了很高興。李友已經有護照了，得辦簽證。王朋說他趕快給旅行社打電話訂飛機票。

Kuài fàng shǔjià le, Wáng Péng de tóngxué yǒude qù shǔqī bān xuéxí, yǒude qù gōngsī shíxí, yǒude huí jiā qù dǎ gōng. Lǐ Yǒu hái méi xiǎng hǎo shǔjià de jìhuà. Wáng Péng yào huí Běijīng kàn fùmǔ, tā gěi Lǐ Yǒu jièshào shuō Běijīng shì Zhōngguó de shǒudū, yě shì Zhōngguó de zhèngzhì, wénhuà zhōngxīn, yǒu hěn duō míngshèng gǔjì, Běijīng de hǎo fànguǎnr duō de bù déliǎo. Lǐ Yǒu qù guo Táiběi hé Xiānggǎng, dànshì méi qù guo Běijīng, tīng le Wáng Péng de jièshào hěn xiǎng qù Běijīng. Wáng Péng ràng Lǐ Yǒu gēn tā yìqǐ huí Běijīng, tā dāng Lǐ Yǒu de dǎoyóu. Lǐ Yǒu tīng le hěn gāoxìng. Lǐ Yǒu yǐjīng yǒu hùzhào le, děi bàn qiānzhèng. Wáng Péng shuō tā gǎnkuài gěi lǚxíngshè dǎ diànhuà dìng fēijī piào.

Dialogue II: Planning an Itinerary

天一旅行社，你好。

你好。請問六月初❶到北京的機票多少錢？

您要買單程票還是往返票？

我要買兩張往返票。

你想買哪家航空公司的？

哪家的便宜，就買哪②家的。

LANGUAGE NOTES

❶ 月初 (yuè chū) refers to the first few days of the month, typically from the 1st to the 5th or 6th. 月中 (yuè zhōng) is for the middle of the month, roughly from the 14th to 16th or 17th. 月底 (yuè dǐ) means the final days of the month, usually from the 27th or 28th. One can also say 年初 (nián chū, beginning of the year), 年中 (nián zhōng, middle of the year), and 年底 (nián dǐ, end of the year). The words 初 (chū, beginning), 中 (zhōng, middle), and 底 (dǐ, end; bottom) usually compound with either 月 (yuè) or 年 (nián) and are never used with 星期 (xīngqī).

請等等，我查一下⋯好幾家航空公司都有航班❷。中國國際航空公司，一千五③，直飛。西北航空公司正在打折③，差不多一千四百六十，可是要轉機。

西北只比國航❹便宜四十幾塊錢❹，我還是買國航吧。

哪一天走❺？哪一天回來？

六月十號走，七月十五號回來。現在可以訂位子嗎？

可以。你們喜歡靠窗戶的還是靠走道的？

靠走道的。對了❻，我朋友吃素，麻煩幫她訂一份素餐。

沒問題⋯您在北京要訂旅館、租車嗎？

不用，謝謝！

❷ In Taiwan, people say 班機 (bānjī) instead of 航班 (hángbān).

❸ The approach to describing a discount in Chinese is different from that in English. In English the emphasis is on the amount that is given as a discount, e.g., 10% off, 20% off, etc. In Chinese, however, the emphasis is on the proportion of the original price that is actually paid. Therefore, 九折 (jiǔ zhé) means that the price is 90% of the original price, or 10% off; 七五折 (qī wǔ zhé) means 75% of the original price; and 對折 (duì zhé) 50% of the original price.

❹ 中國國際航空公司 (Zhōngguó Guójì Hángkōng Gōngsī, literally, "China International Airlines") is often shortened to 國航 (Guóháng). It's known in English as Air China.

❺ As introduced in Lesson 10, the basic meaning of 走 (zǒu) is "to walk." Here 走 (zǒu) means to leave or to depart.

❻ 對了 (duì le) is often used when one suddenly thinks of something. For instance, if a student is saying goodbye to his classmate, and all of a sudden it occurs to him that they need to study for a test the next day, he can say: 明天見。⋯對了，明天考試，別忘了復習。(Míngtiān jiàn....Duì le, míngtiān kǎo shì, bié wàng le fùxí, See you tomorrow. ...Oh yes, we have a test tomorrow. Don't forget to review.)

Tiān Yī lǚxíngshè, nǐ hǎo.

Nǐ hǎo. Qǐng wèn liùyuè chū❶ dào Běijīng de jīpiào duōshao qián?

Nín yào mǎi dānchéng piào háishi wǎngfǎn piào?

Wǒ yào mǎi liǎng zhāng wǎngfǎn piào.

Nǐ xiǎng mǎi nǎ jiā hángkōng gōngsī de?

Nǎ jiā de piányi, jiù mǎi nǎ② jiā de.

Qǐng děng deng, wǒ chá yí xià... Hǎo jǐ jiā hángkōng gōngsī dōu yǒu hángbān❷. Zhōngguó Guójì Hángkōng Gōngsī, yì qiān wǔ③, zhífēi. Xīběi Hángkōng Gōngsī zhèngzài dǎ zhé❸, chàbuduō yì qiān sì bǎi liùshí, kěshì yào zhuǎn jī.

Xīběi zhǐ bǐ Guóháng❹ piányi sìshí jǐ kuài qián④, wǒ háishi mǎi Guóháng ba.

Nǎ yì tiān zǒu❺? Nǎ yì tiān huí lai?

Liùyuè shí hào zǒu, qīyuè shíwǔ hào huí lai. Xiànzài kěyǐ dìng wèizi ma?

Kěyǐ. Nǐmen xǐhuan kào chuānghu de háishi kào zǒudào de?

Kào zǒudào de. Duì le❻, wǒ péngyou chī sù, máfan bāng tā dìng yí fèn sùcān.

Méi wèntí...Nín zài Běijīng yào dìng lǚguǎn, zū chē ma?

Búyòng, xièxie!

這是去哪兒的車票？是單程票還是往返票？
Zhè shì qù nǎr de chēpiào? Shì dānchéng piào háishi wǎngfǎn piào?

VOCABULARY

1.	初	chū	n	beginning
2.	單程	dānchéng	n	one-way trip
3.	往返	wǎngfǎn	v	make a round trip; go there and back
4.	航空	hángkōng	n	aviation
5.	查	chá	v	to check; to look into
6.	航班	hángbān	n	scheduled flight
7.	千	qiān	nu	thousand
8.	直飛	zhí fēi		fly directly
9.	打折	dǎ zhé	vo	to sell at a discount; to give a discount
10.	轉機	zhuǎn jī	vo	change planes
11.	靠	kào	v	to lean on; to lean against; to be next to
12.	窗户	chuānghu	n	window
13.	走道	zǒudào	n	aisle
14.	份	fèn	m	(measure word for meal order, job)
15.	素餐	sùcān	n	vegetarian meal
16.	旅館	lǚguǎn	n	hotel
17.	租	zū	v	to rent

Proper Nouns

18.	中國國際航空公司	Zhōngguó Guójì Hángkōng Gōngsī	Air China
19.	西北航空公司	Xīběi Hángkōng Gōngsī	Northwest Airlines

国内4-8折

上海 深圳 广州 成都 重庆 昆明 西安
海口 厦门 桂林 三亚 福州 武汉 南京
贵阳 济南 青岛 大连 沈阳 长春 哈尔滨

去上海的機票最便宜能打幾折？
Qù Shànghǎi de jīpiào zuì piányí néng dǎ jǐ zhé?

Grammar

2. Question Pronouns as Indefinite References (Whoever, Whatever, etc.)

A question pronoun repeated in two separate but related clauses of the same sentence forms the equivalent of the "question pronoun + -ever" expression in English. Its first occurrence refers to an indefinite person, object, time, place, etc. Its second occurrence then refers to that same person, object, time, place, etc.

 誰想去，誰就去。

Shéi xiǎng qù, shéi jiù qù.

(Whoever wants to go can go.)

❷ 你吃什麼，我就吃什麼。

Nǐ chī shénme, wǒ jiù chī shénme.

(I'll have whatever you're having.)

❸ 哪雙鞋便宜，就買哪雙。

Nǎ shuāng xié piányi, jiù mǎi nǎ shuāng.)

(Buy whichever pair of shoes is the cheapest.)

❹ Taxi Driver: 您想怎麼走？

Nín xiǎng zěnme zǒu?

(Which way do you want to take?)

Passenger:　怎麼近，怎麼走。

Zěnme jìn, zěnme zǒu.

(I'll take whichever is the shortest distance.)

In this kind of sentence, sometimes the two occurrences of the question pronoun play the same grammatical role, i.e, both are subjects, as in (1); or both are objects, as in (2). Sometimes the two occurrences of the question pronoun perform different grammatical functions. In (3), for example, the first 哪雙 (nǎ shuāng) is the subject whereas the second 哪雙 (nǎ shuāng) is the object. The adverb 就 (jiù) often precedes the verb in the second clause, but not always, as shown in (5) and (6) below.

❺　哪兒安靜，我住哪兒。

Nǎr ānjing, wǒ zhù nǎr.

(I'll live wherever it's quiet.)

❻ A:　他找誰幫他搬傢具？

Tā zhǎo shéi bāng tā bān jiājù?

(Who is he going to ask to help him move his furniture?)

B:　誰身體棒，他找誰。

Shéi shēntǐ bàng, tā zhǎo shéi.

(He'll ask whoever is strong.)

3. Numbers over One Thousand

You have already learned how to count in Chinese up to a thousand.

Number	Chinese	Pinyin	English
1	一	yī	one
10	十	shí	ten
100	百	bǎi	hundred
1000	千	qiān	thousand

However, in Chinese the next larger unit after a thousand is not called *十千 (*shí qiān), but 萬 (wàn). Even though the Chinese share the international practice of segmenting a long Arabic number into three-digit sets in writing or in print, they mentally divide the number into four-digit sets instead when they read it. Starting at the fifth digit from the right is the four-digit set of 萬 (wàn), and the next four-digit set is that of 億 (yì). In the examples below, we have artificially indicated such divisions as an aid.

English	Arabic Number	Chinese Mental Division	Chinese	Pinyin
thousand	1,000	1000	（一）千	(yì) qiān
ten thousand	10,000	1'0000	（一）萬	(yí) wàn
hundred thousand	100,000	10'0000	十萬	shí wàn
million	1,000,000	100'0000	（一）百萬	(yì) bǎi wàn
ten million	10,000,000	1000'0000	（一）千萬	(yì) qiān wàn
hundred million	100,000,000	1'0000'0000	（一）億/（一）萬萬	(yí) yì/ (yí) wànwàn
billion	1,000,000,000	10'0000'0000	十億	shí yì

Examples of large numbers:

12,345 (1'2345)

一萬兩千三百四十五

yí wàn liǎng qiān sān bǎi sìshíwǔ

25,000 (2'5000)

兩萬五千

liǎng wàn wǔ qiān

340,876 (34'0876)

三十四萬零八百七十六

sānshísì wàn líng bā bǎi qīshíliù

1,000,900,000 (10'0090'0000)

十億零九十萬

shí yì líng jiǔshí wàn

4. Comparative Sentences with 比 (bǐ) **(II)** [See also Grammar 1 in Lesson 11.]

In a sentence where 比 (bǐ) is used, a numeral + measure word combination can be placed after the adjective to indicate the disparity.

A + 比 (bǐ) + B + Adjective + Numeral + Measure Word + Noun

 我們班比你們班多四個學生。

Wǒmen bān bǐ nǐmen bān duō sì ge xuésheng.

(Our class is larger than yours by four students.)

❷ 這件襯衫比那件襯衫貴二十塊錢。

Zhè jiàn chènshān bǐ nà jiàn chènshān guì èrshí kuài qián.)

(This shirt is twenty dollars more expensive than that shirt.)

❸ 我的房租比你的便宜五百塊。

Wǒ de fángzū bǐ nǐ de piányi wǔ bǎi kuài.

(My rent is five hundred dollars cheaper than yours.)

 我表弟比我小三歲。

Wǒ biǎodì bǐ wǒ xiǎo sān suì.

(My cousin is three years younger than I.)

Language Practice

H. Big Sale

A furniture store is having a big sale. Compare the original prices and the sale prices, and figure out with a partner what discount the store is offering on each item.

EXAMPLE:

→   A: 這張床打幾折？   Zhè zhāng chuáng dǎ jǐ zhé?

B: 這張床打八折。   Zhè zhāng chuáng dǎ bā zhé.

1.

2.

3.

4.

在這個商店買東西，可以打幾折？
Zài zhè ge shāngdiàn mǎi dōngxi, kěyǐ dǎ jǐ zhé?

I. Being Flexible and Accommodating

Mr. Li has just started dating Ms. Wang. He tries to be very nice and asks Ms. Wang what she would like to do, where she would like to go, etc. Ms. Wang is trying to be nice, too, so she leaves it to Mr. Li to decide. Do a role play with a partner, and see if you two can settle on a day, time, place, and activity.

EXAMPLE: Pick a place to go.

→   李先生：你想去
　　　　　哪兒玩兒？

王小姐：你想去哪兒
　　　　玩兒，我就
　　　　去哪兒玩兒。

Lǐ xiānsheng: Nǐ xiǎng qù
　　　　　　nǎr wánr?

Wáng xiǎojiě: Nǐ xiǎng qù nǎr
　　　　　　wánr, wǒ jiù
　　　　　　qù nǎr wánr.

1. Find out what she is interested in.

2. Find out what cuisine she prefers.

3. Find out when she would like to see a movie.

4. Find out which city she would like to travel to.

J. I Almost Forgot!

1. You have just said goodbye to your friend, but suddenly it occurs to you that you need to borrow a Chinese book from him. What do you say?

2. You have been talking to your mom on the phone to ask for more money, and she has granted your request. You've just said "Thanks," but it occurs to you that you should mention your plan to travel to China for the summer and ask for your mom's opinion.

3. You are on the phone with your travel agency and have just booked your flight. Before you hang up the phone, it occurs to you that you should ask for a seat assignment.

K. Who Got a Better Deal?

Compare notes with your partner and find out the differences in what you pay for rent, security deposit, and utilities. Then report to the class.

1. 房租　　　　　　　fángzū

2. 押金　　　　　　　yājīn

3. 水電費　　　　　　shuǐ diàn fèi

L. Don't Leave Any Questions Out!

Divide the class into two groups, one of travelers and the other of travel agents.

Travelers:

As an experienced traveler, what questions will you ask when you make a flight reservation? Make your list as detailed as possible.

1._____

2._____

3._____

4._____

5._____

…

Travel Agents:

As an experienced travel agent, what questions will you ask your customer when he/she books a flight? Make your list as detailed as possible.

1._____

2._____

3._____

4._____

5._____

…

After each group completes its list, the two groups should compare lists and see if any important questions have been left out. Then the whole class decides which list is more satisfactory.

M. Recap and Narrate

Working with a partner, ask and answer the following questions based on Dialogue II.

1. 王朋給哪個旅行社打電話？

   1. Wáng Péng gěi nǎ ge lǚxíngshè dǎ diànhuà?

2. 王朋要買什麼時候、什麼樣的機票？

   2. Wáng Péng yào mǎi shénme shíhou, shénme yàng de jīpiào?

3. 王朋要買哪家航空公司的機票？

   3. Wáng Péng yào mǎi nǎ jiā hángkōng gōngsī de jīpiào?

4. 旅行社的人說機票
   多少錢？

4. Lǚxíngshè de rén shuō jīpiào
   duōshao qián?

5. 王朋買了哪家
   航空公司的機票？

5. Wáng Péng mǎi le nǎ jiā
   hángkōng gōngsī de jīpiào?

6. 王朋和李友哪天
   走，哪天回來？

6. Wáng Péng hé Lǐ Yǒu nǎ tiān
   zǒu, nǎ tiān huí lai?

7. 王朋要什麼樣的
   位子？

7. Wáng Péng yào shénme yàng de
   wèizi?

8. 王朋給李友訂了
   什麼？

8. Wáng Péng gěi Lǐ Yǒu dìng le
   shénme?

Using the words and phrases in blue as prompts, connect your answers above to form a narrative like this example:

王朋打電話給旅行社訂機票。他要買兩張去北京的往返票，六月十號走，七月十五號回來。雖然西北航空公司在打折，但是得轉機，中國國際航空公司只比西北航空公司貴四十塊錢，可是不用轉機，所以他買了國航的票。他訂了靠走道的位子，還給李友訂了一份素餐。

Wáng Péng dǎ diànhuà gěi lǚxíngshè dìng jīpiào. Tā yào mǎi liǎng zhāng qù Běijīng de wǎngfǎn piào, liùyuè shí hào zǒu, qīyuè shíwǔ hào huí lai. Suīrán Xīběi Hángkōng Gōngsī zài dǎ zhé, dànshì děi zhuǎn jī, Zhōngguó Guójì Hángkōng Gōngsī zhǐ bǐ Xīběi Hángkōng Gōngsī guì sìshí kuài qián, kěshì búyòng zhuǎn jī, suǒyǐ tā mǎi le Guóháng de piào. Tā dìng le kào zǒudào de wèizi, hái gěi Lǐ Yǒu dìng le yí fèn sùcān.

HOW ABOUT YOU?

What are the "must haves" when you travel?

1. 現金   xiànjīn   n   cash

2. 證件   zhèngjiàn   n   ID; document

3. 照相機   zhàoxiàngjī   n   camera

Is there anything else you must have when you travel? Please ask your teacher and make a note here:

_____

What would make your flight more comfortable?

1. 頭等艙   tóuděngcāng   n   first class

2. 商務艙   shāngwùcāng   n   business class

3. 阿司匹林   āsīpīlín   n   aspirin

4. 枕頭   zhěntou   n   pillow

5. 毯子   tǎnzi   n   blanket

公務艙就是商務艙。
Gōngwùcāng jiùshì shāngwùcāng.

Any other things that would make your flight more comfortable? Please ask your teacher and make a note here:

_____

Culture Highlights

❶ Most travel agencies in China belong to three travel agency groups targeting different types of tourists: International Travel Agencies (國際旅行社 Guójì Lǚxíngshè) or 國旅 (Guó Lǚ); China Travel Agencies (中國旅行社 Zhōngguó Lǚxīngshè) or 中旅 (Zhōng Lǚ); and Youth Travel Agencies (青年旅行社 Qīngnián Lǚxíngshè) also known as 青旅 (Qīng Lǚ). While 國旅 (Guó Lǚ) and 中旅 (Zhōng Lǚ) mainly serve foreign tourists and overseas Chinese respectively, 青旅 (Qīng Lǚ) is primarily oriented toward Chinese citizens.

❷ The busiest travel season in China is January and February, when millions upon millions of people travel to join their families or friends for the Chinese New Year. Railroad remains the major means of domestic travel. During the Chinese New Year period, all the railroad stations across the country are overcrowded with travelers awaiting their trains or seeking tickets. There are four different classes of train tickets: for carriages with hard seats (硬座 yìng zuò), cushioned seats (軟座 ruǎn zuò), hard sleeping berths (硬臥 yìng wò), or cushioned sleeping berths (軟臥 ruǎn wò). In recent decades, in the wake of the rapid growth of China's aviation industry, airplane travel has become an increasingly competitive option for domestic travelers.

English Text

Dialogue I

Wang Peng: Li You, time flies. It'll be break soon. Some of our classmates are going to summer school; some of them are going to intern at different companies. Some will go home and work. What are your plans?

Li You: I haven't decided. What about you, Wang Peng?

Wang Peng: I plan to go back to Beijing to see my parents.

Li You: Really? I hear that Beijing is a really interesting city.

Wang Peng: Of course. Beijing is China's capital, and it's also China's political and cultural center with lots of famous historic sites.

Li You: That's right. The Great Wall is very famous.

Wang Peng: And there are tons of great restaurants in Beijing.

Li You: Really? I've been to Hong Kong and Taipei, but I've never been to Beijing. I wish I could go to Beijing.

Wang Peng: Why don't you go with me? I could be your guide.

Li You: Really? That would be great! I already have a passport. I'll have to apply for a visa at once.

Wang Peng: I'll give the travel agency a call right away and get the plane tickets.

Dialogue II

Travel Agent: Tianyi Travel Agency, good morning.

Wang Peng: Good morning. How much is a ticket to Beijing for the beginning of June?

Travel Agent: One way or round trip?

Wang Peng: Two round trip tickets.

Travel Agent: Which airline?

Wang Peng: I'll get whichever airline is the least expensive.

Travel Agent: Please wait a moment. Let me check. Quite a few airlines fly there. Air China, $1,500, direct flight. Northwest is having a sale. About $1,460, but you have to change planes.

Wang Peng: Northwest is only $40 cheaper than China Airlines. I'll go with China Airlines.

Travel Agent: What are the dates for departure and return?

Wang Peng: Departing on June 10, returning on July 15. Can I reserve seats now?

Travel Agent: Yes, you can. Do you prefer window or aisle seats?

Wang Peng: Aisle seats. Oh, that's right, my friend is a vegetarian. Could you please order vegetarian meals for her?

Travel Agent: No problem. While in Beijing, do you need to make reservations for a hotel or car rental?

Wang Peng: No, thank you.

PROGRESS CHECKLIST

Before proceeding to Lesson 20, be sure you can complete the following tasks in Chinese:

I am able to—

- ☑ Describe my travel, study, and/or work plans for the summer;
- ☐ Give a basic description of Beijing;
- ☐ Make a travel reservation by giving my travel dates, asking for airfares, and comparing options;
- ☐ Inquire about seat assignments and special meal orders;
- ☐ Express a commercial discount.

這兒賣什麼保險？
Zhèr mài shénme bǎoxiǎn?

LESSON 20

At the Airport

第二十課 在機場

Dì èrshí kè   Zài jīchǎng

LEARNING OBJECTIVES

In this lesson, you will learn to use Chinese to

- Check in at the airport;
- Wish departing friends a safe journey and remind them to keep in touch;
- Greet guests at the airport;
- Compliment someone on his or her language ability;
- Ask about someone's health;
- Remind people to move on to the next event.

RELATE AND GET READY

In your own culture/community—

1. What do people say when seeing someone off on a trip?
2. During the summer, do people prefer to fly or take road trips?
3. What do people say to their guests when greeting them at the airport, train, or bus station?
4. What are some local foods that your guests from elsewhere should try?

Dialogue I: Checking In at the Airport

（在國航的服務台）

 小姐，這是我們的^①機票。

請把護照給我看看。你們有幾件行李要托運？

兩件。這個包不托運，我們帶上飛機。

麻煩❶您把箱子拿上來。

小姐，沒超重吧？

LANGUAGE NOTES

❶ When asking others for help, one polite way is to begin the request with 麻煩 (máfan).

 没有。這是你們的護照、機票，這是登機牌❷。請到五號登機口❸上飛機。

謝謝。

* * *

 哥哥，你們去北京了，就我一個人在這兒。

 小紅，別哭，我們幾個星期就回來，你好好兒地①學英文，別亂跑。

不是幾個星期就回來，是幾個星期以後才回來。

 別擔心，我姐姐小音會照顧你。

對，別擔心。

飛機幾點起飛？

 中午十二點，還有兩個多小時。

白英愛，你什麼時候去紐約實習？

我不去紐約了。文中幫我在加州找了一份實習工作。

❷ The Chinese word for boarding pass is either 登機牌 (dēngjīpái, lit., boarding card) or 登機證 (dēngjīzhèng, lit., boarding certificate).

❸ In mainland China, boarding gates are called 登機口 (dēngjīkǒu). In Taiwan and Hong Kong, they are called 登機門 (dēngjīmén) and 閘口 (zhákǒu) respectively.

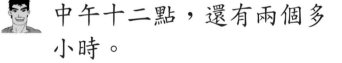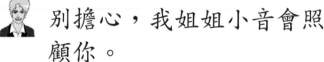

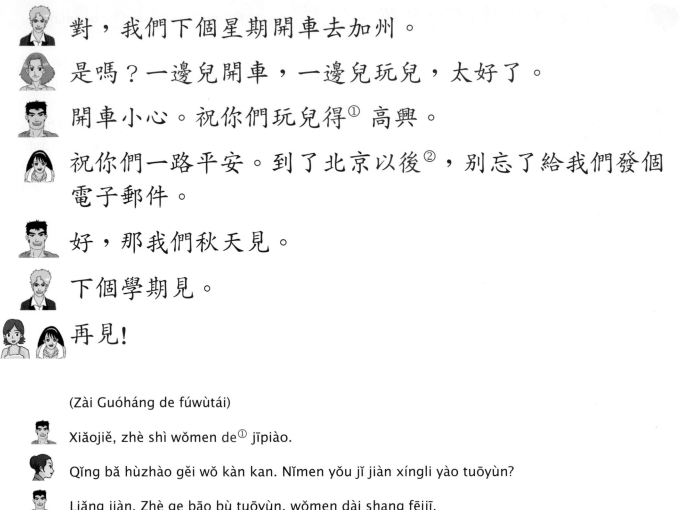

對，我們下個星期開車去加州。

是嗎？一邊兒開車，一邊兒玩兒，太好了。

開車小心。祝你們玩兒得① 高興。

祝你們一路平安。到了北京以後②，別忘了給我們發個電子郵件。

好，那我們秋天見。

下個學期見。

再見!

(Zài Guóháng de fúwùtái)

Xiǎojiě, zhè shì wǒmen de① jīpiào.

Qǐng bǎ hùzhào gěi wǒ kàn kan. Nǐmen yǒu jǐ jiàn xíngli yào tuōyùn?

Liǎng jiàn. Zhè ge bāo bù tuōyùn, wǒmen dài shang fēijī.

Máfan❶ nín bǎ xiāngzi ná shang lai.

Xiǎojiě, méi chāozhòng ba?

Méiyǒu. Zhè shì nǐmen de hùzhào, jīpiào, zhè shì dēngjīpái❷. Qǐng dào wǔ hào dēngjīkǒu❸ shàng fēijī.

Xièxie.

* * *

Gēge, nǐmen qù Běijīng le, jiù wǒ yí ge rén zài zhèr.

Xiǎo Hóng, bié kū, wǒmen jǐ ge xīngqī jiù huí lai, nǐ hǎohāor de① xué Yīngwén, bié luàn pǎo.

Bú shì jǐ ge xīngqī jiù huí lai, shì jǐ ge xīngqī yǐhòu cái huí lai.

Bié dān xīn, wǒ jiějie Xiǎoyīn huì zhàogu nǐ.

Duì, bié dān xīn.

Fēijī jǐ diǎn qǐfēi?

Zhōngwǔ shí'èr diǎn, hái yǒu liǎng ge duō xiǎoshí.

Bái Yīng'ài, nǐ shénme shíhou qù Niǔyuē shíxí?

Wǒ bú qù Niǔyuē le. Wénzhōng bāng wǒ zài Jiāzhōu zhǎo le yí fèn shíxí gōngzuò.

Duì, wǒmen xià ge xīngqī kāi chē qù Jiāzhōu.

Shì ma? Yìbiānr kāi chē, yìbiānr wánr, tài hǎo le.

Kāi chē xiǎoxīn. Zhù nǐmen wánr de[1] gāoxìng.

Zhù nǐmen yí lù píng'ān. Dào le Běijīng yǐhòu[2], bié wàng le gěi wǒmen fā ge diànzǐ yóujiàn.

Hǎo, nà wǒmen qiūtiān jiàn.

Xià ge xuéqī jiàn.

Zàijiàn!

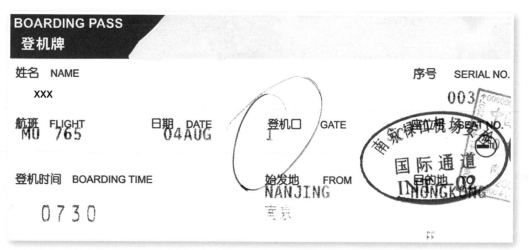

這是一張登機牌。
Zhè shì yì zhāng dēngjīpái.

VOCABULARY

1.	行李	xíngli	n	luggage
2.	托運	tuōyùn	v	to check (luggage)
3.	包	bāo	n	bag; sack; bundle; package
4.	箱子	xiāngzi	n	suitcase; box
5.	超重	chāozhòng	v	to be overweight (of luggage, freight, etc.)
	超	chāo	v	to exceed; to surpass
6.	登機牌	dēngjīpái	n	boarding pass
	牌	pái	n	plate; tablet; card
7.	登機口	dēngjīkǒu	n	boarding gate
	口	kǒu	n	opening; entrance; mouth
8.	哭	kū	v	to cry; to weep
9.	地	de	p	(particle to link adverbial and verb) [See Grammar 1.]
10.	照顧	zhàogu	v	to look after; to care for; to attend to
11.	起飛	qǐfēi	v	(of airplanes) to take off
12.	小心	xiǎoxīn	v	to be careful
13.	一路平安	yí lù píng'ān		have a good trip; bon voyage

Grammar

1. 的 (de), 得 (de), 地 (de) Compared

A. 的 (de) usually follows an attributive but not an adverbial. The attributive can be formed by an adjective, a noun, or a verbal phrase.

❶   漂亮的女孩子

piàoliang de nǔháizi

(pretty girl)

❷   哥哥的公司

gēge de gōngsī

(older brother's company)

❸   我的臥室

wǒ de wòshì

(my bedroom)

❹   剛買的機票

gāng mǎi de jīpiào

(a recently purchased plane ticket)

❺   媽媽給我們做的蛋糕

māma gěi wǒmen zuò de dàngāo

(the cake Mom made for us)

In most cases, 的 (de) is followed by a noun, as seen in (1) to (5), but it can also precede an adjective or verb if that adjective or verb serves as the subject or object in the sentence.

❻   南京的熱[是有名的]。

Nánjīng de rè [shì yǒumíng de].

(Nanjing's heat/That Nanjing is hot [is well-known].)

❼ 他的死 [大家最近才聽說]。

Tā de sǐ [dàjiā zuìjìn cái tīngshuō].

(His death/That he has died [became known to everyone only recently].)

B. 地 (de) links an adverb or adverbial to a following verb. An adjective, an adverb, or a set phrase can serve as an adverbial if followed by 地 (de).

❶ 慢慢兒地吃

mànmānr de chī

(to eat slowly)

❷ 很高興地說

hěn gāoxìng de shuō

(to say happily)

❸ 一直地走

yìzhí de zǒu

(to walk straight forward)

❹ 好好兒地玩兒

hǎohāor de wánr

(to have some real fun)

C. 得 is used after a verb or an adjective to connect it with a descriptive complement or a complement of degree.

❶ 跑得很快

pǎo de hěn kuài

(to run fast)

❷ 做菜做得很好

zuò cài zuò de hěn hǎo

(to cook well)

❸ 高興得跳起來

gāoxìng de tiào qǐ lái

(to leap up with joy)

❹ 危險得不得了

wēixiǎn de bù déliǎo

(unbelievably dangerous)

Compare the following two sentences:

❺ 他高興地唱著歌走回宿舍。

Tā gāoxìng de chàng zhe gē zǒu hui sùshè.

(He sang happily on his way back to the dorm.)

❻ 他高興得唱起歌來了。

Tā gāoxìng de chàng qi gē lai le.

(Hc was so happy that he started to sing.)

In (5) 高興 (gāoxìng) is used to describe the manner of his singing. In (6) 高興 (gāoxìng) is the cause of his singing.

A Quick Reference Table for 的，地，得 **(de, de, de)**

Attributive	+	的 (de)	+	Noun
Adverbial	+	地 (de)	+	Verb
Verb/Adj	+	得 (de)	+	Adj/Verb

2. ⋯的時候 (...de shíhou) and ⋯以後 (...yǐhòu) Compared

In a sentence of the pattern "V1 的時候 (de shíhou),V2...," the second action and the first action take place simultaneously.

❶ 走的時候別忘了帶些錢。

Zǒu de shíhou bié wàng le dài xiē qián.

(Don't forget to take some money with you when you leave.)

❷   我看見他的時候，他正在打球。

Wǒ kàn jiàn tā de shíhou, tā zhèngzài dǎ qiú.

(When I saw him, he was playing ball.)

❸   妹妹看短信的時候，一邊看一邊笑。

Mèimei kàn duǎnxìn de shíhou, yìbiān kàn yìbiān xiào.

(When my little sister was reading the text messages, she smiled as she read along.)

However, in a sentence of the pattern "V1 以後 (yǐhòu), V2...," the second action takes place after the first one.

❹   他走了以後，才想起來忘了帶錢。

Tā zǒu le yǐhòu, cái xiǎng qi lai wàng le dài qián.

(He didn't realize until after he had left that he had forgotten to take any money with him.)

The ···的時候 (de shíhou) structure describes two simultaneous actions. One may say in English, "When I get to China, I will eat Beijing roast duck," when one really means, "After I get to China, I'll eat Beijing roast duck." In Chinese, that idea has to be conveyed with 以後 (yǐhòu):

❺   我到中國以後要吃北京烤鴨。

Wǒ dào Zhōngguó yǐhòu yào chī Běijīng kǎoyā.

(I will eat some Beijing roast duck after I arrive in China.)

[烤鴨   (kǎoyā, roast duck) See Dialogue II.]

(5a)   *我到中國的時候要吃北京烤鴨。

*Wǒ dào Zhōngguó de shíhou yào chī Běijīng kǎoyā.

[This sentence is incorrect because you won't eat Beijing roast duck until *after* you arrive in China.]

Language Practice

A. Rules Are Rules

Parents and teachers always seem to have more rules for their children and students. Work with a partner and figure out what the rules are, based on the visuals.

EXAMPLE:

做功課的時候，

不准／不能看電視。

Zuò gōngkè de shíhou,

bù zhǔn/bù néng kàn diànshì.

1.

2.

3.

4.

B. Before or After

Work with a partner and find out when Wang Peng normally takes a shower, takes his medicine, goes online, and cleans his room.

EXAMPLE:

A: 王朋平常什麼時候做功課？

Wáng Péng píngcháng shénme shíhou zuò gōngkè?

B: 他平常吃了晚飯以後做功課。

Wáng Péng píngcháng chī le wǎnfàn yǐhòu zuò gōngkè.

1.

2.

3.

4.

C. Heading to the Airport

Unlike Li You, you may not have a Chinese friend to accompany you on your trip to China and be your interpreter or tour guide. Work with a partner to make a list of questions and responses that may come in handy when you check in at a Chinese airline counter.

D. Before the School Break

Go around the classroom and ask each of your classmates about his/her summer plans, and how long the activities he/she has planned will last. Remind him/her to keep in touch, and give appropriate good wishes before moving on to the next person.

E. Recap and Narrate

Working with a partner, recap the content of the text:

1. 王朋和李友托運行李了嗎？

1. Wáng Péng hé Lǐ Yǒu tuōyùn xíngli le ma?

2. 他們在幾號登機口上飛機？

2. Tāmen zài jǐ hào dēngjīkǒu shàng fēijī?

3. 誰去機場送王朋和李友？

3. Shéi qù jīchǎng sòng Wáng Péng hé Lǐ Yǒu?

4. 王紅為什麼哭了？

4. Wáng Hóng wèishénme kū le?

5. 王朋讓王紅做什麼？

5. Wáng Péng ràng Wáng Hóng zuò shénme?

6. 王紅覺得王朋和李友去北京的時間長嗎？

6. Wáng Hóng juéde Wáng Péng hé Lǐ Yǒu qù Běijīng de shíjiān cháng ma?

7. 飛機幾點起飛？

7. Fēijī jǐ diǎn qǐfēi?

8. 白英愛和高文中暑假做什麼？

8. Bái Yīng'ài hé Gāo Wénzhōng shǔjià zuò shénme?

9. 王朋和李友上飛機
以前，大家都说了
些什麼？

9. Wáng Péng hé Lǐ Yǒu shàng fēijī yǐqián, dàjiā dōu shuō le xiē shéme?

Using the words and phrases in blue as prompts, connect your answers above to form a narrative like this example:

王朋和李友要去北京了，在機場他們托運了兩件行李，要在五號登機口上飛機。王紅、高文中和白英愛去送他們。王紅哭了，因為她的父母在北京，哥哥也要去北京了。王朋讓妹妹跟小音好好兒練習英文。高文中幫白英愛在加州找了一份工作，他們下個星期要開車去加州。王朋對他們倆説開車要小心，他們對王朋和李友説一路平安。大家説秋天見，下個學期見。

Wáng Péng hé Lǐ Yǒu yào qù Běijīng le, zài jīchǎng tāmen tuōyùn le liǎng jiàn xíngli, yào zài wǔ hào dēngjīkǒu shàng fēijī. Wáng Hóng, Gāo Wénzhōng hé Bái Yīng'ài qù sòng tāmen. Wáng Hóng kū le, yīnwèi tā de fùmǔ zài Běijīng, gēge yě yào qù Běijīng le. Wáng Péng ràng mèimei gēn Xiǎoyīn hǎohāor liànxí Yīngwén. Gāo Wénzhōng bāng Bái Yīng'ài zài Jiāzhōu zhǎo le yí fèn gōngzuò, tāmen xià ge xīngqī yào kāi chē qù Jiāzhōu. Wáng Péng duì tāmen liǎ shuō kāi chē yào xiǎoxīn, tāmen duì Wáng Péng hé Lǐ Yǒu shuō yí lù píng'ān. Dàjiā shuō qiūtiān jiàn, xià ge xuéqī jiàn.

Dialogue II: Arriving in Beijing

（在北京首都機場）

小朋！

爸，媽！

累壞了吧？

還好③。爸，媽，我給你們介紹一下，這是我的同學李友。

叔叔，阿姨④❶，你們好。

歡迎你來北京。

李友，你的中文說得真好。

謝謝。是因為王朋教得好。

LANGUAGE NOTES

❶ One can address a person to whom one is not related as 叔叔 (shūshu, uncle) or 阿姨 (āyí, aunt) if the person is about one's parents' age. These respectful forms of address can be applied even to strangers.

哪裏，是因為你聰明。

哎，你們倆都聰明。

小朋，你好像瘦了點兒。是不是打工太忙，沒有時間吃飯？

我沒瘦。我常常運動，身體比以前棒多了。

小紅怎麼樣？

她很好，英文水平提高了很多。

走吧，我們上車以後，再慢慢兒地聊吧。爺爺、奶奶在烤鴨店等我們呢！

烤鴨店？

(Zài Běijīng Shǒudū Jīchǎng)

Xiǎo Péng!

Bà, mā !

Lèi huài le ba?

Hái hǎo[3]. Bà, mā, wǒ gěi nǐmen jièshao yí xià, zhè shì wǒ de tóngxué Lǐ Yǒu.

Shūshu, āyí[4], nǐmen hǎo.

Huānyíng nǐ lái Běijīng.

Lǐ Yǒu, nǐ de Zhōngwén shuō de zhēn hǎo.

Xièxie. Shì yīnwèi Wáng Péng jiāo de hǎo.

Nǎli, shì yīnwèi nǐ cōngming.

Āi, nǐmen liǎ dōu cōngming.

Xiǎo Péng, nǐ hǎoxiàng shòu le diǎnr. Shì bu shì dǎ gōng tài máng, méiyǒu shíjiān chī fàn?

Wǒ méi shòu. Wǒ chángcháng yùndòng, shēntǐ bǐ yǐqián bàng duō le.

Xiǎo Hóng zěnmeyàng?

Tā hěn hǎo, Yīngwén shuǐpíng tígāo le hěn duō.

Zǒu ba, wǒmen shàng chē yǐhòu, zài mànmānr de liáo ba. Yéye, nǎinai zài kǎoyā diàn děng wǒmen ne!

Kǎoyā diàn?

VOCABULARY

1.	叔叔	shūshu	n	uncle [See Grammar 4.]
2.	阿姨	āyí	n	aunt [See Grammar 4.]
3.	歡迎	huānyíng	v	to welcome
4.	瘦	shòu	adj	thin, slim (usually of a person or animal); lean
5.	爺爺	yéye	n	paternal grandfather [See Grammar 4.]
6.	奶奶	nǎinai	n	paternal grandmother [See Grammar 4.]
7.	烤鴨	kǎoyā	n	roast duck

Proper Noun

| 8. | 首都機場 | Shǒudū Jīchǎng | | the Capital Airport (in Beijing) |

Grammar

3. 還 (hái) + Positive Adjective

還 (hái) when used before a commendatory adjective may indicate that something is acceptable if not truly outstanding.

 A: 你對那家旅館的印象怎麼樣?

Nǐ duì nà jiā lǚguǎn de yìnxiàng zěnmeyàng?

(What was your impression of that hotel?)

B: 還好。

Hái hǎo.

(It's okay.)

 這個廚房還可以,挺乾淨的。

Zhè ge chúfáng hái kěyǐ, tǐng gānjìng de.

(This kitchen is all right. It's pretty clean.)

❸ 那套公寓還行,帶傢具。

Nà tào gōngyù hái xíng, dài jiājù.

(That apartment is not too bad. It's furnished.)

❹ 那個飯館的紅燒牛肉和家常豆腐還不錯。

Nà ge fànguǎn de hóngshāo niúròu hé jiācháng dòufu hái búcuò.

(That restaurant's beef braised in soy sauce and family-style tofu are pretty good.)

4. Kinship Terms

The system of kinship terms in Chinese is rather complicated, especially because Chinese people make a distinction between paternal and maternal relatives, older and younger siblings, even among differently related uncles and aunts, etc. The following is a list of Chinese kinship terms: [f]: indicates a more formal way of address; [n]: northern Chinese usage; [s]: southern Chinese usage.

A. Parents:

father; dad	爸爸	(bàba)	
	父親	(fùqin)	[f]
mother; mom	媽媽	(māma)	
	母親	(mǔqin)	[f]

B. Grandparents:

[paternal] grandfather	爺爺	(yéye)	
	祖父	(zǔfù)	[f]
[paternal] grandmother	奶奶	(nǎinai)	
	祖母	(zǔmǔ)	[f]
[maternal] grandfather	姥爺	(lǎoye)	[n]
	外公	(wàigōng)	[s]
	外祖父	(wàizǔfù)	[f]
[maternal] grandmother	姥姥	(lǎolao)	[n]
	外婆	(wàipó)	[s]
	外祖母	(wàizǔmǔ)	[f]

C. Uncles and aunts:

father's older brother	伯伯	(bóbo)	
	伯父	(bófù)	[f]
father's older brother's wife	大媽	(dàmā)	
	大娘	(dàniáng)	
	伯母	(bómǔ)	[f]
father's younger brother	叔叔	(shūshu)	
	叔父	(shūfù)	[f]
father's younger brother's wife	嬸嬸	(shěnshen)	
	嬸兒	(shěnr)	
father's sister	姑姑	(gūgu)	
	姑媽	(gūmā)	
father's sister's husband	姑父	(gūfù)	
	姑丈	(gūzhàng)	
mother's brother	舅舅	(jiùjiu)	
mother's brother's wife	舅媽	(jiùmā)	

mother's sister	姨	(yí)	[n]
	阿姨	(āyí)	
	姨媽	(yímā)	
mother's sister's husband	姨父	(yífu)	
	姨丈	(yízhàng)	

D. Brothers, sisters and their spouses:

older brother	哥哥	(gēge)
older brother's wife	嫂嫂	(sǎosao)
	嫂子	(sǎozi)
older sister	姐姐	(jiějie)
older sister's husband	姐夫	(jiěfu)
younger brother	弟弟	(dìdi)
younger brother's wife	弟妹	(dìmèi)
younger sister	妹妹	(mèimei)
younger sister's husband	妹夫	(mèifu)

E. Cousins:

father's brother's son older than oneself	堂哥	(tánggē)
father's brother's son younger than oneself	堂弟	(tángdì)
father's brother's daughter older than oneself	堂姐	(tángjiě)
father's brother's daughter younger than oneself	堂妹	(tángmèi)
other male cousin older than oneself	表哥	(biǎogē)
other male cousin younger than oneself	表弟	(biǎodì)
other female cousin older than oneself	表姐	(biǎojiě)
other female cousin younger than oneself	表妹	(biǎomèi)

F. Children and their spouses:

son	兒子	(érzi)
son's wife	兒媳婦	(érxífu)
daughter	女兒	(nǚ'ér)
daughter's husband	女婿	(nǚxu)

H. Grandchildren:

son's son	孫子	(sūnzi)
son's daughter	孫女	(sūnnǚ)
daughter's son	外孫	(wàisūn)
daughter's daughter	外孫女	(wàisūnnǚ)

Language Practice

F. Being Diplomatic

This is your friend Ellen after a complete fashion makeover. She wants your opinion on her new look. You don't like her new style, but you don't want to hurt her feelings, so you try to be tactful.

EXAMPLE:

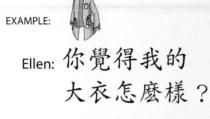

Ellen: 你覺得我的
大衣怎麼樣？

Nǐ juéde wǒ de

dàyī zěnmeyàng?

You: 我覺得你的大衣
還不錯/還行。

Wǒ juéde nǐ de dàyī

hái búcuò/hái xíng.

1.   **2.**   **3.**

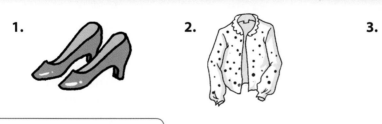

G. My Dear Puppy!

You and your friend just adopted a puppy and are very attentive to its every move. You are extremely careful, and often think the puppy is either losing weight, or gaining weight. You are also worried that the puppy might be 1) tired, 2) thirsty, 3) hungry, 4) having a cold, 5) having a fever, etc. By the way, the puppy's name is 毛毛 (Máomao).

EXAMPLE:

哎，我覺得毛毛
好像瘦了/胖了。

Āi, wǒ juéde Máomao

hǎoxiàng shòu le/pàng le.

What other things will you say when you look at the puppy?

1. _____

2. _____

3. _____

4. _____

5. _____

H. Seeing a Friend Off

Brainstorm with your partner and list the things that people say to each other when saying goodbye at the airport or train station, e.g. "safe journey," "give us a call when you get there," "I'll be back soon," "Don't worry, I'll be fine," etc.

_____

_____

_____

Put the phrases you listed in a logical order. Based on your list, do a role-play of a seeing-off scenario.

I. Greeting Newly Arrived Guests

Brainstorm with your partner and list the things that people say to each other when greeting guests at the airport/train station, e.g. "Welcome to …," "Thank you for picking me up," "You must be exhausted after a long trip," "I'm okay, not too tired," "Let me help you with your luggage," etc.

_____

_____

_____

Put the phrases you listed in a logical order. Based on you list, do a role-play between a guest and a person who comes to pick up the guest.

J. Recap and Narrate

Working with a partner, recap the content of Dialogue II:

1. 誰去北京首都機場接王朋和李友？

   Shéi qù Běijīng Shǒudū Jīchǎng jiē Wáng Péng hé Lǐ Yǒu?

2. 王朋說他累不累？

   Wáng Péng shuō tā lèi bu lèi?

3. 王朋的媽媽說李友的中文怎麼樣？

   Wáng Péng de māma shuō Lǐ Yǒu de Zhōngwén zěnmeyàng?

4. 李友和王朋說李友的中文為什麼這麼好？

   Lǐ Yǒu hé Wáng Péng shuō Lǐ Yǒu de Zhōngwén wèishénme zhème hǎo?

5. 王朋的媽媽覺得王朋的身體怎麼樣？

   Wáng Péng de māma juéde Wáng Péng de shēntǐ zěnmeyàng?

6. 王朋說他的身體怎麼樣？

   Wáng Péng shuō tā de shēntǐ zěnmeyàng?

7. 王朋說他妹妹在美國怎麼樣？

   Wáng Péng shuō tā mèimei zài Měiguó zěnmeyàng?

8. 王朋的爺爺、奶奶在哪兒等他們呢？

   Wáng Péng de yéye, nǎinai zài nǎr děng tāmen ne?

9. 李友聽說要去烤鴨店以後，為什麼說"烤鴨店？"

   Lǐ Yǒu tīngshuō yào qù kǎoyā diàn yǐhòu, wèishénme shuō "kǎoyā diàn?"

Culture Highlights

❶ For domestic flights in China, each passenger is allowed to check only one piece of luggage. Snacks or meals are usually served on domestic flights.

❷ Originally a delicacy on imperial menus, Beijing roast duck boasts a history several centuries long. Now it is arguably the food item most emblematic of the culinary culture of northern China. Indeed, its reputation is well reflected in the Chinese saying that no visit to Beijing is complete without a visit to the Great Wall and a meal at a roast duck restaurant. The most famous roast duck restaurant in Beijing is 全聚德 (Quánjùdé), which was established in 1864.

English Text

Dialogue I

(At the Air China Counter)

Wang Peng: Miss, these are our tickets.

Airline staff: Please show me your passports. How many pieces of checked luggage do you have?

Wang Peng: Two. We won't check this bag. We'll take it on board.

Airline staff: Please put the suitcases up here.

Li You: Miss, they are not over the weight limit, I hope.

Airline staff: No, they're not. Here are your passports and tickets. These are your boarding passes. Please go to Gate 5 to board the plane.

Wang Peng: Thank you.

       *   *   *

Wang Hong: You're both leaving for Beijing. I'll be all alone here.

Wang Peng: Xiao Hong, don't cry. We'll be back in just a few weeks. Work hard on your English. Don't go running around.

Wang Hong: Be back in a few weeks? Won't be back till a few weeks later!

Gao Wenzhong: Don't worry. My sister Xiaoyin will take good care of you.

Li You: That's right. Don't worry.

Bai Ying'ai: When does the plane leave?

Wang Peng: 12:00 noon. There are two hours left.

Li You: Bai Ying'ai, when are you going to New York for your internship?

Bai Ying'ai: I'm not going to New York anymore. Wenzhong helped me get an internship in California.

Gao Wenzhong: That's right. We're driving to California next week.

Li You: Really? Driving and sightseeing at the same time, that's really wonderful.

Wang Peng: Drive carefully. Have fun!

Bai Ying'ai: Have a safe trip. Don't forget to email us after you arrive in Beijing.

Wang Peng: OK. See you in the fall then.

Gao Wenzhong: See you next semester.

Bai Ying'ai and
Wang Hong: Goodbye!

Dialogue II

(At the Beijing Capital Airport)

Wang Peng's Dad: Xiao Peng!

Wang Peng: Dad, Mom!

Mom: You must be really tired.

Wang Peng: Not really. Dad, Mom, let me introduce you… This is my classmate Li You.

Li You: Uncle, Aunt, how do you do?

Dad: Welcome to Beijing.

Mom: Li You, you speak Chinese wonderfully.

Li You: Thank you. It's because Wang Peng is a good teacher.

Wang Peng: You flatter me. It's because you're smart.

Dad: Hey, you're both smart.

Mom: Xiao Peng, you seem to have lost some weight. Is it because you were too busy working and had no time to eat?

Wang Peng: Mom, I haven't lost any weight. I exercise a lot. I'm much stronger than before.

Mom: How is Xiao Hong?

Wang Peng: She's great. Her English has really improved.

Dad: Let's go. We'll talk at leisure after we get in the car. Grandpa and Grandma are waiting for us at the roast duck restaurant.

Li You: Roast duck restaurant?

PROGRESS CHECKLIST

Before proceeding to Level 2, be sure you can complete the following tasks in Chinese:

I am able to—

- ☑ Check in for a flight and check my luggage at the airport counter;
- ☐ Wish others a safe journey;
- ☐ Greet out-of-town guests at the airport;
- ☐ Compliment someone on his/her language ability;
- ☐ Express concern about someone's health;
- ☐ Remind people to move on to the next engagement.

That's How the Chinese Say It!

A Review of Functional Expressions from Lessons 16–20
After gauging your progress and before moving on to the next phase, let's take a break and see how some of the functional expressions that you have encountered in the previous lessons really work!

I. 一言為定 (**yì yán wéi dìng,** it's a deal; it's decided)

You say "一言為定" (yì yán wéi dìng) when you and your friends or business partners have reached a decision. By saying it, you remind all the other parties that the decision should be remembered and honored.

❶   A: 明年我們去中國，怎麼樣？

Míngnián wǒmen qù Zhōngguó, zěnmeyàng?

(We'll go to China next year. How about it?)

B: 好啊！

Hǎo a!

(That's great.)

A: 一言為定。

Yì yán wéi dìng.

(That settles it.)

❷   A: 考完試我們出去玩兒，好嗎？

Kǎo wán shì wǒmen chū qu wánr, hǎo ma?

(After the exam let's go out and have some fun, all right?)

B: 太好了。你開車？

Tài hǎo le. Nǐ kāi chē?

(Wonderful! Will you drive?)

A: 没問題。

Méi wèntí.

(No problem.)

B: 一言為定。

Yì yán wéi dìng.

(It's a deal.)

A: 一言為定。

Yì yán wéi dìng.

(Deal.)

II. "Good," "Very good," "Excellent," "Extraordinary"

Here are some expressions to convey varying degrees of approval, in progressive order of intensity:

❶ 他的中文不錯。

Tā de Zhōngwén búcuò.

(His Chinese is quite good.)

❷ 他的中文很好。

Tā de Zhōngwén hěn hǎo.

(His Chinese is very good.)

❸ 他的中文好得很。

Tā de Zhōngwén hǎo de hěn.

(His Chinese is very, very good.)

❹ 他的中文非常好。

Tā de Zhōngwén fēicháng hǎo.

(His Chinese is unusually good.)

❺ 他的中文好極了。

Tā de Zhōngwén hǎo jí le.

(His Chinese is fantastic.)

❻ 他的中文好得不得了。

Tā de Zhōngwén hǎo de bù dé liǎo.

(His Chinese is extraordinary.)

III. Greetings and Farewells

Greetings

❶ 你好，老師！

Nǐ hǎo, lǎoshī!

(Hello, professor!)

❷ 王先生，早上好！

Wáng xiānsheng, zǎoshang hǎo!

(Good morning, Mr. Wang!)

❸ 早安！

Zǎo'ān!

(Good morning!)

In daily life, however, a common way to greet a person is by asking a casual question about what that person is doing at the moment:

❶ 老李，上課去呀？

Lǎo Lǐ, shàng kè qu ya?

(Lao Li, going to class?)

[It looks like Lao Li is going to class.]

❷ 小王，回家呀？

Xiǎo Wáng, huí jiā ya?

(Little Wang, going home?)

[Upon seeing someone wrapping up his things and leaving the office, or someone on his way home, for instance.]

❸   爸爸，回來了？

Bàba, huí lai le?

(Dad, you're home?)

[Upon seeing one's father walking in the door, for instance.]

Saying goodbye to guests

❶   再見！

Zàijiàn!

(Bye!)

❷   明天見！

Míngtiān jiàn!

(See you tomorrow!)

❸   回頭見！

Huí tóu jiàn!

(See you later!)

❹   慢走！

Màn zǒu!

(Take care!) [Literally, walk carefully!]

Upon finishing a meal before others

❶   慢吃！

Màn chī!

(Take your time [to enjoy the meal]!)

❷   慢用！

Màn yòng!

(Enjoy the meal!)

Any other useful expressions you would like to learn?

Please ask your teacher and make a note here:

_____

_____

_____

Vocabulary Index (Chinese-English)

The Chinese-English index is alphabetized according to *pinyin*. Words containing the same Chinese characters are first grouped together. Homonyms appear in the order of their tonal pronunciation (i.e., first tones first, second tones second, third tones third, fourth tones fourth, and neutral tones last). Proper nouns from the dialogues and readings are shown in green. Supplementary vocabulary from the "How About You?" section is shown in blue.

Traditional	Simplified	Pinyin	Part of Speech	English	Lesson
A					
啊	啊	a	p	(a sentence-final particle)	6
阿司匹林	阿司匹林	āsīpǐlín	n	aspirin	19
阿姨	阿姨	āyí	n	aunt	20
哎	哎	āi	excl	(exclamatory particle to express surprise or dissatisfaction)	13
愛	爱	ài	v	to love; to like; to be fond of	14
安靜	安静	ānjìng	adj	quiet	17
B					
把	把	bǎ	m	(measure word for bunches of things, and chairs)	14
把	把	bǎ	prep	(indicating a thing is disposed of)	15
爸爸	爸爸	bàba	n	father, dad	2
吧	吧	ba	p	(a sentence-final particle)	5
白菜	白菜	báicài	n	bok choy	12
白英愛	白英爱	Bái Yīng'ài	pn	(a personal name)	2
百	百	bǎi	nu	hundred	9
百事可樂	百事可乐	Bǎishìkělè	pn	Pepsi-Cola	5
班	班	bān	n	class	14
搬	搬	bān	v	to move	16
斑馬線	斑马线	bānmǎxiàn	n	zebra crossing; pedestrian crosswalk	13
半	半	bàn	nu	half; half an hour	3
半天	半天	bàntiān		half a day; a long time	18
辦	办	bàn	v	to handle; to do	11
辦法	办法	bànfǎ	n	method; way (of doing something)	15

Traditional	Simplified	Pinyin	Part of Speech	English	Lesson
辦公室	办公室	bàngōngshì	n	office	6
幫	帮	bāng	v	to help	6
棒	棒	bàng	adj	fantastic; super [colloq.]	18
包	包	bāo	n	bag; sack; bundle; package	20
保險	保险	bǎoxiǎn	n	insurance	15
抱	抱	bào	v	to hold or carry in the arms	18
報紙	报纸	bàozhǐ	n	newspaper	17
杯	杯	bēi	m	(measure word for cup and glass)	5
北	北	běi	n	north	13
北京	北京	Běijīng	pn	Beijing	1
被	被	bèi	prep	by	18
本	本	běn	m	(measure word for books)	14
本子	本子	běnzi	n	notebook	7
鼻子	鼻子	bízi	n	nose	14
筆	笔	bǐ	n	pen	7
比	比	bǐ	prep/v	(comparison marker); to compare	11
比賽	比赛	bǐsài	n/v	game; match; competition; to compete	18
遍	遍	biàn	m	(measure word for complete courses of an action or instances of an action)	15
表姐	表姐	biǎojiě	n	older female cousin	14
別	别	bié	adv	don't	6
別人	别人	biérén	n	other people; another person	4
冰茶	冰茶	bīngchá	n	iced tea	12
冰箱	冰箱	bīngxiāng	n	refrigerator	15
餅乾	饼干	bǐnggān	n	cookies; crackers	14
病人	病人	bìngrén	n	patient	15
不	不	bù	adv	not; no	1
不錯	不错	(bùcuò) búcuò	adj	pretty good	4
不但…而且…	不但…而且…	(bùdàn) búdàn…, érqiě…	conj	not only…, but also…	11
不過	不过	(bùguò) búguò	conj	however; but	9
不好意思	不好意思	bù hǎoyìsi		to feel embarrassed	10
不用	不用	(bùyòng) búyòng		need not	9

Traditional	Simplified	Pinyin	Part of Speech	English	Lesson
C					
才	才	cái	adv	not until, only then	5
菜	菜	cài	n	dishes, cuisine	3
參觀	参观	cānguān	vo	to visit a museum	16
博物館	博物馆	bówùguǎn			
餐廳	餐厅	cāntīng	n	dining room, cafeteria	8
草莓	草莓	cǎoméi	n	strawberry	14
廁所	厕所	cèsuǒ	n	restroom, toilet	15
茶	茶	chá	n	tea	5
查	查	chá	v	to check; to look into	19
差不多	差不多	chàbuduō	adv/adj	almost; nearly; similar	17
常常	常常	chángcháng	adv	often	4
常老師	常老师	Cháng lǎoshī	pn	Teacher Chang	6
長城	长城	Chángchéng	pn	the Great Wall	19
長短	长短	chángduǎn	n	length	9
唱歌（兒）	唱歌（儿）	chàng gē(r)	vo	to sing (a song)	4
唱卡拉OK	唱卡拉OK	chàng kǎlā'ōukēi	vo	to sing karaoke	16
場	场	chǎng	n	field	13
超重	超重	chāozhòng	v	to be overweight (of luggage, freight, etc.)	20
潮濕	潮湿	cháoshī	adj	wet; humid	11
吵	吵	chǎo	v/adj	to quarrel; noisy	17
炒麵	炒面	chǎomiàn	n	stir-fried noodles	12
襯衫	衬衫	chènshān	n	shirt	9
成	成	chéng	v	to become	16
城市	城市	chéngshì	n	city	10
吃	吃	chī	v	to eat	3
吃壞	吃坏	chī huài	vc	to get sick because of bad food	15
寵物	宠物	chǒngwù	n	pet	17
初	初	chū	n	beginning	19
出去	出去	chū qu	vc	to go out	11
出租	出租	chūzū	v	to rent out	17
出租汽車	出租汽车	chūzū qìchē	n	taxi	10
廚房	厨房	chúfáng	n	kitchen	17

Traditional	Simplified	Pinyin	Part of Speech	English	Lesson
除了⋯以外	除了⋯以外	chúle...yǐwài	conj	in addition to; besides	8
春天	春天	chūntiān	n	spring	11
穿	穿	chuān	v	to wear; to put on	9
窗戶	窗户	chuānghu	n	window	19
次	次	cì	m	(measure word for frequency)	13
聰明	聪明	cōngming	adj	smart; bright; clever	14
從	从	cóng	prep	from	13
錯	错	cuò	adj	wrong	12

D

Traditional	Simplified	Pinyin	Part of Speech	English	Lesson
打棒球	打棒球	dǎ bàngqiú	vo	to play baseball	18
打車	打车	dǎ chē	vo	to take a taxi	10
打電話	打电话	dǎ diànhuà	vo	to make a phone call	6
打工	打工	dǎ gōng	vo	to work at a temporary job (often part time)	19
打噴嚏	打喷嚏	dǎ pēnti	vo	to sneeze	15
打乒乓球	打乒乓球	dǎ pīngpāngqiú	vo	to play table tennis	18
打球	打球	dǎ qiú	vo	to play ball	4
打掃	打扫	dǎsǎo	v	to clean up (a room, apartment or house)	16
打算	打算	dǎsuàn	v/n	to plan; plan	19
打太極拳	打太极拳	dǎ tàijíquán	vo	to do Tai Chi (a kind of traditional Chinese shadow boxing)	18
打折	打折	dǎ zhé	vo	to sell at a discount; to give a discount	19
打針	打针	dǎ zhēn	vo	to get an injection	15
大	大	dà	adj	big; old	3
大哥	大哥	dàgē	n	eldest brother	2
大家	大家	dàjiā	pr	everybody	7
大姐	大姐	dàjiě	n	eldest sister	2
大小	大小	dàxiǎo	n	size	9
大學生	大学生	dàxuéshēng	n	college student	2
大衣	大衣	dàyī	n	overcoat	9
帶	带	dài	v	to bring; to take; to carry; to come with	12

Traditional	Simplified	Pinyin	Part of Speech	English	Lesson
單程	单程	dānchéng	n	one-way trip	19
單行道	单行道	dānxíngdào	n	one-way street	13
擔心	担心	dān xīn	vo	to worry	18
蛋	蛋	dàn	n	egg	12
蛋糕	蛋糕	dàngāo	n	cake	14
蛋花湯	蛋花汤	dànhuātāng	n	egg drop soup	12
但是	但是	dànshì	conj	but	6
當	当	dāng	v	to serve as; to be	17
當然	当然	dāngrán	adv	of course	18
導遊	导游	dǎoyóu	n	tour guide	19
到	到	dào	v	to go to; to arrive	6
德國	德国	Déguó	pn	Germany	1
德文	德文	Déwén	pn	the German language	6
地	地	de	p	(particle to link adverbial and verb)	20
的	的	de	p	(a possessive or descriptive particle)	2
得	得	de	p	(a structural particle)	7
得	得	děi	mv	must; to have to	6
燈	灯	dēng	n	lamp; light	17
登機口	登机口	dēngjīkǒu	n	boarding gate	20
登機牌	登机牌	dēngjīpái	n	boarding pass	20
等	等	děng	v	to wait; to wait for	6
第	第	dì	prefix	(prefix for ordinal numbers)	7
弟弟	弟弟	dìdi	n	younger brother	2
地方	地方	dìfang	n	place	13
地鐵	地铁	dìtiě	n	subway	10
地圖	地图	dìtú	n	map	13
地下 (通)道	地下 (通)道	dìxià (tōng)dào	n	pedestrian underpass	13
點	点	diǎn	m	o'clock (lit. dot, point, thus "points on the clock")	3
點菜	点菜	diǎn cài	vo	to order food	12
點(兒)	点(儿)	diǎn(r)	m	a little, a bit; some	5

Traditional	Simplified	Pinyin	Part of Speech	English	Lesson
電	电	diàn	n	electricity	16
電腦	电脑	diànnǎo	n	computer	8
電視	电视	diànshì	n	television	4
電影	电影	diànyǐng	n	movie	4
電子郵件	电子邮件	diànzǐ yóujiàn	n	email	10
碟	碟	dié	n	disc; small plate, dish, saucer	11
訂	订	dìng	v	to reserve; to book (a ticket, a hotel room, etc.)	19
東	东	dōng	n	east	13
東京	东京	Dōngjīng	pn	Tokyo	13
東西	东西	dōngxi	n	things; objects	9
冬天	冬天	dōngtiān	n	winter	11
懂	懂	dǒng	v	to understand	7
都	都	dōu	adv	both; all	2
兜風	兜风	dōu fēng	vo	to go for a drive	16
豆腐	豆腐	dòufu	n	tofu; bean curd	12
肚子	肚子	dùzi	n	belly; abdomen	15
對	对	duì	adj	right; correct	4
對不起	对不起	duìbuqǐ	v	sorry	5
多	多	duō	adv	how many/much; to what extent	3
多	多	duō	adj	many; much	7
多少	多少	duōshao	qpr	how much/many	9

E

Traditional	Simplified	Pinyin	Part of Speech	English	Lesson
俄文	俄文	Éwén	pn	the Russian language	6
餓	饿	è	adj	hungry	12
兒子	儿子	érzi	n	son	2
二姐	二姐	èrji	n	second oldest sister	2

F

Traditional	Simplified	Pinyin	Part of Speech	English	Lesson
發短信	发短信	fā duǎnxìn	vo	to send a text message; (lit.) to send a short message	10
發燒	发烧	fā shāo	vo	to have a fever	15
發音	发音	fāyīn	n	pronunciation	8

Traditional	Simplified	Pinyin	Part of Speech	English	Lesson
法國	法国	Fǎguó	pn	France	1
法文	法文	Fǎwén	pn	the French language	6
飯	饭	fàn	n	meal; (cooked) rice	3
飯館(兒)	饭馆(儿)	fànguǎn(r)	n	restaurant	12
飯卡	饭卡	fànkǎ	n	meal card	12
飯桌	饭桌	fànzhuō	n	dining table	17
方便	方便	fāngbiàn	adj	convenient	6
房間	房间	fángjiān	n	room	16
房租	房租	fángzū	n	rent	17
放	放	fàng	v	to put; to place	12
放假	放假	fàng jià	vo	go on vacation; have time off	19
非常	非常	fēicháng	adv	very, extremely, exceedingly	11
飛機	飞机	fēijī	n	airplane	10
(飛)機場	(飞)机场	(fēi)jīchǎng	n	airport	10
費	费	fèi	v	to spend; to take (effort)	16
費	费	fèi	n	fee; expenses	17
分	分	fēn	m	(measure word for 1/100 of a kuai, cent)	9
分鐘	分钟	fēnzhōng	n	minute	17
粉紅色	粉红色	fěnhóngsè	n	pink	9
份	份	fèn	m	(measure word for meal order, job)	19
風	风	fēng	n	wind	11
封	封	fēng	m	(measure word for letters)	8
服務員	服务员	fúwùyuán	n	waiter; attendant	12
附近	附近	fùjìn	n	vicinity; neighborhood; nearby area	17
父母	父母	fùmǔ	n	parents; father and mother	19
父親節	父亲节	Fùqīnjié	pn	Father's Day	3
付錢	付钱	fù qián	vo	to pay money	9
復習	复习	fùxí	v	to review	7

Traditional	Simplified	Pinyin	Part of Speech	English	Lesson
G					
乾淨	干净	gānjìng	adj	clean	17
感恩節	感恩节	Gǎn'ēnjié	pn	Thanksgiving	3
感冒	感冒	gǎnmào	v	to have a cold	15
趕快	赶快	gǎnkuài	adv	right away; quickly; in a hurry	15
剛	刚	gāng	adv	just	12
剛才	刚才	gāngcái	t	just now; a moment ago	11
鋼筆	钢笔	gāngbǐ	n	fountain pen	7
高速公路	高速公路	gāosù gōnglù	n	highway	10
高文中	高文中	Gāo Wénzhōng	pn	(a personal name)	2
高小音	高小音	Gāo Xiǎoyīn	pn	(a personal name)	5
高興	高兴	gāoxìng	adj	happy, pleased	5
告訴	告诉	gàosu	v	to tell	8
哥哥	哥哥	gēge	n	older brother	2
個	个	gè/ge	m	(a measure word for many common everyday objects)	2
給	给	gěi	v	to give	5
給	给	gěi	prep	to; for	6
跟	跟	gēn	prep	with	6
更	更	gèng	adv	even more	11
宮保雞丁	宫保鸡丁	gōngbǎo jīdīng	n	Kung Pao chicken	12
工程師	工程师	gōngchéngshī	n	engineer	2
工人	工人	gōngrén	n	worker	2
工商管理	工商管理	gōngshāng guǎnlǐ	n	business management	8
工作	工作	gōngzuò	n/v	job; to work	2
公共汽車	公共汽车	gōnggòng qìchē	n	bus	10
公司	公司	gōngsī	n	company	19
公寓	公寓	gōngyù	n	apartment	17
公園	公园	gōngyuán	n	park	11
功課	功课	gōngkè	n	homework; schoolwork	7
狗	狗	gǒu	n	dog	14
夠	够	gòu	adj	enough	12
拐	拐	guǎi	v	to turn	13
廣告	广告	guǎnggào	n	advertisement	17

Traditional	Simplified	Pinyin	Part of Speech	English	Lesson
逛街	逛街	guàng jiē	vo	to windowshop	4
貴	贵	guì	adj	honorable; expensive	1
櫃子	柜子	guìzi	n	cabinet; cupboard	17
國際	国际	guójì	adj	international	18
果汁	果汁	guǒzhī	n	fruit juice	5
過	过	guò	v	to pass	13
過敏	过敏	guòmǐn	v	to be allergic to	15
過	过	guo	p	(particle used after a verb to indicate a past experience)	13

H

還	还	hái	adv	also; too; as well	3
還是	还是	háishi	conj	or	3
孩子	孩子	háizi	n	child	2
海報	海报	hǎibào	n	poster	17
海關	海关	hǎiguān	n	customs	20
海倫	海伦	Hǎilún	pn	Helen	14
韓國	韩国	Hánguó	pn	South Korea	1
韓文	韩文	Hánwén	pn	the Korean language	6
寒假	寒假	hánjià	n	winter vacation	10
漢字	汉字	Hànzì	n	Chinese characters	7
航班	航班	hángbān	n	scheduled flight	19
航空	航空	hángkōng	n	aviation	19
航站樓	航站楼	hángzhànlóu	n	concourse (of airport)	20
好	好	hǎo	adj	fine; good; nice; O.K.; it's settled	1
好吃	好吃	hǎochī	adj	delicious	12
好幾	好几	hǎo jǐ		quite a few	15
好久	好久	hǎo jiǔ		a long time	4
好玩兒	好玩儿	hǎowánr	adj	fun, amusing, interesting	11
好像	好像	hǎoxiàng	v	to seem; to be like	12
號	号	hào	m	(measure word for number in a series; day of the month)	3
號	号	hào	n	size	9
號碼	号码	hàomǎ	n	number	16
喝	喝	hē	v	to drink	5

Traditional	Simplified	Pinyin	Part of Speech	English	Lesson
和	和	hé	conj	and	2
合適	合适	héshì	adj	suitable	9
黑	黑	hēi	adj	black	9
很	很	hěn	adv	very	3
紅	红	hóng	adj	red	9
紅綠燈	红绿灯	hónglǜdēng	n	traffic light	13
紅燒	红烧	hóngshāo	v	to braise in soy sauce	12
後來	后来	hòulái	t	later	8
後天	后天	hòutiān	t	the day after tomorrow	16
胡蘿蔔	胡萝卜	húluóbo	n	carrot	12
護照	护照	hùzhào	n	passport	19
花	花	huā	v	to spend	10
花	花	huā	n	flower	14
花粉	花粉	huāfěn	n	pollen	15
花生	花生	huāshēng	n	peanuts	15
滑冰	滑冰	huá bīng	vo	to ice skate	11
畫畫兒	画画儿	huà huàr	vo	to draw; to paint	4
化學	化学	huàxué	n	chemistry	8
歡迎	欢迎	huānyíng	v	to welcome	20
還	还	huán	v	to return (something)	17
換	换	huàn	v	to exchange; to change	9
黃	黄	huáng	adj	yellow	9
黃瓜	黄瓜	huánggua	n	cucumber	12
灰塵	灰尘	huīchén	n	dust	15
灰色	灰色	huīsè	n	gray	9
回家	回家	huí jiā	vo	to go home	5
回來	回来	huí lai	vc	to come back	6
回去	回去	huí qu	vc	to go back; to return	11
會	会	huì	mv	can; know how to	8
會	会	huì	mv	will	11
活動	活动	huódòng	n	activity	13
或者	或者	huòzhě	conj	or	10
護士	护士	hùshi	n	nurse	2

Traditional	Simplified	Pinyin	Part of Speech	English	Lesson
J					
雞	鸡	jī	n	chicken	12
極	极	jí	adv	extremely	12
幾	几	jǐ	nu	how many; some; a few	2
記得	记得	jìde	v	to remember	16
計劃	计划	jìhuà	n/v	plan; to plan	19
家	家	jiā	n	family; home	2
家常	家常	jiācháng	n	home-style	12
傢具	家具	jiājù	n	furniture	17
加拿大	加拿大	Jiā'nádà	pn	Canada	1
加州	加州	Jiāzhōu	pn	California	1, 11
夾克	夹克	jiákè	n	jacket	9
檢查	检查	jiǎnchá	v	to examine	15
簡單	简单	jiǎndān	adj	simple	18
件	件	jiàn	m	(measure word for shirts, dresses, jackets, coats, etc.)	9
見	见	jiàn	v	to see	3
見面	见面	jiàn miàn	vo	to meet up; to meet with	6
健康	健康	jiànkāng	adj/n	healthy; health	15
教	教	jiāo	v	to teach	7
腳	脚	jiǎo	n	foot	18
餃子	饺子	jiǎozi	n	dumplings (with vegetable and/or meat filling)	12
叫	叫	jiào	v	to be called; to call	1
教室	教室	jiàoshì	n	classroom	8
教授	教授	jiàoshòu	n	professor	2
接	接	jiē	v	to catch; to meet; to welcome	14
節	节	jié	m	(measure word for class periods)	6
姐姐	姐姐	jiějie	n	older sister	2
介紹	介绍	jièshào	v	to introduce	5
今年	今年	jīnnián	t	this year	3
今天	今天	jīntiān	t	today	3
緊張	紧张	jǐnzhāng	adj	nervous, anxious	10
近	近	jìn	adj	near	13

Traditional	Simplified	Pinyin	Part of Speech	English	Lesson
進	进	jìn	v	to enter	5
進來	进来	jìn lai	vc	to come in	5
經濟	经济	jīngjì	n	economics	8
經理	经理	jīnglǐ	n	manager	2
九月	九月	jiǔyuè	n	September	3
就	就	jiù	adv	precisely; exactly	6
就	就	jiù	adv	just; only (indicating a small number)	16
橘子	橘子	júzi	n	tangerine	14
橘紅色	橘红色	júhóngsè	n	orange (color)	9
覺得	觉得	juéde	v	to feel; to think	4
軍人	军人	jūnrén	n	soldier; military officer	2

K

Traditional	Simplified	Pinyin	Part of Speech	English	Lesson
咖啡	咖啡	kāfēi	n	coffee	5
咖啡色	咖啡色	kāfēisè	n	brown; coffee color	9
卡片	卡片	kǎpiàn	n	card	14
開車	开车	kāi chē	vo	to drive a car	10
開會	开会	kāi huì	vo	to have a meeting	6
開始	开始	kāishǐ	v/n	to begin, to start; beginning	7
看	看	kàn	v	to watch; to look; to read	4
看病	看病	kàn bìng	vo	to see a doctor; (of a doctor) to see a patient	15
考試	考试	kǎo shì	vo/n	to give or take a test; test	6
烤鴨	烤鸭	kǎoyā	n	roast duck	20
靠	靠	kào	v	to lean on; to lean against; to be next to	19
咳嗽	咳嗽	késòu	v	to cough	15
渴	渴	kě	adj	thirsty	12
可愛	可爱	kě'ài	adj	cute; lovable	14
可口可樂	可口可乐	Kěkǒukělè	pn	Coca-Cola	5
可樂	可乐	kělè	n	[Coke or Pepsi] cola	5
可能	可能	kěnéng	adv/adj	maybe; possible	17
可是	可是	kěshì	conj	but	3
可以	可以	kěyǐ	mv	can; may	5
刻	刻	kè	m	quarter (of an hour)	3

Traditional	Simplified	Pinyin	Part of Speech	English	Lesson
課	课	kè	n	class; course; lesson	6
課本	课本	kèběn	n	textbook	7
課文	课文	kèwén	n	text of a lesson	7
客氣	客气	kèqi	adj	polite	6
客廳	客厅	kètīng	n	living room	17
空(兒)	空(儿)	kòng(r)	n	free time	6
口	口	kǒu	m	(measure word for number of family members)	2
哭	哭	kū	v	to cry; to weep	20
酷	酷	kù	adj	cool	7
褲子	裤子	kùzi	n	pants	9
快	快	kuài	adv/adj	quickly; fast, quick	5
快樂	快乐	kuàilè	adj	happy	10
塊	块	kuài	m	(measure word for the basic Chinese monetary unit)	9
礦泉水	矿泉水	kuàngquánshuǐ	n	mineral water	5

L

Traditional	Simplified	Pinyin	Part of Speech	English	Lesson
拉丁文	拉丁文	Lādīngwén	pn	the Latin language	6
來	来	lái	v	to come	5
藍	蓝	lán	adj	blue	10
籃球	篮球	lánqiú	n	basketball	18
懶	懒	lǎn	adj	lazy	15
老師	老师	lǎoshī	n	teacher	1
了	了	le	p	(a dynamic particle)	5
累	累	lèi	adj	tired	8
冷	冷	lěng	adj	cold	11
離	离	lí	prep	away from	13
梨	梨	lí	n	pear	14
裏邊	里边	lǐbian	n	inside	13
禮物	礼物	lǐwù	n	gift; present	14
李友	李友	Lǐ Yǒu	pn	(a personal name)	1
力氣	力气	lìqi	n	strength; effort	16
歷史	历史	lìshǐ	n	history	8

Traditional	Simplified	Pinyin	Part of Speech	English	Lesson
倆	俩	liǎ	nu+m	(coll.) two	16
連	连	lián	prep	even	17
臉	脸	liǎn	n	face	14
練習	练习	liànxí	v	to practice	6
練習本	练习本	liànxíběn	n	exercise book	7
涼拌	凉拌	liángbàn	v	(of food) cold "blended"; cold tossed	12
涼快	凉快	liángkuai	adj	pleasantly cool	11
兩	两	liǎng	nu	two; a couple of	2
聊天(兒)	聊天(儿)	liáo tiān(r)	vo	to chat	5
零食	零食	língshí	n	snacks	14
另外	另外	lìngwài	conj	furthermore; in addition	17
流鼻涕	流鼻涕	liú bítì	vo	to have a runny nose	15
樓	楼	lóu	n	multi-storied building; floor (of a multi-level building)	14
路口	路口	lùkǒu	n	intersection	13
錄音	录音	lùyīn	n/vo	sound recording; to record	7
旅館	旅馆	lǚguǎn	n	hotel	19
旅行	旅行	lǚxíng	v	to travel	16
旅行社	旅行社	lǚxíngshè	n	travel agency	19
綠	绿	lǜ	adj	green	10
律師	律师	lǜshī	n	lawyer	2
亂	乱	luàn	adv	randomly; arbitrarily; messily	15

M

Traditional	Simplified	Pinyin	Part of Speech	English	Lesson
媽媽	妈妈	māma	n	mother, mom	2
馬上	马上	mǎshàng	adv	immediately; right away	19
嗎	吗	ma	qp	(question particle)	1
麻煩	麻烦	máfan	adj	troublesome	10
麻婆豆腐	麻婆豆腐	mápó dòufu	n	Mapo tofu	12
買	买	mǎi	v	to buy	9
賣完	卖完	mài wán	vc	to be sold out	12
慢	慢	màn	adj	slow	7
慢跑	慢跑	mànpǎo	v/n	to jog; jogging	18
忙	忙	máng	adj	busy	3

Traditional	Simplified	Pinyin	Part of Speech	English	Lesson
貓	猫	māo	n	cats	15
毛	毛	máo	m	(measure word for 1/10 of a kuai, dime (for US money))	9
毛筆	毛笔	máobǐ	n	writing brush	7
毛衣	毛衣	máoyī	n	woolen sweater	9
帽子	帽子	màozi	n	hat; cap	9
沒	没	méi	adv	not	2
沒關係	没关系	méi guānxi		it doesn't matter	12
每	每	měi	pr	every; each	10
美國	美国	Měiguó	pn	America	1
美式	美式	Měishì	adj	American-style	18
美元	美元	Měiyuán	n	U.S. currency	17
妹妹	妹妹	mèimei	n	younger sister	2
悶熱	闷热	mēnrè	adj	hot and stifling	11
米飯	米饭	mǐfàn	n	cooked rice	12
免稅商店	免税商店	miǎn shuì shāngdiàn	n	duty-free shop	20
面試	面试	miànshì	v/n	to interview; interview	11
明天	明天	míngtiān	t	tomorrow	3
名勝古蹟	名胜古迹	míngshèng gǔjì		famous scenic spots and historic sites	19
名字	名字	míngzi	n	name	1
墨西哥	墨西哥	Mòxīgē	pn	Mexico	1
母親節	母亲节	Mǔqīnjié	pn	Mother's Day	3

N

Traditional	Simplified	Pinyin	Part of Speech	English	Lesson
拿	拿	ná	v	to take; to get	13
哪	哪	nǎ/něi	qpr	which	6
哪裏	哪里	nǎli	pr	where	7
哪兒	哪儿	nǎr	qpr	where	5
那	那	nà	pr	that	2
那	那	nà	conj	in that case; then	4
那裏	那里	nàli	pr	there	17
那麼	那么	nàme	pr	(indicating degree) so, such	11
那兒	那儿	nàr	pr	there	8

Traditional	Simplified	Pinyin	Part of Speech	English	Lesson
奶奶	奶奶	nǎinai	n	paternal grandmother	20
男	男	nán	adj	male	2
南	南	nán	n	south	13
難	难	nán	adj	difficult	7
難受	难受	nánshòu	adj	hard to bear; uncomfortable	18
呢	呢	ne	qp	(question particle)	1
能	能	néng	mv	can; to be able to	8
你	你	nǐ	pr	you	1
年級	年级	niánjí	n	grade in school	6
念	念	niàn	v	to read aloud	7
您	您	nín	pr	you (honorific for 你)	6
牛肉	牛肉	niúròu	n	beef	12
紐約	纽约	Niǔyuē	pn	New York	1
農民	农民	nóngmín	n	farmer; peasant	2
暖和	暖和	nuǎnhuo	adj	warm	11
女	女	nǚ	adj	female	2
女兒	女儿	nǚ'ér	n	daughter	2

P

Traditional	Simplified	Pinyin	Part of Speech	English	Lesson
怕	怕	pà	v	to fear; to be afraid of	18
拍	拍	pāi	n	racket	18
盤	盘	pán	n	plate; dish	12
旁邊	旁边	pángbiān	n	side	13
胖	胖	pàng	adj	fat	18
跑步	跑步	pǎo bù	vo	to jog	18
朋友	朋友	péngyou	n	friend	3
篇	篇	piān	m	(measure word for essays, articles, etc.)	8
便宜	便宜	piányi	adj	cheap; inexpensive	9
片	片	piàn	m	(measure word for tablet; slice)	15
票	票	piào	n	ticket	10
漂亮	漂亮	piàoliang	adj	pretty	5
瓶	瓶	píng	m/n	(measure word for bottles); bottle	5
平常	平常	píngcháng	adv	usually	7

Traditional	Simplified	Pinyin	Part of Speech	English	Lesson
蘋果	苹果	píngguǒ	n	apple	14
葡萄	葡萄	pútao	n	grape	14
葡萄牙文	葡萄牙文	Pútáoyáwén	pn	the Portuguese language	6
Q					
騎摩托車	骑摩托车	qí mótuōchē	vo	to ride a motorcycle	10
騎自行車	骑自行车	qí zìxíngchē	vo	to ride a bicycle	10
起床	起床	qǐ chuáng	vo	to get up	8
起飛	起飞	qǐfēi	v	(of airplanes) to take off	20
氣球	气球	qìqiú	n	balloons	14
汽水(兒)	汽水(儿)	qìshuǐ(r)	n	soft drink; soda pop	5, 14
千	千	qiān	nu	thousand	19
鉛筆	铅笔	qiānbǐ	n	pencil	7
簽證	签证	qiānzhèng	n	visa	19
錢	钱	qián	n	money	9
前	前	qián	n	forward; ahead	13
前面	前面	qiánmian	n	ahead; in front of	13
青菜	青菜	qīngcài	n	green/leafy vegetable	12
清楚	清楚	qīngchu	adj	clear	12
情人節	情人节	Qíngrénjié	pn	Valentine's Day	3
晴天	晴天	qíngtiān	n	sunny day	11
請	请	qǐng	v	please (polite form of request); to treat or to invite (somebody)	1
請客	请客	qǐng kè	vo	to invite someone (to dinner, coffee, etc.); to play the host	4
秋天	秋天	qiūtiān	n	autumn; fall	11
去	去	qù	v	to go	4
去年	去年	qùnián	t	last year	14
裙子	裙子	qúnzi	n	skirt	9
R					
然後	然后	ránhòu	adv	then	10
讓	让	ràng	v	to allow or cause (somebody to do something)	10
熱	热	rè	adj	hot	11

Traditional	Simplified	Pinyin	Part of Speech	English	Lesson
人	人	rén	n	people; person	1
人民幣	人民币	rénmínbì	n	renminbi (RMB, Chinese currency)	17
認識	认识	rènshi	v	to be acquainted with; recognize	3
日本	日本	Rìběn	pn	Japan	1, 13
日記	日记	rìjì	n	diary	8
日文	日文	Rìwén	pn	the Japanese language	6, 13
容易	容易	róngyì	adj	easy	7
肉	肉	ròu	n	meat	12
如果…的話	如果…的话	rúguǒ... de huà	conj	if	9

S

Traditional	Simplified	Pinyin	Part of Speech	English	Lesson
沙發	沙发	shāfā	n	sofa	17
商店	商店	shāngdiàn	n	store; shop	9
商人	商人	shāngrén	n	merchant; businessperson	2
商務艙	商务舱	shāngwùcāng	n	business class	19
上	上	shàng	v	to go [colloq.]	13
上菜	上菜	shàng cài	vo	to serve food	12
上次	上次	shàng cì		last time	15
上大學	上大学	shàng dàxué	vo	to attend college/university	18
上個	上个	shàng ge		the previous one	7
上海	上海	Shànghǎi	pn	Shanghai	1, 12
上課	上课	shàng kè	vo	to go to a class; to start a class; to be in class	7
上網	上网	shàng wǎng	vo	to go online; to surf the internet	8
上午	上午	shàngwǔ	t	morning	6
上衣	上衣	shàngyī	n	upper garment	9
誰	谁	shéi	qpr	who	2
身體	身体	shēntǐ	n	body; health	15
什麼	什么	shénme	qpr	what	1
生病	生病	shēng bìng	vo	to get sick	15
生詞	生词	shēngcí	n	new words; vocabulary	7
生日	生日	shēngrì	n	birthday	3
師傅	师傅	shīfu	n	master worker	12

Traditional	Simplified	Pinyin	Part of Speech	English	Lesson
十八	十八	shíbā	nu	eighteen	3
十二	十二	shí'èr	nu	twelve	3
時候	时候	shíhou	n	(a point in) time; moment; (a duration of) time	4
時間	时间	shíjiān	n	time	6
實習	实习	shíxí	v	to intern	19
試	试	shì	v	to try	9
是	是	shì	v	to be	1
事(兒)	事(儿)	shì(r)	n	matter; affair; event	3
收	收	shōu	v	to receive; to accept	9
手	手	shǒu	n	hand	18
手機	手机	shǒujī	n	cell phone	10
首都	首都	shǒudū	n	capital city	19
首都機場	首都机场	Shǒudū Jīchǎng	pn	the Capital Airport (in Beijing)	20
瘦	瘦	shòu	adj	thin, slim (usually of a person or animal); lean	20
售貨員	售货员	shòuhuòyuán	n	shop assistant; salesclerk	9
書	书	shū	n	book	4
書店	书店	shūdiàn	n	bookstore	13
書架	书架	shūjià	n	bookcase; bookshelf	17
書桌	书桌	shūzhuō	n	desk	17
舒服	舒服	shūfu	adj	comfortable	11
叔叔	叔叔	shūshu	n	uncle	20
屬	属	shǔ	v	to belong to	14
暑假	暑假	shǔjià	n	summer vacation	19
暑期	暑期	shǔqī	n	summer term	14
數學	数学	shùxué	n	mathematics	8
刷卡	刷卡	shuā kǎ	vo	to pay with a credit card	9
帥	帅	shuài	adj	handsome	7
雙	双	shuāng	m	(measure word for a pair)	9
水	水	shuǐ	n	water	5
水果	水果	shuǐguǒ	n	fruit	14
水平	水平	shuǐpíng	n	level; standard	18
睡覺	睡觉	shuì jiào	vo	to sleep	4
說	说	shuō	v	to say; to speak	6

Traditional	Simplified	Pinyin	Part of Speech	English	Lesson
說話	说话	shuō huà	vo	to talk	7
送	送	sòng	v	to see off or out; to take (someone somewhere)	10
送	送	sòng	v	to give as a gift	14
素	素	sù	adj	vegetarian; made from vegetables	12
素餐	素餐	sùcān	n	vegetarian meal	19
宿舍	宿舍	sùshè	n	dormitory	8
酸	酸	suān	adj	sour	12
酸辣湯	酸辣汤	suānlàtāng	n	hot and sour soup	12
算了	算了	suàn le		forget it; never mind	4
雖然	虽然	suīrán	conj	although	9
歲	岁	suì	n	year (of age)	3
所以	所以	suǒyǐ	conj	so	4

T

Traditional	Simplified	Pinyin	Part of Speech	English	Lesson
T恤衫	T恤衫	T-xùshān	n	T-shirt	9
他	他	tā	pr	he; him	2
她	她	tā	pr	she; her	2
它	它	tā	pr	it	9
台北	台北	Táiběi	pn	Taipei	19
太…了	太…了	tài...le		too; extremely	3
毯子	毯子	tānzi	n	blanket	19
湯姆	汤姆	Tāngmǔ	pn	Tom	14
糖醋魚	糖醋鱼	tángcùyú	n	fish in sweet and sour sauce	12
糖（果）	糖（果）	táng (guǒ)	n	candy	14
躺下	躺下	tǎng xia	vc	to lie down	15
桃兒	桃儿	táor	n	peach	14
套	套	tào	m	(measure word for suite or set)	17
特別	特别	tèbié	adv	especially	10
疼死	疼死	téng sǐ	adj+c	really painful	15
踢	踢	tī	v	to kick	18
提高	提高	tígāo	v	to improve; to raise; to heighten	18
天	天	tiān	n	day	3
天氣	天气	tiānqì	n	weather	11

Traditional	Simplified	Pinyin	Part of Speech	English	Lesson
天橋	天桥	tiānqiáo	n	pedestrian overpass	13
甜	甜	tián	adj	sweet	12
條	条	tiáo	m	(measure word for pants and long, thin objects)	9
跳舞	跳舞	tiào wǔ	vo	to dance	4
聽	听	tīng	v	to listen	4
聽説	听说	tīngshuō	v	to be told; to hear of	13
聽音樂會	听音乐会	tīng yīnyuèhuì	vo	to go to a concert	16
挺	挺	tǐng	adv	very; rather	9
同	同	tóng	adj	same; alike	16
同學	同学	tóngxué	n	classmate	3
頭等艙	头等舱	tóuděngcāng	n	first class	19
頭疼	头疼	tóu téng		to have a headache	15
圖書館	图书馆	túshūguǎn	n	library	5
托運	托运	tuōyùn	v	to check (luggage)	20

W

Traditional	Simplified	Pinyin	Part of Speech	English	Lesson
襪子	袜子	wàzi	n	socks	9
外國	外国	wàiguó	n	foreign country	4
外套	外套	wàitào	n	outer garment; coat; jacket	9
玩(兒)	玩(儿)	wán(r)	v	to have fun; to play	5
玩遊戲機	玩游戏机	wán yóuxìjī	vo	to play videogames	4
碗	碗	wǎn	n	bowl	12
晚	晚	wǎn	adj	late	7
晚飯	晚饭	wǎnfàn	n	dinner; supper	3
晚上	晚上	wǎnshang	t/n	evening; night	3
王紅	王红	Wáng Hóng	pn	(a personal name)	14
王朋	王朋	Wáng Péng	pn	(a personal name)	1
往	往	wǎng	prep	towards	13
往返	往返	wǎngfǎn	v	make a round trip; go there and back	19
網球	网球	wǎngqiú	n	tennis	18
網上	网上	wǎng shang		on the internet	11
忘	忘	wàng	v	to forget	12

Traditional	Simplified	Pinyin	Part of Speech	English	Lesson
危險	危险	wēixiǎn	adj	dangerous	18
喂	喂	wéi/wèi	interj	(on telephone) Hello!; Hey!	6
位	位	wèi	m	(polite measure word for people)	6
位子	位子	wèizi	n	seat	12
味精	味精	wèijīng	n	monosodium glutamate (MSG)	12
為了	为了	wèile	prep	for the sake of	18
為什麼	为什么	wèishénme	qpr	why	3
衛生間	卫生间	wèishēngjiān	n	bathroom	17
文化	文化	wénhuà	n	culture	19
問	问	wèn	v	to ask (a question)	1
問題	问题	wèntí	n	question; problem	6
我	我	wǒ	pr	I; me	1
我們	我们	wǒmen	pr	we	3
臥室	卧室	wòshì	n	bedroom	17
午飯	午饭	wǔfàn	n	lunch, midday meal	8
舞會	舞会	wǔhuì	n	dance party; ball	14
物理	物理	wùlǐ	n	physics	8

X

Traditional	Simplified	Pinyin	Part of Speech	English	Lesson
西	西	xī	n	west	13
西班牙文	西班牙文	Xībānyáwén	pn	the Spanish language	6
西北航空公司	西北航空公司	Xīběi Hángkōng Gōngsī	pn	Northwest Airlines	19
西瓜	西瓜	xīgua	n	watermelon	14
西裝	西装	xīzhuāng	n	(western-style) suit	9
希臘文	希腊文	Xīlàwén	pn	the Greek language	6
希望	希望	xīwàng	v/n	to hope; hope	8
喜歡	喜欢	xǐhuan	v	to like	3
洗澡	洗澡	xǐ zǎo	vo	to take a bath/shower	8
蝦	虾	xiā	n	shrimp	12
下車	下车	xià chē	vo	to get off (a bus, train, etc.)	10
下個	下个	xià ge		next one	6
下棋	下棋	xià qí	vo	to play chess	4
下午	下午	xiàwǔ	t	afternoon	6

Traditional	Simplified	Pinyin	Part of Speech	English	Lesson
下雪	下雪	xià xuě	vo	to snow	11
下雨	下雨	xià yǔ	vo	to rain	11
夏天	夏天	xiàtiān	n	summer	11
夏威夷	夏威夷	Xiàwēiyí	pn	Hawaii	1
先	先	xiān	adv	first	10
先生	先生	xiānsheng	n	Mr.; husband; teacher	1
線	线	xiàn	n	line	10
現金	现金	xiànjīn	n	cash	19
現在	现在	xiànzài	t	now	3
香港	香港	Xiānggǎng	pn	Hong Kong	19
香蕉	香蕉	xiāngjiāo	n	banana	14
箱子	箱子	xiāngzi	n	suitcase; box	20
想	想	xiǎng	mv	to want to; would like to; to think	4
想起來	想起来	xiǎng qi lai	vc	to remember; to recall	16
像	像	xiàng	v	to be like; to look like; to take after	14
小	小	xiǎo	adj	small; little	4
小姐	小姐	xiǎojiě	n	Miss; young lady	1
小時	小时	xiǎoshí	n	hour	15
小心	小心	xiǎoxīn	v	to be careful	20
笑	笑	xiào	v	to laugh at; to laugh; to smile	8
些	些	xiē	m	(measure word for an indefinite amount); some	12
鞋	鞋	xié	n	shoes	9
寫	写	xiě	v	to write	7
謝謝	谢谢	xièxie	v	to thank	3
新	新	xīn	adj	new	8
新年	新年	xīnnián	n	new year	10
信	信	xìn	n	letter (correspondence)	8
信用卡	信用卡	xìnyòngkǎ	n	credit card	9
星期	星期	xīngqī	n	week	3
星期四	星期四	xīngqīsì	n	Thursday	3
行	行	xíng	v	all right; O.K.	6

Traditional	Simplified	Pinyin	Part of Speech	English	Lesson
行李	行李	xíngli	n	luggage	20
姓	姓	xìng	v/n	(one's) surname is...; to be surnamed; surname	1
興趣	兴趣	xìngqù	n	interest	17
休息	休息	xiūxi	v	to take a break; to rest	15
學	学	xué	v	to study; to learn	7
學期	学期	xuéqī	n	school term; semester/quarter	8
學生	学生	xuésheng	n	student	1
學習	学习	xuéxí	v	to study; to learn	7
學校	学校	xuéxiào	n	school	5
雪碧	雪碧	Xuěbì	pn	Sprite	5

Y

Traditional	Simplified	Pinyin	Part of Speech	English	Lesson
壓	压	yā	v	to press; to hold down; to weigh down	18
押金	押金	yājīn	n	security deposit	17
亞洲研究	亚洲研究	Yàzhōu yánjiū	n	Asian studies	8
呀	呀	ya	p	(interjectory particle used to soften a question)	5
淹死	淹死	yān sǐ	vc	to drown	18
鹽	盐	yán	n	salt	12
顏色	颜色	yánsè	n	color	9
演	演	yǎn	v	to show (a film); to perform	16
眼睛	眼睛	yǎnjing	n	eye	14
洋葱	洋葱	yángcōng	n	onion	12
羊肉	羊肉	yángròu	n	lamb; mutton	12
養	养	yǎng	v	to raise	17
癢	痒	yǎng	adj	itchy	15
樣子	样子	yàngzi	n	style	9
藥	药	yào	n	medicine	15
藥店	药店	yàodiàn	n	pharmacy	15
要	要	yào	v	to want	5
要	要	yào	mv	will, to be going to; to want to, to have a desire to	6
要不然	要不然	yàobùrán	conj	otherwise	15
要是	要是	yàoshi	conj	if	6

Traditional	Simplified	Pinyin	Part of Speech	English	Lesson
爺爺	爷爷	yéye	n	paternal grandfather	20
也	也	yě	adv	too; also	1
野餐	野餐	yěcān	v	to picnic	16
夜裏	夜里	yèli	n	at night	15
一邊	一边	(yībiān) yìbiān	adv	simultaneously; at the same time	8
一定	一定	(yīdìng) yídìng	adj/adv	certain(ly); definite(ly)	14
一房一廳	一房一厅	(yī fáng yī tīng) yì fáng yì tīng		one bedroom and one living room	17
一共	一共	(yīgòng) yígòng	adv	altogether	9
一路平安	一路平安	(yī lù píng'ān) yí lù píng'ān		have a good trip; bon voyage	20
一起	一起	(yīqǐ) yìqǐ	adv	together	5
一下	一下	(yī xià) yí xià	n+m	once; a bit	5
一言為定	一言为定	(yī yán wéi dìng) yì yán wéi dìng		it's a deal, that settles it; it's decided	16
一樣	一样	(yīyàng) yíyàng	adj	same; alike	9
一直	一直	(yīzhí) yìzhí	adv	straight; continuously	13
衣服	衣服	yīfu	n	clothes	9
醫生	医生	yīshēng	n	doctor; physician	2
醫院	医院	yīyuàn	n	hospital	15
以後	以后	yǐhòu	t	after	6
以前	以前	yǐqián	t	before	8
以為	以为	yǐwéi	v	to assume erroneously	14
已經	已经	yǐjīng	adv	already	8
椅子	椅子	yǐzi	n	chair	17
意大利文	意大利文	Yìdàlìwén	pn	the Italian language	6
陰天	阴天	yīntiān	n	overcast day	11
因為	因为	yīnwèi	conj	because	3
音響	音响	yīnxiǎng	n	stereo system	17
音樂	音乐	yīnyuè	n	music	4
音樂會	音乐会	yīnyuèhuì	n	concert	8
飲料	饮料	yǐnliào	n	beverage	14
飲水器	饮水器	yǐnshuǐqì	n	water dispenser	20
印度	印度	Yìndù	pn	India	1
印象	印象	yìnxiàng	n	impression	16
應該	应该	yīnggāi	mv	should; ought to	18

Traditional	Simplified	Pinyin	Part of Speech	English	Lesson
英國	英国	Yīngguó	pn	Britain; England	3
英文	英文	Yīngwén	pn	English (language)	2
用	用	yòng	v	to use	8
用功	用功	yònggōng	adj	hard-working; diligent; studious	14
游泳	游泳	yóu yǒng	vo	to swim	18
有	有	yǒu	v	to have; to exist	2
有的	有的	yǒude	pr	some	4
有名	有名	yǒumíng	adj	famous; well-known	19
有意思	有意思	yǒu yìsi	adj	interesting	4
又	又	yòu	adv	again	11
右	右	yòu	n	right	13
魚	鱼	yú	n	fish	12
語法	语法	yǔfǎ	n	grammar	7
語言學	语言学	yǔyánxué	n	linguistics	8
預報	预报	yùbào	v	to forecast	11
預習	预习	yùxí	v	to preview	7
元	元	yuán	m	(measure word for the basic Chinese monetary unit); *yuan*	17
圓	圆	yuán	adj	round	14
圓珠筆	圆珠笔	yuánzhūbǐ	n	ballpoint pen	7
遠	远	yuǎn	adj	far	13
願意	愿意	yuànyì	av	to be willing	18
約	约	yuē	v	to make an appointment	11
月	月	yuè	n	month	3
越來越	越来越	yuè lái yuè	adv	more and more	15
越南	越南	Yuènán	pn	Vietnam	1
運動	运动	yùndòng	n	sports	13
運動服	运动服	yùndòngfú	n	sportswear; athletic clothing	18

Z

在	在	zài	prep	at; in; on	5
在	在	zài	v	to be present; to be at (a place)	6
再	再	zài	adv	again	9
再見	再见	zàijiàn	v	goodbye; see you again	3

Traditional	Simplified	Pinyin	Part of Speech	English	Lesson
再說	再说	zàishuō	conj	moreover	15
糟糕	糟糕	zāogāo	adj	in a terrible mess; how terrible	11
早	早	zǎo	adj	early	7
早飯	早饭	zǎofàn	n	breakfast	8
早上	早上	zǎoshang	t	morning	7
怎麼	怎么	zěnme	qpr	how; how come	7
怎麼樣	怎么样	zěnmeyàng	qpr	Is it O.K.? How is that? How does that sound?	3
站	站	zhàn	m	(measure word for stops of bus, train, etc.)	10
張	张	zhāng	m	(measure word for flat objects, paper, pictures, etc.)	7
長	长	zhǎng	v	to grow; to appear	14
長大	长大	zhǎng dà	vc	to grow up	14
找	找	zhǎo	v	to look for	4
找(錢)	找(钱)	zhǎo (qián)	v(o)	to give change	9
照顧	照顾	zhàogu	v	to look after; to care for; to attend to	20
照片	照片	zhàopiàn	n	picture; photo	2
照相機	照相机	zhàoxiàngjī	n	camera	19
這	这	zhè	pr	this	2
這麼	这么	zhème	pr	so; such	7
這兒	这儿	zhèr	pr	here	9
真	真	zhēn	adv	really	7
枕頭	枕头	zhěntou	n	pillow	19
整理	整理	zhěnglǐ	v	to put in order	16
證件	证件	zhèngjiàn	n	ID; document	19
正在	正在	zhèngzài	adv	in the middle of (doing something)	8
政治	政治	zhèngzhì	n	politics	19
枝	枝	zhī	m	(measure word for long, thin, inflexible objects, pens, rifles, etc.)	7
知道	知道	zhīdào	v	to know	8
直飛	直飞	zhí fēi		fly directly	19

Traditional	Simplified	Pinyin	Part of Speech	English	Lesson
植物	植物	zhíwù	n	plant	17
只	只	zhǐ	adv	only	4
紙	纸	zhǐ	n	paper	7
中	中	zhōng	adj	medium; middle	9
中國	中国	Zhōngguó	pn	China	1
中國城	中国城	Zhōngguóchéng	n	Chinatown	13
中國國際航空公司	中国国际航空公司	Zhōngguó Guójì Hángkōng Gōngsī	pn	Air China	19
中間	中间	zhōngjiān	n	middle	13
中文	中文	Zhōngwén	pn	Chinese (language)	6
中午	中午	zhōngwǔ	n	noon	8
中心	中心	zhōngxīn	n	center	13
中學	中学	zhōngxué	n	middle school ; secondary school	14
鐘頭	钟头	zhōngtóu	n	hour	14
種	种	zhǒng	m	(measure word for kinds, sorts, types)	9
重	重	zhòng	adj	heavy; serious	14
週末	周末	zhōumò	n	weekend	4
豬肉	猪肉	zhūròu	n	pork	12
住	住	zhù	v	to live (in a certain place)	14
祝	祝	zhù	v	to wish (well)	8
專業	专业	zhuānyè	n	major (in college); specialty	8
轉機	转机	zhuǎn jī	vo	change planes	19
准	准	zhǔn	v	to allow; to be allowed	17
準備	准备	zhǔnbèi	v	to prepare	6
桌子	桌子	zhuōzi	n	table	12
紫色	紫色	zǐsè	n	purple	9
字	字	zì	n	character	7
字典	字典	zìdiǎn	n	dictionary	7
自己	自己	zìjǐ	pr	oneself	10
走	走	zǒu	v	to go by way of; to walk	10
走道	走道	zǒudào	n	aisle	19
走路	走路	zǒu lù	vo	to walk	10, 17
租	租	zū	v	to rent	19

Traditional	Simplified	Pinyin	Part of Speech	English	Lesson
足球	足球	zúqiú	n	soccer; football	18
嘴	嘴	zuǐ	n	mouth	14
最	最	zuì	adv	most, (of superlative degree) -est	14
最好	最好	zuìhǎo	adv	had better	15
最後	最后	zuìhòu		final; last	10
最近	最近	zuìjìn	t	recently	8
昨天	昨天	zuótiān	t	yesterday	4
左	左	zuǒ	n	left	13
做	做	zuò	v	to do	2
做飯	做饭	zuò fàn	vo	to cook; to prepare a meal	17
做瑜伽	做瑜伽	zuò yújiā	vo	to do yoga	18
坐	坐	zuò	v	to sit	5
坐	坐	zuò	v	to travel by	10
坐船	坐船	zuò chuán	vo	to travel by ship; to take a boat	10
坐電車	坐电车	zuò diànchē	vo	to take a cable car, trolley bus, or tram	10
坐火車	坐火车	zuò huǒchē	vo	to travel by train	10
坐計程車	坐计程车	zuò jìchéngchē	vo	to take a taxi (in Taiwan)	10

Vocabulary Index (English-Chinese)

Proper nouns from the dialogues and readings are shown in green. Supplementary vocabulary from the "How About You?" section is shown in blue.

English	Characters	Pinyin	Part of Speech	Lesson
A				
a little, a bit; some	點(兒)	diǎn(r)	m	5
a long time	好久	hǎo jiǔ		4
activity	活動	huódòng	n	13
advertisement	廣告	guǎnggào	n	17
after	以後	yǐhòu	t	6
afternoon	下午	xiàwǔ	t	6
again	再	zài	adv	9
again	又	yòu	adv	11
ahead; in front of	前面	qiánmian	n	13
Air China	中國國際航空公司	Zhōngguó Guójì Hángkōng Gōngsī	pn	19
airplane	飛機	fēijī	n	10
airport	(飛)機場	(fēi)jīchǎng	n	10
aisle	走道	zǒudào	n	19
all right; O.K.	行	xíng	v	6
allow; be allowed	准	zhǔn	v	17
allow or cause (somebody to do something)	讓	ràng	v	10
almost; nearly; similar	差不多	chàbuduō	adv/adj	17
already	已經	yǐjīng	adv	8
also; too; as well	還	hái	adv	3
although	雖然	suīrán	conj	9
altogether	一共	yígòng	adv	9
America	美國	Měiguó	pn	1
American-style	美式	Měishì	adj	18
and	和	hé	conj	2
apartment	公寓	gōngyù	n	17
apple	蘋果	píngguǒ	n	14

English	Characters	Pinyin	Part of Speech	Lesson
Asian studies	亞洲研究	Yàzhōu yánjiū	n	8
ask (a question)	問	wèn	v	1
aspirin	阿司匹林	āsīpǐlín	n	19
assume erroneously	以為	yǐwéi	v	14
at; in; on	在	zài	prep	5
at night	夜裏	yèli	n	15
aunt	阿姨	āyí	n	20
autumn; fall	秋天	qiūtiān	n	11
aviation	航空	hángkōng	n	19
away from	離	lí	prep	13

B

English	Characters	Pinyin	Part of Speech	Lesson
bag; sack; bundle; package	包	bāo	n	20
Bai Ying'ai	白英愛	Bái Yīng'ài (apersonal name)	pn	2
balloons	氣球	qìqiú	n	14
ballpoint pen	圓珠筆	yuánzhūbǐ	n	7
banana	香蕉	xiāngjiāo	n	14
basketball	籃球	lánqiú	n	18
bathroom	衛生間	wèishēngjiān	n	17
be	是	shì	v	1
be acquainted with; recognize	認識	rènshi	v	3
be allergic to	過敏	guòmǐn	v	15
be called; call	叫	jiào	v	1
be careful	小心	xiǎoxīn	v	20
be like; look like; take after	像	xiàng	v	14
be overweight (of luggage, freight, etc.)	超重	chāozhòng	v	20
be present; be at (a place)	在	zài	v	6
be sold out	賣完	mài wán	vc	12
be told; hear of	聽說	tīngshuō	v	13
be willing	願意	yuànyì	av	18
because	因為	yīnwèi	conj	3
become	成	chéng	v	16
bedroom	臥室	wòshì	n	17

English	Characters	Pinyin	Part of Speech	Lesson
beef	牛肉	niúròu	n	12
before	以前	yǐqián	t	8
begin, start; beginning	開始	kāishǐ	v/n	7
beginning	初	chū	n	19
Beijing	北京	Běijīng	pn	1
belly; abdomen	肚子	dùzi	n	15
belong to	屬	shǔ	v	14
beverage	飲料	yǐnliào	n	14
big; old	大	dà	adj	3
birthday	生日	shēngrì	n	3
black	黑	hēi	adj	9
blanket	毯子	tǎnzi	n	19
blue	藍	lán	adj	10
boarding gate	登機口	dēngjīkǒu	n	20
boarding pass	登機牌	dēngjīpái	n	20
body; health	身體	shēntǐ	n	15
bok choy	白菜	báicài	n	12
book	書	shū	n	4
bookcase; bookshelf	書架	shūjià	n	17
bookstore	書店	shūdiàn	n	13
both; all	都	dōu	adv	2
bowl	碗	wǎn	n	12
braise in soy sauce	紅燒	hóngshāo	v	12
breakfast	早飯	zǎofàn	n	8
bring; take; carry; come with	帶	dài	v	12
Britain; England	英國	Yīngguó	pn	3
brown; coffee colored	咖啡色	kāfēisè	n	9
bus	公共汽車	gōnggòng qìchē	n	10
business class	商務艙	shāngwùcāng	n	19
business management	工商管理	gōngshāng guǎnlǐ	n	8
busy	忙	máng	adj	3
but	但是	dànshì	conj	6
but	可是	kěshì	conj	3
buy	買	mǎi	v	9
by	被	bèi	prep	18

English	Characters	Pinyin	Part of Speech	Lesson
C				
cabinet; cupboard	櫃子	guìzi	n	17
cake	蛋糕	dàngāo	n	14
California	加州	Jiāzhōu	pn	1, 11
camera	照相機	zhàoxiàngjī	n	19
can; able to	能	néng	mv	8
can; know how to	會	huì	mv	8
can; may	可以	kěyǐ	mv	5
Canada	加拿大	Jiā'nádà	pn	1
candy	糖（果）	táng (guǒ)	n	14
Capital Airport (in Beijing)	首都機場	Shǒudū Jīchǎng	pn	20
capital city	首都	shǒudū	n	19
card	卡片	kǎpiàn	n	14
carrot	胡蘿蔔	húluóbo	n	12
cash	現金	xiànjīn	n	19
catch; meet; welcome	接	jiē	v	14
cats	貓	māo	n	15
cell phone	手機	shǒujī	n	10
center	中心	zhōngxīn	n	13
certain(ly); definite(ly)	一定	yídìng	adj/adv	14
chair	椅子	yǐzi	n	17
change planes	轉機	zhuǎn jī	vo	19
character	字	zì	n	7
chat	聊天(兒)	liáo tiān(r)	vo	5
cheap; inexpensive	便宜	piányi	adj	9
check; look into	查	chá	v	19
check (luggage)	托運	tuōyùn	v	20
chemistry	化學	huàxué	n	8
chicken	雞	jī	n	12
child	孩子	háizi	n	2
China	中國	Zhōngguó	pn	1
Chinatown	中國城	Zhōngguóchéng	n	13
Chinese characters	漢字	Hànzì	n	7
Chinese (language)	中文	Zhōngwén	pn	6

English	Characters	Pinyin	Part of Speech	Lesson
city	城市	chéngshì	n	10
class	班	bān	n	14
class; course; lesson	課	kè	n	6
classmate	同學	tóngxué	n	3
classroom	教室	jiàoshì	n	8
clean	乾淨	gānjìng	adj	17
clean up (a room, apartment or house)	打掃	dǎsǎo	v	16
clear	清楚	qīngchu	adj	12
clothes	衣服	yīfu	n	9
Coca-Cola	可口可樂	Kěkǒukělè	pn	5
coffee	咖啡	kāfēi	n	5
[Coke or Pepsi] cola	可樂	kělè	n	5
cold	冷	lěng	adj	11
(of food) cold "blended"; cold tossed	涼拌	liángbàn	v	12
college student	大學生	dàxuéshēng	n	2
color	顏色	yánsè	n	9
come	來	lái	v	5
come back	回來	huí lai	vc	6
come in	進來	jìn lai	vc	5
comfortable	舒服	shūfu	adj	11
company	公司	gōngsī	n	19
(comparison marker); compare	比	bǐ	prep/v	11
computer	電腦	diànnǎo	n	8
concert	音樂會	yīnyuèhuì	n	8
concourse (of airport)	航站樓	hángzhànlóu	n	20
convenient	方便	fāngbiàn	adj	6
cook; prepare a meal	做飯	zuò fàn	vo	17
cooked rice	米飯	mǐfàn	n	12
cookies; crackers	餅乾	bǐnggān	n	14
cool	酷	kù	adj	7
cough	咳嗽	késòu	v	15
credit card	信用卡	xìnyòngkǎ	n	9
cry; weep	哭	kū	v	20

English	Characters	Pinyin	Part of Speech	Lesson
cucumber	黃瓜	huánggua	n	12
culture	文化	wénhuà	n	19
customs	海關	hǎiguān	n	20
cute; lovable	可愛	kě'ài	adj	14

D

English	Characters	Pinyin	Part of Speech	Lesson
dance	跳舞	tiào wǔ	vo	4
dance party; ball	舞會	wǔhuì	n	14
dangerous	危險	wēixiǎn	adj	18
daughter	女兒	nǚ'ér	n	2
day	天	tiān	n	3
day after tomorrow	後天	hòutiān	t	16
delicious	好吃	hǎochī	adj	12
desk	書桌	shūzhuō	n	17
diary	日記	rìjì	n	8
dictionary	字典	zìdiǎn	n	7
difficult	難	nán	adj	7
dining room, cafeteria	餐廳	cāntīng	n	8
dining table	飯桌	fànzhuō	n	17
dinner; supper	晚飯	wǎnfàn	n	3
disc; small plate, dish, saucer	碟	dié	n	11
dishes, cuisine	菜	cài	n	3
do	做	zuò	v	2
do Tai Chi (a kind of traditional Chinese shadow boxing)	打太極拳	dǎ tàijíquán	vo	18
do yoga	做瑜伽	zuò yújiā	vo	18
doctor; physician	醫生	yīshēng	n	2
dog	狗	gǒu	n	14
don't	別	bié	adv	6
dormitory	宿舍	sùshè	n	8
draw; paint	畫畫兒	huà huàr	vo	4
drink	喝	hē	v	5
drive a car	開車	kāi chē	vo	10
drown	淹死	yān sǐ	vc	18

English	Characters	Pinyin	Part of Speech	Lesson
dumplings (with vegetable and/or meat filling)	餃子	jiǎozi	n	12
dust	灰塵	huīchén	n	15
duty-free shop	免稅商店	miǎn shuì shāngdiàn	n	20
(dynamic particle)	了	le	p	5

E

English	Characters	Pinyin	Part of Speech	Lesson
early	早	zǎo	adj	7
easy	容易	róngyì	adj	7
east	東	dōng	n	13
eat	吃	chī	v	3
economics	經濟	jīngjì	n	8
egg	蛋	dàn	n	12
egg drop soup	蛋花湯	dànhuātāng	n	12
eighteen	十八	shíbā	nu	3
eldest brother	大哥	dàgē	n	2
eldest sister	大姐	dàjiě	n	2
electricity	電	diàn	n	16
email	電子郵件	diànzǐ yóujiàn	n	10
engineer	工程師	gōngchéngshī	n	2
England; Britain	英國	Yīngguó	pn	3
English (language)	英文	Yīngwén	pn	2
enough	夠	gòu	adj	12
enter	進	jìn	v	5
especially	特別	tèbié	adv	10
even	連	lián	prep	17
even more	更	gèng	adv	11
evening; night	晚上	wǎnshang	t/n	3
every; each	每	měi	pr	10
everybody	大家	dàjiā	pr	7
examine	檢查	jiǎnchá	v	15
exchange; change	換	huàn	v	9
(exclamatory particle to express surprise or dissatisfaction)	哎	āi	excl	13

English	Characters	Pinyin	Part of Speech	Lesson
exercise book	練習本	liànxíběn	n	7
extremely	極	jí	adv	12
eye	眼睛	yǎnjing	n	14

F

English	Characters	Pinyin	Part of Speech	Lesson
face	臉	liǎn	n	14
family; home	家	jiā	n	2
famous; well-known	有名	yǒumíng	adj	19
famous scenic spots and historic sites	名勝古蹟	míngshèng gǔjì		19
fantastic; super [colloq.]	棒	bàng	adj	18
far	遠	yuǎn	adj	13
farmer; peasant	農民	nóngmín	n	2
fat	胖	pàng	adj	18
father, dad	爸爸	bàba	n	2
Father's Day	父親節	Fùqīnjié	pn	3
fear; be afraid of	怕	pà	v	18
fee; expenses	費	fèi	n	17
feel; think	覺得	juéde	v	4
feel embarrassed	不好意思	bù hǎoyìsi		10
female	女	nǚ	adj	2
field	場	chǎng	n	13
final; last	最後	zuìhòu		10
fine; good; nice; O.K.; it's settled	好	hǎo	adj	1
first	先	xiān	adv	10
first class	頭等艙	tóuděngcāng	n	19
fish	魚	yú	n	12
fish in sweet and sour sauce	糖醋魚	tángcùyú	n	12
flower	花	huā	n	14
fly directly	直飛	zhí fēi		19
foot	腳	jiǎo	n	18
for the sake of	為了	wèile	prep	18
forecast	預報	yùbào	v	11
foreign country	外國	wàiguó	n	4

English	Characters	Pinyin	Part of Speech	Lesson
forget	忘	wàng	v	12
forget it; never mind	算了	suàn le		4
forward; ahead	前	qián	n	13
fountain pen	鋼筆	gāngbǐ	n	7
France	法國	Fǎguó	pn	1
free time	空(兒)	kòng(r)	n	6
French language	法文	Fǎwén	n	6
friend	朋友	péngyou	n	3
from	從	cóng	prep	13
fruit	水果	shuǐguǒ	n	14
fruit juice	果汁	guǒzhī	n	5
fun, amusing, interesting	好玩兒	hǎowánr	adj	11
furniture	傢具	jiājù	n	17
furthermore; in addition	另外	lìngwài	conj	17

G

English	Characters	Pinyin	Part of Speech	Lesson
game; match; competition; to compete	比賽	bǐsài	n/v	18
Gao Wenzhong	高文中	Gāo Wénzhōng	pn	2
Gao Xiaoyin	高小音	Gāo Xiǎoyīn	pn	5
Germany	德國	Déguó	pn	1
German language	德文	Déwén	pn	6
get an injection	打針	dǎ zhēn	vo	15
get off (a bus, train, etc.)	下車	xià chē	vo	10
get sick	生病	shēng bìng	vo	15
get sick because of bad food	吃壞	chī huài	vc	15
get up	起床	qǐ chuáng	vo	8
gift; present	禮物	lǐwù	n	14
give	給	gěi	v	5
give as a gift	送	sòng	v	14
give change	找（錢）	zhǎo (qián)	v(o)	9
give or take a test; test	考試	kǎo shì	vo/n	6
go	去	qù	v	4
go [colloq.]	上	shàng	v	13
go back; return	回去	huí qu	vc	11

English	Characters	Pinyin	Part of Speech	Lesson
go by way of; walk	走	zǒu	v	10
go for a drive	兜風	dōu fēng	vo	16
go home	回家	huí jiā	vo	5
go on vacation; have time off	放假	fàng jià	vo	19
go online; surf the internet	上網	shàng wǎng	vo	8
go out	出去	chū qu	vc	11
go to; arrive	到	dào	v	6
go to a class; start a class; be in class	上課	shàng kè	vo	7
go to a concert	聽音樂會	tīng yīnyuèhuì	vo	16
goodbye; see you again	再見	zàijiàn	v	3
grade in school	年級	niánjí	n	6
grammar	語法	yǔfǎ	n	7
grape	葡萄	pútao	n	14
gray	灰色	huīsè	n	9
Great Wall	長城	Chángchéng	pn	19
Greek language	希臘文	Xīlàwén	pn	6
green	綠	lǜ	adj	10
green/leafy vegetable	青菜	qīngcài	n	12
grow; appear	長	zhǎng	v	14
grow up	長大	zhǎng dà	vc	14

H

had better	最好	zuìhǎo	adv	15
half; half an hour	半	bàn	nu	3
half a day; a long time	半天	bàntiān		18
hand	手	shǒu	n	18
handle; do	辦	bàn	v	11
handsome	帥	shuài	adj	7
happy	快樂	kuàilè	adj	10
happy, pleased	高興	gāoxìng	adj	5
hard to bear; uncomfortable	難受	nánshòu	adj	18
hard-working; diligent; studious	用功	yònggōng	adj	14
hat; cap	帽子	màozi	n	9
have; exist	有	yǒu	v	2

English	Characters	Pinyin	Part of Speech	Lesson
have a cold	感冒	gǎnmào	v	15
have a fever	發燒	fā shāo	vo	15
have a good trip; bon voyage	一路平安	yí lù píng'ān		20
have a headache	頭疼	tóu téng		15
have a meeting	開會	kāi huì	vo	6
have a runny nose	流鼻涕	liú bítì	vo	15
have fun; play	玩(兒)	wán(r)	v	5
Hawaii	夏威夷	Xiàwēiyí	pn	1
he; him	他	tā	pr	2
healthy; health	健康	jiànkāng	adj/n	15
heavy; serious	重	zhòng	adj	14
Helen	海倫	Hǎilún	pn	14
Hello!; Hey! (on telephone)	喂	wéi/wèi	interj	6
help	幫	bāng	v	6
here	這兒	zhèr	pr	9
highway	高速公路	gāosù gōnglù	n	10
history	歷史	lìshǐ	n	8
hold or carry in the arms	抱	bào	v	18
home-style	家常	jiācháng	n	12
homework; schoolwork	功課	gōngkè	n	7
Hong Kong	香港	Xiānggǎng	pn	19
honorable; expensive	貴	guì	adj	1
hope; hope	希望	xīwàng	v/n	8
hospital	醫院	yīyuàn	n	15
hot	熱	rè	adj	11
hot and sour soup	酸辣湯	suānlàtāng	n	12
hot and stifling	悶熱	mēnrè	adj	11
hotel	旅館	lǚguǎn	n	19
hour	小時	xiǎoshí	n	15
hour	鐘頭	zhōngtóu	n	14
how; how come	怎麼	zěnme	qpr	7
how many; some; a few	幾	jǐ	nu	2
how many/much; to what extent	多	duō	adv	3
how much/many	多少	duōshao	qpr	9

English	Characters	Pinyin	Part of Speech	Lesson
however; but	不過	búguò	conj	9
hundred	百	bǎi	nu	9
hungry	餓	è	adj	12

I

English	Characters	Pinyin	Part of Speech	Lesson
I; me	我	wǒ	pr	1
ice skate	滑冰	huá bīng	vo	11
iced tea	冰茶	bīngchá	n	12
ID; document	證件	zhèngjiàn	n	19
if	要是	yàoshi	conj	6
if	如果…的話	rúguǒ… de huà	conj	9
immediately; right away	馬上	mǎshàng	adv	19
impression	印象	yìnxiàng	n	16
improve; raise; heighten;	提高	tígāo	v	18
in a terrible mess; how terrible	糟糕	zāogāo	adj	11
in addition to; besides	除了…以外	chúle…yǐwài	conj	8
in that case; then	那	nà	conj	4
in the middle of (doing something)	正在	zhèngzài	adv	8
India	印度	Yìndù	pn	1
(indicating a thing is disposed of)	把	bǎ	prep	15
inside	裏邊	lǐbian	n	13
insurance	保險	bǎoxiǎn	n	15
interest	興趣	xìngqù	n	17
interesting	有意思	yǒu yìsi	adj	4
(interjectory particle used to soften a question)	呀	ya	p	5
intern	實習	shíxí	v	19
international	國際	guójì	adj	18
intersection	路口	lùkǒu	n	13
interview	面試	miànshì	v/n	11
introduce	介紹	jièshào	v	5
invite someone (to dinner, coffee, etc.); play the host	請客	qǐng kè	vo	4
Is it O.K.? How is that? How does that sound?	怎麼樣	zěnmeyàng	qpr	3
it	它	tā	pr	9

English	Characters	Pinyin	Part of Speech	Lesson
it doesn't matter	没關係	méi guānxi		12
it's a deal, that settles it; it's decided	一言為定	yì yán wéi dìng		16
Italian language	意大利文	Yìdàlìwén	pn	6
itchy	癢	yǎng	adj	15
J				
jacket	夾克	jiákè	n	9
Japan	日本	Rìběn	pn	1, 13
Japanese (language)	日文	Rìwén	pn	6, 13
job; work	工作	gōngzuò	n/v	2
jog	跑步	pǎo bù	vo	18
jog; jogging	慢跑	mànpǎo	v/n	18
just	剛	gāng	adv	12
just; only (indicating a small number)	就	jiù	adv	16
just now; a moment ago	剛才	gāngcái	t	11
K				
kick	踢	tī	v	18
kitchen	廚房	chúfáng	n	17
know	知道	zhīdào	v	8
Korea (South)	韓國	Hánguó	pn	1
Korean language	韓文	Hánwén	pn	6
Kung Pao chicken	宮保雞丁	gōngbǎo jīdīng	n	12
L				
lamb; mutton	羊肉	yángròu	n	12
lamp; light	燈	dēng	n	17
last time	上次	shàng cì		15
last year	去年	qùnián	t	14
late	晚	wǎn	adj	7
later	後來	hòulái	t	8
Latin language	拉丁文	Lādīngwén	pn	6
laugh at; laugh; smile	笑	xiào	v	8

English	Characters	Pinyin	Part of Speech	Lesson
lawyer	律師	lǜshī	n	2
lazy	懶	lǎn	adj	15
lean on; lean against; be next to	靠	kào	v	19
left	左	zuǒ	n	13
length	長短	chángduǎn	n	9
letter (correspondence)	信	xìn	n	8
level; standard	水平	shuǐpíng	n	18
Li You	李友	Lǐ Yǒu	pn	1
library	圖書館	túshūguǎn	n	5
lie down	躺下	tǎng xia	vc	15
like	喜歡	xǐhuan	v	3
line	線	xiàn	n	10
linguistics	語言學	yǔyánxué	n	8
listen	聽	tīng	v	4
live (in a certain place)	住	zhù	v	14
living room	客廳	kètīng	n	17
look after; care for; attend to	照顧	zhàogu	v	20
look for	找	zhǎo	v	4
love; like; be fond of	愛	ài	v	14
luggage	行李	xíngli	n	20
lunch, midday meal	午飯	wǔfàn	n	8

M

English	Characters	Pinyin	Part of Speech	Lesson
major (in college); specialty	專業	zhuānyè	n	8
make a phone call	打電話	dǎ diànhuà	vo	6
make a round trip; go there and back	往返	wǎngfǎn	v	19
make an appointment	約	yuē	v	11
male	男	nán	adj	2
manager	經理	jīnglǐ	n	2
many; much	多	duō	adj	7
map	地圖	dìtú	n	13
mapo tofu	麻婆豆腐	mápó dòufu	n	12

English	Characters	Pinyin	Part of Speech	Lesson
master worker	師傅	shīfu	n	12
mathematics	數學	shùxué	n	8
matter; affair; event	事（兒）	shì(r)	n	3
maybe; possible	可能	kěnéng	adv/adj	17
meal; (cooked) rice	飯	fàn	n	3
meal card	飯卡	fànkǎ	n	12
(measure word for a pair)	雙	shuāng	m	9
(measure word for an indefinite amount); some	些	xiē	m	12
(measure word for books)	本	běn	m	14
(measure word for bottles); bottle	瓶	píng	m/n	5
(measure word for bunches of things, and chairs)	把	bǎ	m	14
(measure word for class periods)	節	jié	m	6
(measure word for complete courses of an action or instances of an action)	遍	biàn	m	15
(measure word for cup and glass)	杯	bēi	m	5
(measure word for essays, articles, etc.)	篇	piān	m	8
(measure word for flat objects, paper, pictures, etc.)	張	zhāng	m	7
(measure word for frequency)	次	cì	m	13
(measure word for kinds, sorts, types)	種	zhǒng	m	9
(measure word for letters)	封	fēng	m	8
(measure word for long, thin, inflexible objects, pens, rifles, etc.)	枝	zhī	m	7
(measure word for many common everyday objects)	個	gè/ge	m	2
(measure word for meal order, job)	份	fèn	m	19
(measure word for number in a series; day of the month)	號	hào	m	3
(measure word for number of family members)	口	kǒu	m	2
(measure word for 1/100 of a kuai, cent)	分	fēn	m	9

English	Characters	Pinyin	Part of Speech	Lesson
(measure word for 1/10 of a kuai, dime (for US money))	毛	máo	m	9
(measure word for pants and long, thin objects)	條	tiáo	m	9
(measure word for people (polite))	位	wèi	m	6
(measure word for quarter (of an hour))	刻	kè	m	3
(measure word for shirts, dresses, jackets, coats, etc.)	件	jiàn	m	9
(measure word for stops of a bus, train, etc.)	站	zhàn	m	10
(measure word for suite or set)	套	tào	m	17
(measure word for tablet; slice)	片	piàn	m	15
(measure word for the basic Chinese monetary unit)	塊	kuài	m	9
(measure word for the basic Chinese monetary unit); *yuan*	元	yuán	m	17
meat	肉	ròu	n	12
medicine	藥	yào	n	15
medium; middle	中	zhōng	adj	9
meet up; meet with	見面	jiàn miàn	vo	6
merchant; businessperson	商人	shāngrén	n	2
method; way (of doing something)	辦法	bànfǎ	n	15
Mexico	墨西哥	Mòxīgē	pn	1
middle	中間	zhōngjiān	n	13
middle school; secondary school	中學	zhōngxué	n	14
mineral water	礦泉水	kuàngquánshuǐ	n	5
minute	分鐘	fēnzhōng	n	17
Miss; young lady	小姐	xiǎojiě	n	1
money	錢	qián	n	9
monosodium glutamate (MSG)	味精	wèijīng	n	12
month	月	yuè	n	3
more and more	越來越	yuè lái yuè	adv	15
moreover	再說	zàishuō	conj	15
morning	上午	shàngwǔ	t	6

English	Characters	Pinyin	Part of Speech	Lesson
morning	早上	zǎoshang	t	7
most, (of superlative degree) -est	最	zuì	adv	14
mother, mom	媽媽	māma	n	2
Mother's Day	母親節	Mǔqīnjié	pn	3
mouth	嘴	zuǐ	n	14
move	搬	bān	v	16
movie	電影	diànyǐng	n	4
Mr.; husband; teacher	先生	xiānsheng	n	1
multi-storied building; floor (of a multi-level building)	樓	lóu	n	14
music	音樂	yīnyuè	n	4
must; have to	得	děi	mv	6

N

English	Characters	Pinyin	Part of Speech	Lesson
name	名字	míngzi	n	1
near	近	jìn	adj	13
need not	不用	búyòng		9
nervous, anxious	緊張	jǐnzhāng	adj	10
new	新	xīn	adj	8
new words; vocabulary	生詞	shēngcí	n	7
new year	新年	xīnnián	n	10
New York	紐約	Niǔyuē	pn	1
newspaper	報紙	bàozhǐ	n	17
next one	下個	xià ge		6
noon	中午	zhōngwǔ	n	8
north	北	běi	n	13
Northwest Airlines	西北航空公司	Xīběi Hángkōng Gōngsī	pn	19
nose	鼻子	bízi	n	14
not	沒	méi	adv	2
not; no	不	bù	adv	1
not only..., but also...	不但…而且…	búdàn..., érqiě...	conj	11
not until, only then	才	cái	adv	5
notebook	本子	běnzi	n	7

English	Characters	Pinyin	Part of Speech	Lesson
now	現在	xiànzài	t	3
number	號碼	hàomǎ	n	16
nurse	護士	hùshi	n	2
O				
o'clock (lit. dot, point, thus "points on the clock")	點	diǎn	m	3
of course	當然	dāngrán	adv	18
office	辦公室	bàngōngshì	n	6
often	常常	chángcháng	adv	4
older brother	哥哥	gēge	n	2
older female cousin	表姐	biǎojiě	n	14
older sister	姐姐	jiějie	n	2
on the internet	網上	wǎng shang		11
once; a bit	一下	yí xià	n+m	5
one bedroom and one living room	一房一廳	yì fáng yì tīng		17
one-way street	單行道	dānxíngdào	n	13
one-way trip	單程	dānchéng	n	19
oneself	自己	zìjǐ	pr	10
onion	洋葱	yángcōng	n	12
only	只	zhǐ	adv	4
or	還是	háishi	conj	3
or	或者	huòzhě	conj	10
orange (color)	橘紅色	júhóngsè	n	9
order food	點菜	diǎn cài	vo	12
other people; another person	別人	biérén	n	4
otherwise	要不然	yàobùrán	conj	15
outer garment; coat; jacket	外套	wàitào	n	9
overcast day	陰天	yīntiān	n	11
overcoat	大衣	dàyī	n	9
P				
pants	褲子	kùzi	n	9
paper	紙	zhǐ	n	7
parents; father and mother	父母	fùmǔ	n	19

English	Characters	Pinyin	Part of Speech	Lesson
park	公園	gōngyuán	n	11
(particle to link adverbial and verb)	地	de	p	20
(particle used after a verb to indicate a past experience)	過	guo	p	13
pass	過	guò	v	13
passport	護照	hùzhào	n	19
paternal grandfather	爺爺	yéye	n	20
paternal grandmother	奶奶	nǎinai	n	20
patient	病人	bìngrén	n	15
pay money	付錢	fù qián	vo	9
pay with a credit card	刷卡	shuā kǎ	vo	9
peach	桃兒	táor	n	14
peanuts	花生	huāshēng	n	15
pear	梨	lí	n	14
pedestrian overpass	天橋	tiānqiáo	n	13
pedestrian underpass	地下(通)道	dìxià (tōng)dào	n	13
pen	筆	bǐ	n	7
pencil	鉛筆	qiānbǐ	n	7
people; person	人	rén	n	1
Pepsi-Cola	百事可樂	Bǎishìkělè	pn	5
pet	寵物	chǒngwù	n	17
pharmacy	藥店	yàodiàn	n	15
physics	物理	wùlǐ	n	8
picnic	野餐	yěcān	v	16
picture; photo	照片	zhàopiàn	n	2
pillow	枕頭	zhěntou	n	19
pink	粉紅色	fěnhóngsè	n	9
place	地方	dìfang	n	13
plan; plan	打算	dǎsuàn	v/n	19
plan; plan	計劃	jìhuà	n/v	19
plant	植物	zhíwù	n	17
plate; dish	盤	pán	n	12
play ball	打球	dǎ qiú	vo	4
play baseball	打棒球	dǎ bàngqiú	vo	18

English	Characters	Pinyin	Part of Speech	Lesson
play chess	下棋	xià qí	vo	4
play table tennis	打乒乓球	dǎ pīngpāngqiú	vo	18
play videogames	玩遊戲機	wán yóuxìjī	vo	4
pleasantly cool	涼快	liángkuai	adj	11
please (polite form of request); treat or invite (somebody)	請	qǐng	v	1
polite	客氣	kèqi	adj	6
politics	政治	zhèngzhì	n	19
pollen	花粉	huāfěn	n	15
pork	豬肉	zhūròu	n	12
Portuguese language	葡萄牙文	Pútáoyáwén	pn	6
(possessive or descriptive particle)	的	de	p	2
poster	海報	hǎibào	n	17
practice	練習	liànxí	v	6
precisely; exactly	就	jiù	adv	6
(prefix for ordinal numbers)	第	dì	prefix	7
prepare	準備	zhǔnbèi	v	6
press; hold down; weigh down	壓	yā	v	18
pretty	漂亮	piàoliang	adj	5
pretty good	不錯	búcuò	adj	4
preview	預習	yùxí	v	7
previous one	上個	shàng ge		7
professor	教授	jiàoshòu	n	2
pronunciation	發音	fāyīn	n	8
purple	紫色	zǐsè	n	9
put; place	放	fàng	v	12
put in order	整理	zhěnglǐ	v	16

Q

English	Characters	Pinyin	Part of Speech	Lesson
quarrel; noisy	吵	chǎo	v/adj	17
quarter (of an hour)	刻	kè	m	4
question; problem	問題	wèntí	n	6
(question particle)	嗎	ma	qp	1
(question particle)	呢	ne	qp	1
quickly, fast, quick	快	kuài	adv/adj	5

English	Characters	Pinyin	Part of Speech	Lesson
quiet	安靜	ānjìng	adj	17
quite a few	好幾	hǎo jǐ		15

R

English	Characters	Pinyin	Part of Speech	Lesson
racket	拍	pāi	n	18
rain	下雨	xià yǔ	vo	11
raise	養	yǎng	v	17
randomly; arbitrarily; messily	亂	luàn	adv	15
read aloud	念	niàn	v	7
really	真	zhēn	adv	7
really painful	疼死	téng sǐ	adj+c	15
receive; accept	收	shu	v	9
recently	最近	zuìjìn	t	8
red	紅	hóng	adj	9
refrigerator	冰箱	bīngxiāng	n	15
remember	記得	jìde	v	16
remember; recall	想起來	xiǎng qi lai	vc	16
renminbi (RMB, Chinese currency)	人民幣	rénmínbì	n	17
rent	房租	fángzū	n	17
rent	租	zū	v	19
rent out	出租	chūzū	v	17
reserve; book (a ticket, a hotel room, etc.)	訂	dìng	v	19
restaurant	飯館(兒)	fànguǎn(r)	n	12
restroom, toilet	廁所	cèsuǒ	n	15
return (something)	還	huán	v	17
review	復習	fùxí	v	7
ride a bicycle	騎自行車	qí zìxíngchē	vo	10
ride a motorcycle	騎摩托車	qí mótuōchē	vo	10
right	右	yòu	n	13
right; correct	對	duì	adj	4
right away; quickly; in a hurry	趕快	gǎnkuài	adv	15
roast duck	烤鴨	kǎoyā	n	20
room	房間	fángjiān	n	16
round	圓	yuán	adj	14
Russian language	俄文	Éwén	pn	6

English	Characters	Pinyin	Part of Speech	Lesson
S				
salt	鹽	yán	n	12
same; alike	同	tóng	adj	16
same; alike	一樣	yíyàng	adj	9
say; speak	說	shuō	v	6
scheduled flight	航班	hángbān	n	19
school	學校	xuéxiào	n	5
school term; semester/quarter	學期	xuéqī	n	8
seat	位子	wèizi	n	12
second oldest sister	二姐	èrjiě	n	2
security deposit	押金	yājīn	n	17
see	見	jiàn	v	3
see a doctor; (of a doctor) to see a patient	看病	kàn bìng	vo	15
see off or out; take (someone somewhere)	送	sòng	v	10
seem; be like	好像	hǎoxiàng	v	12
sell at a discount; give a discount	打折	dǎ zhé	vo	19
send a text message; (lit.) send a short message	發短信	fā duǎnxìn	vo	10
(sentence-final particle)	啊	a	p	6
(sentence-final particle)	吧	ba	p	5
September	九月	jiǔyuè	n	3
serve as; to be	當	dāng	v	17
serve food	上菜	shàng cài	vo	12
Shanghai	上海	Shànghǎi	pn	1, 12
she; her	她	tā	pr	2
shirt	襯衫	chènshān	n	9
shoes	鞋	xié	n	9
shop assistant; salesclerk	售貨員	shòuhuòyuán	n	9
should; ought to	應該	yīnggāi	mv	18
show (a film); perform	演	yǎn	v	16
shrimp	蝦	xiā	n	12
side	旁邊	pángbiān	n	13
simple	簡單	jiǎndān	adj	18

English	Characters	Pinyin	Part of Speech	Lesson
simultaneously; at the same time	一邊	yìbiān	adv	8
sing (a song)	唱歌（兒）	chàng gē(r)	vo	4
sing karaoke	唱卡拉OK	chàng kǎlā'ōukēi	vo	16
sit	坐	zuò	v	5
size	大小	dàxiǎo	n	9
size	號	hào	n	9
skirt	裙子	qúnzi	n	9
sleep	睡覺	shuì jiào	vo	4
slow	慢	màn	adj	7
small; little	小	xiǎo	adj	4
smart; bright; clever	聰明	cōngming	adj	14
snacks	零食	língshí	n	14
sneeze	打噴嚏	dǎpēnti	vo	15
snow	下雪	xià xuě	vo	11
so	所以	suǒyǐ	conj	4
so; such	這麼	zhème	pr	7
(indicating degree) so, such	那麼	nàme	pr	11
soccer; football	足球	zúqiú	n	18
socks	襪子	wàzi	n	9
sofa	沙發	shāfā	n	17
soft drink; soda pop	汽水（兒）	qìshuǐ(r)	n	5, 14
soldier; military officer	軍人	jūnrén	n	2
some	有的	yǒude	pr	4
son	兒子	érzi	n	2
sorry	對不起	duìbuqǐ	v	5
sound recording; record	錄音	lùyīn	n/vo	7
sour	酸	suān	adj	12
south	南	nán	n	13
Spanish language	西班牙文	Xībānyáwén	pn	6
spend	花	huā	v	10
spend; take (effort)	費	fèi	v	16
sports	運動	yùndòng	n	13
sportswear; athletic clothing	運動服	yùndòngfú	n	18
spring	春天	chūntiān	n	11

English	Characters	Pinyin	Part of Speech	Lesson
Sprite	雪碧	Xuěbì	pn	5
stereo system	音響	yīnxiǎng	n	17
stir-fried noodles	炒麵	chǎomiàn	n	12
store; shop	商店	shāngdiàn	n	9
straight; continuously	一直	yìzhí	adv	13
strawberry	草莓	cǎoméi	n	14
strength; effort	力氣	lìqi	n	16
(structural particle)	得	de	p	7
student	學生	xuésheng	n	1
study; learn	學	xué	v	7
study; learn	學習	xuéxí	v	7
style	樣子	yàngzi	n	9
subway	地鐵	dìtiě	n	10
suit (western-style)	西裝	xīzhuāng	n	9
suitable	合適	héshì	adj	9
suitcase; box	箱子	xiāngzi	n	20
summer	夏天	xiàtiān	n	11
summer term	暑期	shǔqī	n	14
summer vacation	暑假	shǔjià	n	19
(one's) surname is...; be surnamed; surname	姓	xìng	v/n	1
sunny day	晴天	qíngtiān	n	11
sweater (woolen)	毛衣	máoyī	n	9
sweet	甜	tián	adj	12
swim	游泳	yóu yǒng	vo	18

T

English	Characters	Pinyin	Part of Speech	Lesson
T-shirt	T恤衫	T-xùshān	n	9
table	桌子	zhuōzi	n	12
Taipei	台北	Táiběi	pn	19
take; get	拿	ná	v	13
take a bath/shower	洗澡	xǐ zǎo	vo	8
take a break; to rest	休息	xiūxi	v	15
take a cable car, trolley bus, or tram	坐電車	zuò diànchē	vo	10

English	Characters	Pinyin	Part of Speech	Lesson
take a taxi	打車	dǎ chē	vo	10
take a taxi (in Taiwan)	坐計程車	zuò jìchéngchē	vo	10
(of airplanes) take off	起飛	qǐfēi	v	20
talk	説話	shuō huà	vo	7
tangerine	橘子	júzi	n	14
taxi	出租汽車	chūzū qìchē	n	10
tea	茶	chá	n	5
teach	教	jiāo	v	7
teacher	老師	lǎoshī	n	1
Teacher Chang	常老師	Cháng lǎoshī	pn	6
television	電視	diànshì	n	4
tell	告訴	gàosu	v	8
tennis	網球	wǎngqiú	n	18
textbook	課本	kèběn	n	7
text of a lesson	課文	kèwén	n	7
thank	謝謝	xièxie	v	3
Thanksgiving	感恩節	Gǎn'ēnjié	pn	3
that	那	nà	pr	2
then	然後	ránhòu	adv	10
there	那裏	nàli	pr	17
there	那兒	nàr	pr	8
thin, slim (usually of a person or animal); lean	瘦	shòu	adj	20
things; objects	東西	dōngxi	n	9
thirsty	渴	kě	adj	12
this	這	zhè	pr	2
this year	今年	jīnnián	t	3
thousand	千	qiān	nu	19
Thursday	星期四	xīngqīsì	n	3
ticket	票	piào	n	10
time	時間	shíjiān	n	6
time (a point in); moment; time (a duration of)	時候	shíhou	n	4
tired	累	lèi	adj	8
to; for	給	gěi	prep	6

English	Characters	Pinyin	Part of Speech	Lesson
today	今天	jīntiān	t	3
tofu; bean curd	豆腐	dòufu	n	12
together	一起	yìqǐ	adv	5
Tokyo	東京	Dōngjīng	pn	13
Tom	湯姆	Tāngmǔ	pn	14
tomorrow	明天	míngtiān	t	3
too; also	也	yě	adv	1
too; extremely	太…了	tài…le		3
tour guide	導遊	dǎoyóu	n	19
towards	往	wǎng	prep	13
traffic light	紅綠燈	hónglǜdēng	n	13
travel	旅行	lǚxíng	v	16
travel agency	旅行社	lǚxíngshè	n	19
travel by	坐	zuò	v	10
travel by train	坐火車	zuò huǒchē	vo	10
travel by ship; take a boat	坐船	zuò chuán	vo	10
troublesome	麻煩	máfan	adj	10
try	試	shì	v	9
turn	拐	guǎi	v	13
twelve	十二	shí'èr	nu	3
(coll.) two	倆	liǎ	nu+m	16
two; a couple of	兩	liǎng	nu	2

U

English	Characters	Pinyin	Part of Speech	Lesson
uncle	叔叔	shūshu	n	20
understand	懂	dǒng	v	7
upper garment	上衣	shàngyī	n	9
U.S. currency	美元	Měiyuán	n	17
use	用	yòng	v	8
usually	平常	píngcháng	adv	7

V

English	Characters	Pinyin	Part of Speech	Lesson
Valentine's Day	情人節	Qíngrénjié	pn	3
vegetarian; made from vegetables	素	sù	adj	12
vegetarian meal	素餐	sùcān	n	19

English	Characters	Pinyin	Part of Speech	Lesson
very	很	hěn	adv	3
very, extremely, exceedingly	非常	fēicháng	adv	11
very; rather	挺	tǐng	adv	9
vicinity; neighborhood; nearby area	附近	fùjìn	n	17
Vietnam	越南	Yuènán	pn	1
visa	簽證	qiānzhèng	n	19
visit a museum	參觀博物館	cānguān bówùguǎn	vo	16

W

English	Characters	Pinyin	Part of Speech	Lesson
wait; wait for	等	děng	v	6
waiter; attendant	服務員	fúwùyuán	n	12
walk	走路	zǒu lù	vo	10, 17
Wang Hong	王紅	Wáng Hóng	pn	14
Wang Peng	王朋	Wáng Péng	pn	1
want	要	yào	v	5
want to; would like to; think	想	xiǎng	mv	4
warm	暖和	nuǎnhuo	adj	11
watch; look; read	看	kàn	v	4
water	水	shuǐ	n	5
water dispenser	飲水器	yǐnshuǐqì	n	20
watermelon	西瓜	xīgua	n	14
we	我們	wǒmen	pr	3
wear; put on	穿	chuān	v	9
weather	天氣	tiānqì	n	11
week	星期	xīngqī	n	3
weekend	週末	zhōumò	n	4
welcome	歡迎	huānyíng	v	20
west	西	xī	n	13
wet; humid	潮濕	cháoshī	adj	11
what	什麼	shénme	qpr	1
where	哪裏	nǎli	pr	7
where	哪兒	nǎr	qpr	5
which	哪	nǎ/něi	qpr	6

English	Characters	Pinyin	Part of Speech	Lesson
who	誰	shéi	qpr	2
why	為什麼	wèishénme	qpr	3
will	會	huì	mv	11
will; be going to; want to, have a desire to	要	yào	mv	6
wind	風	fēng	n	11
window	窗戶	chuānghu	n	19
windowshop	逛街	guàng jiē	vo	4
winter	冬天	dōngtiān	n	11
winter vacation	寒假	hánjià	n	10
wish (well)	祝	zhù	v	8
with	跟	gēn	prep	6
work at a temporary job (often part time)	打工	dǎ gōng	vo	19
worker	工人	gōngrén	n	2
worry	擔心	dān xīn	vo	18
write	寫	xiě	v	7
writing brush	毛筆	máobǐ	n	7
wrong	錯	cuò	adj	12

Y

English	Characters	Pinyin	Part of Speech	Lesson
year (of age)	歲	suì	n	3
yellow	黃	huáng	adj	9
yesterday	昨天	zuótiān	t	4
you	你	nǐ	pr	1
you (honorific for 你)	您	nín	pr	6
younger brother	弟弟	dìdi	n	2
younger sister	妹妹	mèimei	n	2

Z

English	Characters	Pinyin	Part of Speech	Lesson
zebra crossing; pedestrian crosswalk	斑馬線	bānmǎxiàn	n	13

Vocabulary by Grammar Category and by Lesson

Lesson & Section	noun	measure word	pronoun	numeral	verb	modal verb
L11-1	天氣 公園 碟				下雪 約 滑冰 預報 辦	會
L11-2	冬天 夏天 春天 秋天		那麼		出去 下雨 下面 回去 試	
L12-1	飯館(兒) 位子 服務員 桌子 盤 餃子 家常 豆腐 肉 碗 酸辣湯 味精 鹽 白菜 青菜 冰茶	些			好像 服務 點菜 放 賣完 上菜	
L12-2	師傅 糖醋魚 牛肉 魚 黃瓜 米飯 飯卡				紅燒 涼拌 忘 帶	

	adjective	adverb	preposition	conjunction	time word	particle	others	proper noun
	暖和 冷	更	比	不但…， 而且…	剛才		網上	
	好玩兒 糟糕 熱 舒服	非常 又						加州
	素 渴 夠 餓	剛						
	好吃 甜 酸 錯 清楚	極					沒關係	

Lesson & Section	noun	measure word	pronoun	numeral	verb	modal verb
L13-1	中心 運動場 旁邊 活動 中間 書店 地方 裏邊				上 聽説	
L13-2	中國城 地圖 南 路口 西 東 北 前 紅綠燈 右 左 前面	次			拿 過 拐	
L14-1	舞會 表姐 中學 禮物 飲料 水果 花 蘋果 梨 西瓜 樓	本 把			送 愛 住 接	
L14-2	鐘頭 暑期 班 去年 狗 臉 眼睛 嘴 蛋糕				以為 長 屬 像 長大	

adjective	adverb	preposition	conjunction	time word	particle	others	proper noun
遠 近		離					
	一直	從 往			過	哎	文 京 東 本 日 日
重							王 紅
聰 明 用 功 可 愛 圓	一定 最	離					倫 海 姆 湯

Lesson & Section	noun	measure word	pronoun	numeral	verb	modal verb
L15-1	醫院 病人 肚子 夜裏 廁所 冰箱 藥 小時 辦法	片 遍			看病 發燒 躺下 檢查 吃 壞 打針	
L15-2	身體 藥店 保險				感冒 生病 過敏 休息	
L16-1	印象 力氣				成 演 費	
L16-2	號碼 房間 電				記得 想起來 搬 打掃 整理 旅行	
L17-1	報紙 廣告 附近 公寓 分鐘 臥室 廚房 衛生間 客廳 傢具	套			吵 做飯 出租 走路	
L17-2	沙發 飯桌 椅子 書桌 書架 書房 租 美元 人民幣 費 金 押 寵物 興趣	元	那裏		還 准 養	

adjective	adverb	preposition	conjunction	time word	particle	others	proper noun
疼死	最好	把				好幾	
癢 健康 懶 亂	趕快 越來越		要不然 再説	後天		上次 一言為定	
同	就					倆	
	可能	連					
乾淨 安靜	差不多		另外			一房一廳	

Lesson & Section	noun	measure word	pronoun	numeral	verb	modal verb
L18-1	網球 拍 籃球				怕 跑步 游泳 淹死	願意
L18-2	水平 足球 比賽 腳 手 運動服				上大學 提高 踢 抱 壓 擔心	應該
L19-1	公司 計劃 暑假 父母 首都 政治 文化 導遊 護照 簽證 旅行社				放假 實習 打工 打算 訂	
L19-2	初 單程 航空 航班 窗戶 走道 素餐 旅館	份		千	往返 查 打折 轉機 靠 租	
L20-1	行李 包 箱子 登機牌 登機口				托運 重 起 照顧 哭 起飛 小心	
L20-2	叔叔 阿姨 爺爺 奶奶 烤鴨				歡迎	

adjective	adverb	preposition	conjunction	time word	particle	others	proper noun
胖 簡單 難受 危險	當然						
國際 美式 棒		為了 被				半天	
有名	馬上					名勝古蹟	長城 香港 台北
						直飛	中國國際航空公司 西北航空公司
					地	一路平安	
瘦							首都機場

Alternate Characters
(Texts in Simplified Form)

Lesson 11

Dialogue I: Tomorrow's Weather Will Be Even Better!

(Gao Xiaoyin is looking out the window.)

今天天气比^①昨天好，不下雪了^②。

我约了朋友明天去公园滑冰，不知道天气会^③怎么样？

我刚才看了网上的天气预报，明天天气比今天更好。不但不会下雪，而且❶会暖和一点儿^④。

是吗？太好了！

你约了谁去滑冰？

白英爱。

你约了白英爱？可是她今天早上坐飞机去纽约了。

真的啊？那我明天怎么办？

你还是在家看碟❷吧！

Dialogue II: The Weather Here Is Awful!

（高文中在网上找白英爱聊天儿。）

英爱，纽约那么好玩儿，你怎么在网上，没出去？

这儿的天气非常糟糕。

怎么了？❶

昨天下大雨，今天又⑤下雨了。

这个周末这儿天气很好，你快一点儿回来吧。

这个周末纽约也会暖和一点儿。我下个星期有一个面试，还不能回去。

我在加州找了一个工作，你也去吧。加州冬天不冷，夏天不热，春天和秋天更舒服。

加州好是好⑥，可是我更喜欢纽约。

Lesson 12

Dialogue I: Dining Out

（在饭馆儿）

请进，请进。

人怎么这么❶多？好像一个位子都①没有了。

服务员❷，请问，还有没有位子？

有，有，有。那张桌子没有人。

*　*　*

两位想吃点儿什么？

王朋，你点菜吧。

好。先给我们两盘饺子，要素的。

除了饺子以外，还要什么？

李友，你说呢？

还要一盘家常豆腐，不要放肉，我吃素。

我们的家常豆腐没有肉。

还要两碗酸辣汤③，请别放味精，少②放点儿盐。有小白菜吗？

对不起，小白菜刚③卖完④。

那就不要青菜了。

那喝点儿④什么呢？

我要一杯冰茶。李友，你喝什么？

我很渴，请给我一杯可乐，多放点儿冰。

好，两盘饺子，一盘家常豆腐，两碗酸辣汤，一杯冰茶，一杯可乐，多放冰。还要别的吗？

不要别的了，这些够⑤了。服务员，我们都饿了，请上菜快一点儿。

没问题，菜很快就能做好⑤。

Dialogue II: Eating in a Cafeteria

（今天是星期四，学生餐厅有中国菜，师傅是上海人。）

师傅❶，请问今天晚饭有什么好吃的？

我们今天有糖醋鱼，甜甜的⑥、酸酸的，好吃极了❷，你买一个吧。

好。今天有没有红烧牛肉？

没有。你已经要鱼了，别吃肉了。来⑦个凉拌黄瓜吧？

好。再来一碗米饭。一共多少钱？

糖醋鱼，四块五，凉拌黄瓜，一块七；一碗米饭，五毛钱。一共六块七。

师傅，糟糕，我忘了带饭卡了。这是十块钱。

找你三块三。

师傅，钱你找错了，多找了我一块钱。

对不起，我没有看清楚。

没关系❸。

下个星期四再来。

好，再见。

Lesson 13

Dialogue I: Where Are You Off To?

小白，下课了？上哪儿去❶？

您好，常老师。我想去学校的电脑中心，不知道怎么走，听说就在运动场旁边①。

电脑中心没有②运动场那么③远。你知道学校图书馆在哪里❷吗？

知道，离王朋的宿舍不远。

电脑中心离图书馆很近，就在图书馆和学生活动中心中间。

常老师，您去哪儿呢？

我想到学校书店去买书④。

书店在什么地方❸？

就在学生活动中心里边。我们一起走吧。

好。

Dialogue II: Going to Chinatown

我们去中国城吃中国饭吧！

我没去过⑤中国城，不知道中国城在哪儿。

没问题❶，你开车，我告诉你怎么走。

你有地图吗？给我看看⑥。

地图在宿舍里，我忘了拿来了。

没有地图，走错了怎么办？

没有地图没关系，中国城我去过很多次，不用地图也能找到⑦。你从这儿一直往南开，过三个路口，往西一拐❷就⑧到了。

哎，我不知道东南西北❸。

那你一直往前开，过三个红绿灯，往右一拐就到了。

（过了三个路口）

不对，不对。你看，这个路口只能往左拐，不能往右拐。

那就是下一个路口。往右拐，再往前开。到了，到了，你看见了吗？前面有很多中国字。

那不是中文，那是日文，我们到了小东京了。

是吗？那我们不吃中国饭了，吃日本饭吧！

Lesson 14

Dialogue I: Let's Go to a Party!

（李友给王朋打电话。）

王朋，你做什么呢①？

我看书呢。

今天高小音过生日❶，晚上我们在她家开舞会，你能去吗？

能去。几点？

七点。我们先吃饭，吃完饭再唱歌跳舞。

有哪些人？

小音和她的男朋友，小音的表姐❷，白英爱，你妹妹王红，听说还有小音的中学同学。

你要送给小音什么生日礼物？

我买了一本书送给她。

那我带什么东西？

饮料或者水果都可以。

那我带一些饮料，再买一把花儿。

小音爱吃水果，我再买一些苹果、梨和西瓜吧。

你住的地方② 离小音家很远，水果很重，我开车来接你，我们一起去吧。

好，我六点半在楼下等你。

Dialogue II: Attending a Birthday Party

（在高小音家）

王朋，李友，快进来。

小音，祝你生日快乐！这是送给你的生日礼物。

谢谢！ (She opens the gift.) 太好了！我一直想买这本书。带这么多东西，你们太客气了。

哥哥，李友，你们来了❶。

啊。小红，你怎么样？

我很好。每天都在学英文。

小红，你每天练习英文练习多长时间③？

三个半钟头❷。还看两个钟头的英文电视。

哎，你们两个是什么时候到的④？

刚到。

白英爱没跟你们一起来吗？

她还⑤没来？我以为❸她已经来了。

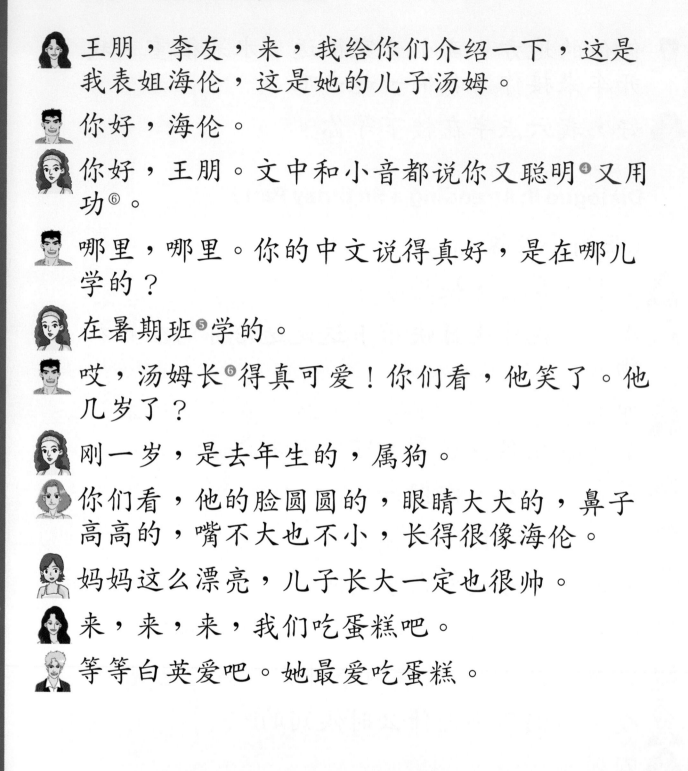

王朋，李友，来，我给你们介绍一下，这是我表姐海伦，这是她的儿子汤姆。

你好，海伦。

你好，王朋。文中和小音都说你又聪明❹又用功⑥。

哪里，哪里。你的中文说得真好，是在哪儿学的？

在暑期班❺学的。

哎，汤姆长❻得真可爱！你们看，他笑了。他几岁了？

刚一岁，是去年生的，属狗。

你们看，他的脸圆圆的，眼睛大大的，鼻子高高的，嘴不大也不小，长得很像海伦。

妈妈这么漂亮，儿子长大一定也很帅。

来，来，来，我们吃蛋糕吧。

等等白英爱吧。她最爱吃蛋糕。

Lesson 15

Dialogue I: My Stomachache Is Killing Me!

（病人去医院看病）

医生，我肚子疼死①了。

你昨天吃什么东西了？

我姐姐上个星期过生日，蛋糕没吃完。昨天晚上我吃了几口②，夜里肚子就疼起来了③，今天早上上了好几次②厕所。

你把④蛋糕放在哪儿了？

放在冰箱里了。

放了几天了？

五、六❶天了。

发烧吗？

不发烧。

你躺下。先检查一下。

* * *

你吃蛋糕把肚子吃坏了。

要不要打针？

不用打针，吃这种药❷就可以。一天三次，一次两片。

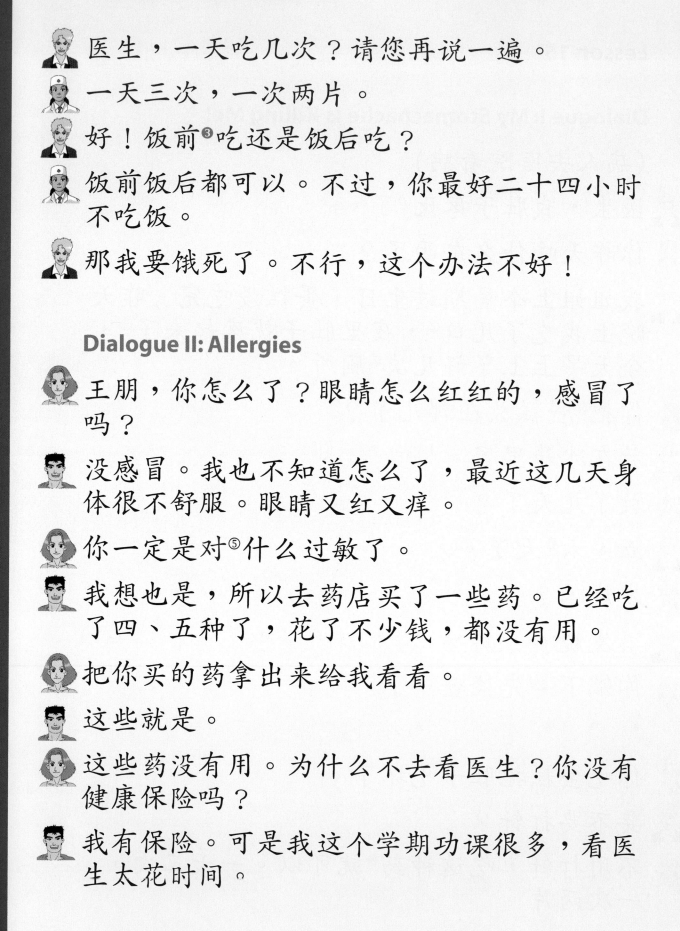

医生，一天吃几次？请您再说一遍。

一天三次，一次两片。

好！饭前❸吃还是饭后吃？

饭前饭后都可以。不过，你最好二十四小时不吃饭。

那我要饿死了。不行，这个办法不好！

Dialogue II: Allergies

王朋，你怎么了？眼睛怎么红红的，感冒了吗？

没感冒。我也不知道怎么了，最近这几天身体很不舒服。眼睛又红又痒。

你一定是对⑤什么过敏了。

我想也是，所以去药店买了一些药。已经吃了四、五种了，花了不少钱，都没有用。

把你买的药拿出来给我看看。

这些就是。

这些药没有用。为什么不去看医生？你没有健康保险吗？

我有保险。可是我这个学期功课很多，看医生太花时间。

那你也得赶快去看医生❶。要不然病会越来越⑥重。

我想再吃点儿别的药试试❷。我上次生病，没去看医生，休息两天，最后也好了。

不行，不行，你太懒了。再说⑦，你不能自己乱吃药。走，我跟你看病去。

Lesson 16

Dialogue I: Seeing a Movie

王朋跟李友在同一个学校学习，他们认识已经快半年了。王朋常常帮李友练习说中文。他们也常常一起出去玩儿，每次都玩儿得①很高兴。李友对王朋的印象❶很好，王朋也很喜欢李友，他们成了好朋友。

＊　＊　＊

这个周末学校演②一个中国电影，我们一起去看，好吗？

好啊！不过，听说看电影的人很多，买得到②票吗？

票已经买好了，我费了很大的力气才买到。

好极了！我早③就想看中国电影了。还有别人跟我们一起去吗？

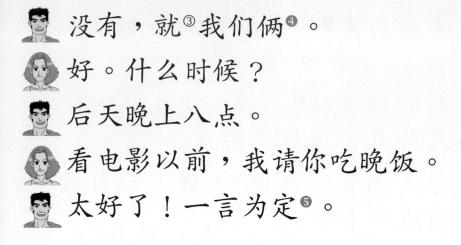

没有，就③我们俩④。

好。什么时候？

后天晚上八点。

看电影以前，我请你吃晚饭。

太好了！一言为定⑤。

Dialogue II: Turning Down an Invitation

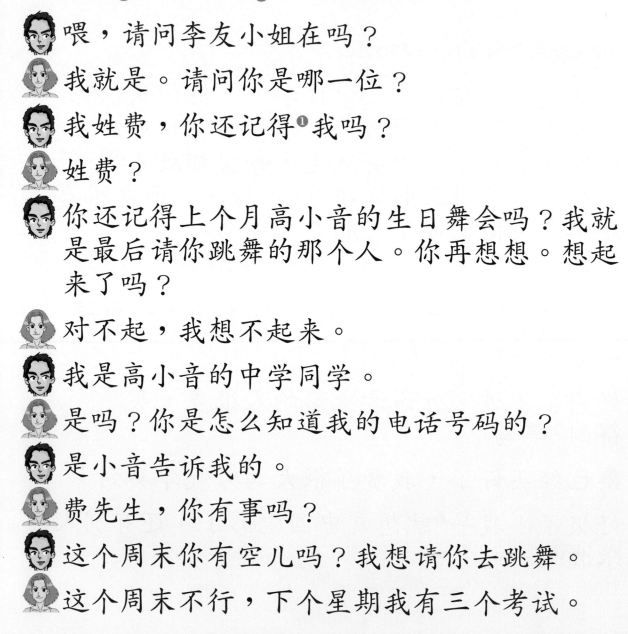

喂，请问李友小姐在吗？

我就是。请问你是哪一位？

我姓费，你还记得❶我吗？

姓费？

你还记得上个月高小音的生日舞会吗？我就是最后请你跳舞的那个人。你再想想。想起来了吗？

对不起，我想不起来。

我是高小音的中学同学。

是吗？你是怎么知道我的电话号码的？

是小音告诉我的。

费先生，你有事吗？

这个周末你有空儿吗？我想请你去跳舞。

这个周末不行，下个星期我有三个考试。

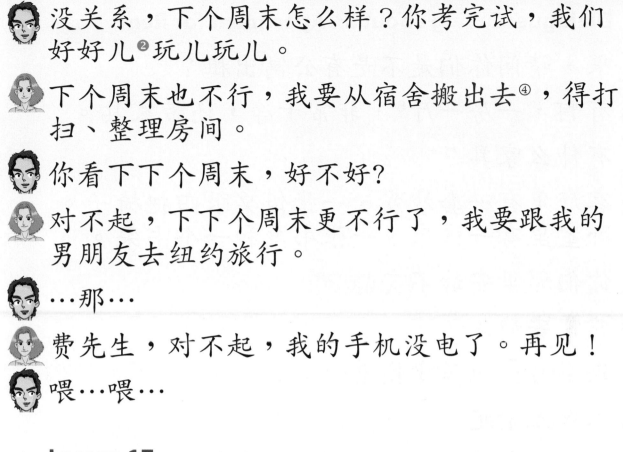

没关系，下个周末怎么样？你考完试，我们好好儿❷玩儿玩儿。

下个周末也不行，我要从宿舍搬出去④，得打扫、整理房间。

你看下下个周末，好不好？

对不起，下下个周末更不行了，我要跟我的男朋友去纽约旅行。

…那…

费先生，对不起，我的手机没电了。再见！

喂…喂…

Lesson 17

Narrative: Finding a Better Place

王朋在学校的宿舍住了两个学期了①。他觉得宿舍太吵，睡不好觉，房间太小，连电脑都②放不下③，再说也没有地方可以做饭，很不方便，所以准备下个学期搬出去住。他找房子找了一个多④月了，可是还没有找到合适的。刚才他在报纸上看到了一个广告，说学校附近有一套公寓出租，离学校很近，走路只要五分钟，很方便。公寓有一个卧室，一个厨房，一个卫生间❶，一个客厅，还带家具。王朋觉得这套公寓可能对他很合适。

Dialogue: Calling about an Apartment for Rent

喂，请问你们是不是有公寓出租？

有啊，一房一厅❶，非常干净，还带家具。

有什么家具？

客厅里有一套沙发、一张饭桌跟四把椅子。卧室里有一张床、一张书桌和一个书架。

你们那里安静不安静？

非常安静。

每个月房租多少钱？

八百五十元。

八百五十美元？人民币差不多是…有一点儿贵，能不能便宜点儿？

那你不用付水电费。

要不要付押金？

要多付一个月的房租当押金，搬出去的时候还给你。另外，我们公寓不准养宠物。

没关系，我对养宠物没有兴趣❷，什么宠物都⑤不养。

那太好了。你今天下午来看看吧。

好。

Lesson 18

Dialogue I: My Gut Keeps Getting Bigger and Bigger!

你看，我的肚子越来越大了。

你平常吃得那么多，又❶不运动，当然越来越胖了。

那怎么办呢？

如果怕胖，你一个星期运动两、三次，每次半个小时，肚子就会小了。

我两年没运动了①，做什么运动呢？

最简单的运动是跑步。

冬天那么冷，夏天那么热，跑步太难受②了。

你打网球吧。

打网球得买网球拍、网球鞋，你知道，网球拍、网球鞋贵极了！

找几个人打篮球吧。买个篮球很便宜。

那每次都得打电话约人，麻烦死了。

你去游泳吧。不用找人，也不用花很多钱，什么时候去都可以。

游泳？我怕水，太危险了，淹死了怎么办？

我也没办法了。你不愿意运动，那就胖下去③吧。

Dialogue II: Watching American Football

王朋的妹妹王红刚从北京来，要在美国上大学❶，现在住在高小音家里学英文。为了❷提高英文水平，她每天都看两个小时的电视④。

* * *

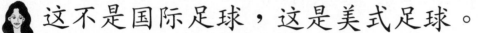 快把电视打开，足球比赛开始了。

是吗？我也喜欢看足球赛❸。⋯这是什么足球④啊？怎么不是圆的？

这不是国际足球，这是美式足球。

足球应该用脚踢，为什么那个人用手抱着③跑呢？

美式足球可以用手。

你看，你看，那么多人都压在一起，下面的人不是要被⑥压坏了吗？

别担心，他们的身体都很棒，而且还穿特别的运动服，没问题。

我看了半天⑤也看不懂。还是看别的吧。

你在美国住半年就会喜欢了。我男朋友看美式足球的时候，常常连饭都忘了吃。

Lesson 19

Dialogue I: Traveling to Beijing

李友，时间过得真快，马上就要放假了，我们的同学，有的去暑期班学习，有的去公司实习，有的回家打工，你有什么计划？

我还没有想好。你呢，王朋？

我暑假打算❶回北京去看父母。

是吗？我听说北京这个城市很有意思。

当然。北京是中国的首都，也是中国的政治、文化中心，有很多名胜古迹。

对啊，长城很有名。

还有，北京的好饭馆多得不得了①。

真的？我去过香港、台北，还没去过北京，要是能去北京就好了。

那你跟我一起回去吧，我当你的导游。

真的吗？那太好了！护照我已经有了，我得赶快办签证❷。

那我马上给旅行社打电话订飞机票。

Dialogue II: Planning an Itinerary

天一旅行社，你好。

你好。请问六月初❶到北京的机票多少钱？

您要买单程票还是往返票？

我要买两张往返票。

你想买哪家航空公司的？

哪家的便宜，就买哪②家的。

请等等，我查一下…好几家航空公司都有航班❷。中国国际航空公司，一千五③，直飞。西北航空公司正在打折❸，差不多一千四百六十，可是要转机。

西北只比国航❹便宜四十几块钱④，我还是买国航吧。

哪一天走❺？哪一天回来？

六月十号走，七月十五号回来。现在可以订位子吗？

可以。你们喜欢靠窗户的还是靠走道的？

靠走道的。对了❻，我朋友吃素，麻烦帮她订一份素餐。

没问题…您在北京要订旅馆、租车吗？

不用，谢谢！

Lesson 20

Dialogue I: Checking In at the Airport

（在国航的服务台）

小姐，这是我们的①机票。

请把护照给我看看。你们有几件行李要托运？

两件。这个包不托运，我们带上飞机。

麻烦❶您把箱子拿上来。

小姐，没超重吧？

没有。这是你们的护照、机票，这是登机牌❷。请到五号登机口❸上飞机。

谢谢。

*　　*　　*

哥哥，你们去北京了，就我一个人在这儿。

小红，别哭，我们几个星期就回来，你好好儿地①学英文，别乱跑。

不是几个星期就回来，是几个星期以后才回来。

别担心，我姐姐小音会照顾你。

对，别担心。

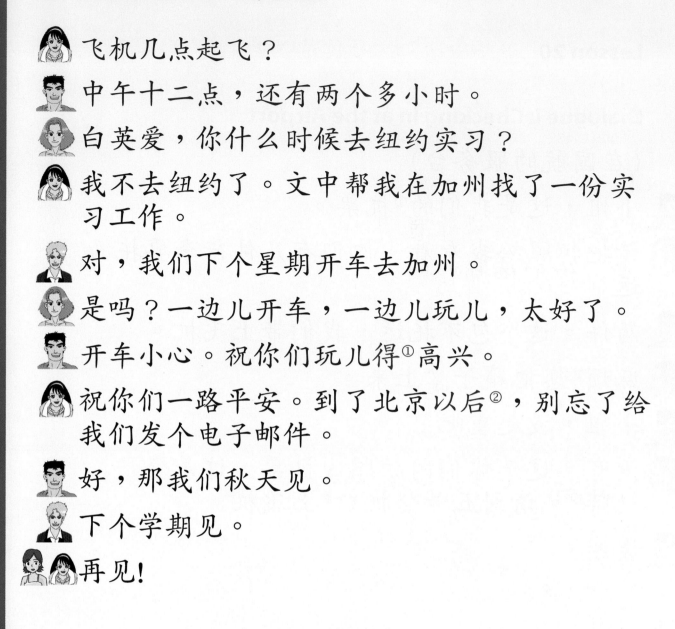

飞机几点起飞？

中午十二点，还有两个多小时。

白英爱，你什么时候去纽约实习？

我不去纽约了。文中帮我在加州找了一份实习工作。

对，我们下个星期开车去加州。

是吗？一边儿开车，一边儿玩儿，太好了。

开车小心。祝你们玩儿得①高兴。

祝你们一路平安。到了北京以后②，别忘了给我们发个电子邮件。

好，那我们秋天见。

下个学期见。

再见！

Dialogue II: Arriving in Beijing

（在北京首都机场）

小朋！

爸，妈！

累坏了吧？

还好③。爸，妈，我给你们介绍一下，这是我的同学李友。

叔叔，阿姨④❶，你们好。

欢迎你来北京。

李友，你的中文说得真好。

谢谢。是因为王朋教得好。

哪里，是因为你聪明。

哎，你们俩都聪明。

小朋，你好像瘦了点儿。是不是打工太忙，没有时间吃饭？

我没瘦。我常常运动，身体比以前棒多了。

小红怎么样？

她很好，英文水平提高了很多。

走吧，我们上车以后，再慢慢儿地聊吧。爷爷、奶奶在烤鸭店等我们呢！

烤鸭店？